HARRY G. JOHNSON ON TRADE STRATEGY & ECONOMIC POLICY

Volume 1

T0331324

ECONOMIC POLICIES TOWARDS LESS DEVELOPED COUNTRIES

ECONOMIC POLICIES TOWARDS LESS DEVELOPED COUNTRIES

HARRY G. JOHNSON

LONDON AND NEW YORK

First published in Great Britain in 1967 by George Allen & Unwin Ltd.

This edition first published in 2021
by Routledge
4 Park Square, Milton Park, Abingdon, Oxon OX14 4RN
605 Third Avenue, New York, NY 10017

Routledge is an imprint of the Taylor & Francis Group, an informa business

British Library Cataloguing in Publication Data
A catalogue record for this book is available from the British Library

ISBN: 978-1-03-204939-7 (Set)
ISBN: 978-1-00-319597-9 (Set) (ebk)
ISBN: 978-1-03-205008-9 (Volume 1) (hbk)
ISBN: 978-1-03-205018-8 (Volume 1) (pbk)
ISBN: 978-1-00-319563-4 (Volume 1) (ebk)

Publisher's Note
The publisher has gone to great lengths to ensure the quality of this reprint but points out that some imperfections in the original copies may be apparent.

Disclaimer
The publisher has made every effort to trace copyright holders and would welcome correspondence from those they have been unable to trace.

HARRY G. JOHNSON

Economic Policies Towards Less Developed Countries

A Brookings Institution study
LONDON: GEORGE ALLEN & UNWIN LTD
RUSKIN HOUSE MUSEUM STREET

FIRST PUBLISHED IN GREAT BRITAIN IN 1967
SECOND IMPRESSION 1968
THIRD IMPRESSION 1969

© 1967 by
THE BROOKINGS INSTITUTION
1775 Massachusetts Avenue, N.W.
Washington, D.C.

SBN 04 330036 7

PRINTED IN GREAT BRITAIN
BY PHOTOLITHOGRAPHY
UNWIN BROTHERS LIMITED
WOKING AND LONDON

THE BROOKINGS INSTITUTION is an independent organization devoted to nonpartisan research, education, and publication in
economics, government, foreign policy, and the social sciences
generally. Its principal purposes are to aid in the development of sound public
policies and to promote public understanding of issues of national importance.

The Institution was founded December 8, 1927, to merge the activities of
the Institute for Government Research, founded in 1916, the Institute of
Economics, founded in 1922, and the Robert Brookings Graduate School of
Economics and Government, founded in 1924.

The general administration of the Institution is the responsibility of a self-
perpetuating Board of Trustees. The trustees are likewise charged with maintaining the independence of the staff and fostering the most favorable conditions for creative research and education. The immediate direction of the
policies, program, and staff of the Institution is vested in the President, as-
sisted by the division directors and an advisory council, chosen from the
professional staff of the Institution.

In publishing a study, the Institution presents it as a competent treatment
of a subject worthy of public consideration. The interpretations and conclusions in such publications are those of the author or authors and do not pur-
port to represent the views of the other staff members, officers, or trustees of
the Brookings Institution.

Foreword

The United Nations Conference on Trade and Development, which met in Geneva in the spring of 1964, represented a turning point in relations between the less developed and the more developed nations of the world. A three-month seminar involving more than 2,000 delegates from 120 countries, UNCTAD was one of the largest and most wide-ranging international economic conferences ever held. Existing policies, objectives, and institutional arrangements were subjected to severe criticism by representatives of the less developed countries, and the United States found itself virtually isolated among the developed countries as a defender of the present principles governing international trade.

The United States is consequently faced with the necessity of reconsidering both its policies toward the less developed countries and its views on the general principles by which international trade should be governed, especially since a second Conference on Trade and Development will be held in 1967. As a contribution to this process, the present study surveys the main issues now confronting the United States in its relations with the less developed countries and explores the alternatives among which some choice must be made.

The first chapter is oriented toward the international politics of relations among the United States, the other developed countries, and the less developed countries. It provides necessary political, economic, and institutional background, discusses the 1964 conference and its outcome, and summarizes the chief issues requiring policy decisions. Chapter II deals with the broad economics—and some of the political and economic sociology—of the development problem and with the economics of foreign participation of various kinds in the development process. Chapter III surveys the impediments to efficient development of the world economy imposed by commercial and other economic policies in both the less developed and the more developed countries. The next three chapters deal with specific policy alternatives: the possibilities of providing more external resources to the less developed countries within the existing international institutional framework; the various possibilities for action to increase the flow of external resources by new arrangements in the field of commodity trade; and the issues raised by the new proposals at UNCTAD for giving preferences to exports of manufactured products by less developed countries in the markets of the developed countries and among groups of less developed countries.

Chapter VII departs from the main theme to present some reflections on reform of the international monetary system and its relation to the problem of economic development. The concluding chapter offers some retrospective thoughts on the study—a summary of the main outlines of the argument, some suggestions on specific policy measures that might be adopted, and some ideas on further research that might be undertaken to extend knowledge relevant to this important area of economic policy.

The Brookings Institution considers itself fortunate to have enlisted as author of the study an outstanding international economist and incisive analyst of international economic problems, Professor Harry G. Johnson, who has taught at leading Canadian, British, and American universities. He has been Professor of Economics at the University of Chicago since 1959, and has served as the Editor of the *Journal of Political Economy* and President of the Canadian Economic and Political Science Association. In the autumn of 1966, he became Professor of Economics at the London School of Economics and Political Science. The present volume is an important addition to Professor Johnson's numerous contributions to the analysis of international economic problems and policies.

This project was a joint venture of the Division of Economic Studies and the Division of Foreign Policy Studies at Brookings, directed respectively by Joseph A. Pechman and H. Field Haviland, Jr. The draft manuscript served as a basis for a conference of specialists in trade and development from universities, government agencies, and international organizations, held at the Institution on December 9 and 10, 1965. The conference was organized by Robert E. Asher and Walter S. Salant of the Brookings Senior Staff, who also served as a Reading Committee on the manuscript.

The Institution is grateful to the conferees for their many penetrating comments, to the others mentioned in the Author's Acknowledgments, to Alice M. Carroll for editing the manuscript, and to Charlene Semer for preparing the index.

The views expressed in this book are, of course, those of the author and do not necessarily represent the views of those consulted during its preparation. Neither should they be construed as reflecting the views of the trustees, the officers, or other staff members of the Brookings Institution.

ROBERT D. CALKINS
President

October 1966
Washington, D.C.

Author's Acknowledgments

I should like to express my gratitude to the Brookings Institution for offering me the opportunity to undertake a comprehensive study of trade and development. The question has long interested me, but this was a unique challenge to attempt to integrate pure economic theory, empirical knowledge, and the study of economic policy into the exploration of a policy problem of outstanding importance to the country and the world. I would like in particular to express my thanks to the research officers of the Brookings Institution for their encouragement, advice, and help: to Joseph A. Pechman, for his always comforting assumption that research can indeed be completed according to its planned timetable; to Walter S. Salant and Robert E. Asher, for their always available wisdom, the meticulous care with which they read the manuscript, and their gentle insistence that it should say what it meant; and to Lawrence B. Krause, for his patience in answering innumerable queries about data sources and research findings and in discussing fine theoretical points while engaged in an exacting major research project of his own. I should also like to thank John Pincus, of the RAND Corporation, who read the manuscript carefully as it was produced and made many helpful suggestions; Richard N. Cooper of the Department of State; Robert A. Mundell, Rockefeller Foundation Visiting Research Professor of International Economics at the Brookings Institution; and David Meiselman and O. H. Brownlee of the Office of the Comptroller of the Currency—all of whom made useful suggestions about parts of the manuscript.

As reported by Dr. Calkins in the Foreword, the first draft of this book formed the agenda for a conference of experts on international trade and development policy convened at Brookings on December 9 and 10, 1965. Their comments were extremely useful in revising the first draft for publication. I am particularly grateful to the following people, who commented in writing or in interviews: Bela A. Balassa of Yale University; Bernard R. Bell, former Economic Consultant in Washington who is now with the International Bank for Reconstruction and Development; Richard Caves of Harvard University; Gerard Curzon of the Institute Universitaire de Hautes Etudes Internationales; J. Marcus Fleming of the International Monetary Fund; Theodore Geiger of the National Planning Association; Gottfried Haberler and Albert O. Hirschman of Harvard University; Andrew M. Kamarck of the International Bank for Reconstruction and Development; Hal B. Lary of the National Bureau of Economic Research; Grant L. Reuber of the University of Western Ontario; and Hans W. Singer of the United Nations.

HARRY G. JOHNSON

Contents

I

The Political
and Economic Setting

One of the most important and fundamental changes in the political
and economic structure of international relations in the past twenty
years has been the emergence of the former colonies and dependent
territories of the major European powers as independent national
states. With political independence has come the urge for economic development, as a means both of raising living standards in countries
that are extremely poor by comparison with European and North
American nations and of creating the material foundations of national
identity and self-respect. This urge has been shared by other nations,
neither "new" nor yet "developed," such as those of Latin America and
the Near and Middle East. As a result most of these countries have
adopted programs for the planning, and planned acceleration, of their
economic growth.

The developed nations have recognized an obligation to assist and
facilitate the economic development of the less developed countries.
Their motivations have been a mixture of general humanitarian considerations and more narrow specific national interests. In some cases,
notably France and the United Kingdom, a major motivation has been
a sense of responsibility to, and desire to maintain the political support of, former colonial territories, on which development assistance
has been concentrated. For the French there is an explicit desire to
strengthen and extend their culture, while for the United Kingdom
and other advanced Commonwealth countries such as Canada and
Australia the motivation derives rather from a common historical and
cultural background and similar political and legal institutions. In
other cases, such as Germany, the long-run commercial and political

A

advantages of the goodwill obtainable by generosity to the developing nations are regarded as important. In the case of the United States, broad humanitarianism and the moral obligation of the rich to assist the poor have been inextricably intermingled with the belief in rapid economic development as a potent strengthener of resistance to domestic communist influences and generosity in development assistance as an effective means of commanding the political and military support—or at least neutrality—of the less developed nations.

UNITED STATES POLICY
AND THE LESS DEVELOPED NATIONS

Though some elements of its rationale for development assistance are debatable, and there has been increasingly serious questioning of the effectiveness of and necessity for the foreign aid program in recent years, the United States government has repeatedly reaffirmed its commitment to assist the development of the less developed countries. This commitment has been expressed in a substantial flow of real resources to these countries through the foreign aid, military assistance, surplus commodity, and other programs. In absolute terms, the United States is by far the largest donor of development assistance in the world. However, its predominance is largely a consequence of its size and wealth. If development aid is measured as a proportion of national income, and especially if loans are reckoned at the value of the real resources they transfer instead of their nominal value, the U. S. contribution is only about half as large as that of France, though over double that of any other leading noncommunist aid donor.[1] If aid contributions are compared with what would be assessed on the basis of an income tax on individual citizens as progressive as the average national tax system, the United States does not appear to be bearing a disproportionately large share of the aid burden.[2]

[1] See John A. Pincus, "The Cost of Foreign Aid," *Review of Economics and Statistics*, Vol. 45 (November 1963), pp. 360-67, especially p. 364. Pincus estimates French aid commitments in 1962 at 1.32 percent of gross national product, U.S. at 0.66 or 0.55 percent (depending on whether P.L. 480 aid is valued at official prices or at world market prices), and German, Dutch, and U.K. commitments at 0.27, with Japan, Portugal, Canada, and Italy being committed for successively smaller proportions of their gross national products.
[2] See I. B. Kravis and M. W. S. Davenport, "The Political Arithmetic of International Burden-Sharing," *Journal of Political Economy*, Vol. 71 (August 1963), pp. 309-30.

Foreign Aid

Foreign aid in the form of grants, loans, and sales of surplus agricultural commodities for local currencies, together with technical assistance, has been the prime means through which the United States has contributed to the economic development of the poor countries of the world. The general technique, developed to meet the postwar reconstruction needs of the European countries during the period of dollar shortage, was transferred to the new problem of promoting economic development as the demands for such assistance became more pressing and Europe's problems were overcome. The fact that the two problems were essentially different was scarcely appreciated at the time, and failure to recognize the fundamental difference in their amenability to quick solution by foreign aid is largely responsible for the growing disenchantment with development aid. Europe possessed industrial skills, modern technology and entrepreneurial ability and could be revitalized by marginal contributions of real resources and foreign exchange supplied over a limited period. The less developed countries must modernize their economies by accumulating stocks of "human" capital as well as material capital, starting from a low level of virtually every asset.[3] Limited contributions of aid can scarcely have a catalytic effect on these economies, for the process of getting economic development started is bound to be prolonged, expensive, and grossly inefficient by the standards of investment productivity normally applied in developed countries.

Despite the burden that the transfer of resources through foreign aid places on the U.S. taxpayer and the U.S. economy—a substantially lighter burden than is indicated by the money amounts involved in surplus disposal under Public Law 480 or total aid during periods of abnormally high unemployment—primary reliance on foreign aid in policy toward the less developed countries represents a "soft option" for both parties, not merely the recipient country.[4] For the beneficiary of aid, the real resources and foreign exchange provided reduce the pressure to develop industries that can compete efficiently with those

[3] For discussions of economic development as a generalized process of capital accumulation, see Harry G. Johnson, *The Canadian Quandary* (Toronto: McGraw-Hill, 1963), Chap. 14, and T. W. Schultz, *Transforming Traditional Agriculture* (Yale University Press, 1964).

[4] P. T. Bauer and J. B. Wood, "Foreign Aid: The Soft Option," *Banca Nazionale del Lavoro*, No. 59 (December 1961), pp. 403-18.

of the developed countries in the domestic and foreign markets. Aid in the form of surplus agricultural products reduces the incentives to increase productivity in agriculture (which tends anyway to be starved of investment resources by planners interested in industrialization) even though it is typically the largest, and an obviously backward, sector in the less developed countries. For the donors the giving of aid excuses the maintenance or adoption of commercial and domestic economic policies that restrict the opportunities for less developed countries to develop on the basis of exporting to their rich and growing markets. Aid in the form of agricultural surpluses enables a domestic problem to be shifted to the world market under the guise of charity. In short, the giving and receipt of aid permits both parties to avoid harder choices involving conflicts between the requirements of economic efficiency and other objectives of economic policy.

An incidental but significant consequence is that some part of the potential contribution of aid to development is nullified by the greater inefficiency that aid permits both sides to tolerate. In addition—a matter of importance in view of the value attached by the United States to the free enterprise system—the process of aid giving inevitably obliges the donor to insist that the recipient practice some sort of central economic planning, since this appears to provide a relatively simple basis for testing aid-worthiness. Moreover, the administration of aid given directly by one country to another places officials of the donor country in the recipient country in a rich-man/poor-man relationship that is scarcely conducive to mutual respect and political amity.

In the early stages of promotion of development through assistance—broadly speaking, the 1950's—the U.S. policy of concentrating on the provision of loans and grants meshed reasonably closely with the demands of the less developed countries and with the requirements indicated by the prevailing theory of the development problem. Nationalistic development policies, modeling themselves on the examples of the United States and especially the Soviet Union, aimed at the creation of a self-contained modern industrial economy. Such an economy was to be created by transferring labor from the traditional export industries and the subsistence sector to an industrial sector, which was to be developed by investing resources obtained through foreign aid and the taxation of traditional exports in "economic infrastructure" and in domestic production of industrial goods formerly imported—the policy of development through import substitution. The prevailing theory of development, derived from the Keynesian theory of unemployment in advanced economies and the extension of it into a growth model by Harrod and others, stressed the necessity of material investment to draw supposedly surplus labor from the subsistence sector into productive industrial employment, and of foreign aid to fill the gap between the available domestic savings and the investment required for a satisfactory rate of economic growth. Since both policy and theory emphasized development of production for the domestic market, on the simplistic assumption that the shortage of capital and the absence of economic planning were the root causes of underdevelopment, it appeared that all the developed countries could usefully contribute was foreign aid coupled with technical assistance in planning and executing its investment.

Demands for New Trade Policies

With the accumulation of experience of the development problem, the growth in the number of countries claiming assistance, and the steady increase in the rate of economic growth to which those countries aspire, however, it has become clear that foreign aid is no longer a sufficient means of promoting economic growth. The less developed countries and their sympathizers have thus begun to press for other forms of assistance. In the first place, the prospective requirements of the less developed countries for external resources to implement their target rates of development are substantially greater than the amount of aid the developed countries are likely to provide. This has led on the one hand to growing pressure both for increases in the amount of aid provided and for changes in the form and terms of aid designed to increase its real value. On the other hand, and of more fundamental significance, it has generated a new interest in the possibilities of obtaining external resources through trade rather than aid. The variety of demands on the developed countries for changes in their policies that directly or indirectly affect their foreign trade ranges from demands for higher prices for the primary products on whose export the less developed countries depend for most of their foreign exchange earnings (to be achieved by international commodity agreements) to modification of policies associated with agricultural protectionsim that restrict the market for such exports. In the second place, those less developed countries that have achieved sufficient progress to be capable of exporting industrial products and are anxious to expand such exports as a means of earning external resources have become aware that the developed countries place serious obstacles, both tariff and non-tariff barriers, in the way of such export expansion. They, and other less developed countries expecting or hoping to arrive at a comparable stage of development, have been voicing demands for reduction of these barriers and beyond that for preferential treatment of their exports of manufactured and semimanufactured goods.

These criticisms of the approach of the developed countries to assistance for the less developed countries, and recommendations of changes in trade policy to benefit the latter, have been mounting in volume and seriousness through the 1960's. They have increasingly occupied the attention of GATT (the General Agreement on Tariffs and Trade, the international body concerned with the rules of commercial policy and the conduct of trade negotiations) where they have been the subject of sharp divisions both between the less developed and the developed nations and among the latter. They culminated in the convening of the United Nations Conference on Trade and Development (UNCTAD), held in Geneva from March to June 1964, which served as a forum for the expression of the views and demands of the less developed countries (they were all somewhat euphemistically rechristened "developing countries" before the occasion) and which has since been made a permanent organ of the United Nations.

Modifications of U.S. Policy

The United States has modified its policy in certain respects in recent years in response to the evolving views and demands of the less developed countries and also as a result of its special commitment to the economic development of Latin America. Its previously rigid opposition to international commodity agreements intended to raise and control prices has been modified, as evidenced by U.S. participation in the international coffee agreement. Within GATT, the United States has affirmed its general sympathy with the evolving program for unilateral action by the developed countries to assist the export endeavors of the less developed countries. This sympathy was reflected concretely in certain provisions of the Trade Expansion Act of 1962, notably the authority to eliminate tariffs of 5 percent or less, the authority to eliminate duties on tropical agricultural products and hardwoods if the European Economic Community would do the same, and the authority to bargain about nontariff barriers to trade. On the other hand, in the past few years the United States (like some other developed members of GATT) has continued to take policy actions particularly harmful to the export interests of less developed countries, such as the imposition of more restrictive sugar quotas, restriction of imports of cotton textiles, and the imposition of quotas on meat imports and petroleum.

The modifications of U. S. policy have been extremely minor by comparison both with the changes sought by the less developed countries and with those the other developed countries have shown themselves prepared to contemplate. Increasingly the United States has appeared to be isolated from the general trend of thinking and discussion about problems of the less developed countries, a lone voice of negation confronting a chorus of hopeful positive suggestions. This was certainly the impression registered on the other participants and the observers and commentators at UNCTAD. The United States appeared as the most forceful (and often the only) opponent of the less developed countries' proposals for new arrangements to increase their export earnings. In particular, it flatly rejected any proposal for preferences for their exports—the most novel and appealing proposal that had emerged both from the discussions of GATT and from the preparatory work for UNCTAD.[5]

After the experience of UNCTAD, it is virtually an international political impossibility for the United States to maintain its traditional economic policies toward the less developed countries. In the first place, its political objectives cannot be promoted by an adamantly negative attitude toward policy changes whose desirability has been endorsed by the less developed nations acting as a cohesive political group in the United Nations setting—especially when its stance has not been supported by the other developed countries of the West with which the United States must ultimately work in concert and which have offered positive alternatives for consideration. The United States must, if it is to serve those political objectives, evaluate and propound solutions for the problems of the less developed countries as those

---

[5] "The United States Delegation appeared to lack both an understanding of the basic needs of the less developed countries (the LDC's) and any desire to gain one. An American observer remarked of the chief delegate of his country: 'He had nothing to offer and so he offered nothing.' The U.S. became clearly identified as the least willing of the industrial countries to even consider a 'new' international division of labour which would permit the developing countries to industrialize." J. C. Mills, "Canada at UNCTAD," *The International Journal,* Vol. 20 (Spring 1965), p. 214.

countries, and not the United States alone, understand them. Secondly, though the solutions proposed at UNCTAD and elsewhere for those problems are in many cases highly questionable from an economic point of view or politically and administratively not feasible, the problems themselves are genuine and deserve serious consideration, analysis, and remedial action. The position of leadership of the United States imposes a responsibility to formulate constructive policies to deal with them. Thirdly, the United States cannot evade the demand for action in the trade field by offering substantial increases in foreign aid, which appears to have been its strategy at UNCTAD and is clearly unacceptable to the less developed countries. That course, even if it were possible, appears to be precluded, at least for the present, by domestic political opposition to further enlargement of the aid program and by the mounting cost of the war in Vietnam.

THE INSTITUTIONAL FRAMEWORK OF WESTERN COMMERCE AND THE POLITICAL REALITIES

In formulating and executing its international economic policies the United States, like other leading Western nations, cannot operate autonomously. Its freedom of action is circumscribed by its responsibilities to the various international institutions that facilitate and regulate international economic relations and in whose establishment and evolution the United States has played a leading part. Moreover, and to an extent which is difficult for the outside observer fully to appreciate, there has developed within and around these institutions a system of regular consultations among the officials of the various governments concerned and between these officials and those of the international institutions themselves. From these consultations, which provide a forum for the regular examination and criticism of the policies of the individual countries, informal codes for the conduct of national economic policy have gradually been emerging. Central to the determination of what goes on in the international institutions, however, are the political and economic objectives of the leading nations and groupings of nations.

International Institutions

The basis of present international economic institutional arrangements was laid in the formation after World War II of three new international institutions: the International Monetary Fund, designed to provide a stable international monetary system by supplementing the world supply of monetary gold with additional international liquidity based on credit and providing machinery for agreed changes in exchange rates in cases of fundamental disequilibrium; the International Bank for Reconstruction and Development, designed to provide long-term credit for economic development on somewhat better than commercial terms; and an International Trade Organization, based on a charter setting forth a code of fair practices in international trade and intended to serve as the medium for the restoration of a liberal world trading system. The first two of these institutions were actually established. The International Trade Organization was never ratified by the U. S. Congress; however, its intended functions have been assumed to a large extent by the General Agreement on Tariffs and Trade (GATT), originally established as a stop-gap arrangement pending the creation of a formal international institution to regulate international trade and commercial policy.

For reasons inherent in the evolution of postwar political and economic history, these three institutions have come to play a different role in the world economy than their postwar planners intended. Moreover, some of their intended functions have come to be performed either by direct nation-to-nation arrangements or through new less comprehensive international institutions.[6] The growth of bilateral foreign aid has dwarfed the International Bank as a supplier of capital for the development of the less developed countries. The postwar dollar shortage in the European countries and the initiation of the Marshall Plan by the United States gave birth to the Organization for European Economic Cooperation, a regional arrangement with American (and Canadian) participation which during the period of dollar shortage substituted for the functions of the international institutions in the fields of money, trade, and international finance. Subsequently the OEEC was transformed into the Organization for Economic Cooperation and Development (OECD), again a regional arrangement whose main functions are the coordination of the development aid policies of the Western countries and the surveillance of members' balance-of-payments and related domestic policies. The emergence of the U.S. dollar as an international reserve currency, and the international monetary

[6] For a more detailed account of the by-passing of these three institutions, see Harry G. Johnson, *The World Economy at the Crossroads* (Oxford: The Clarendon Press, 1965).

difficulties associated with the period of persistent U.S. balance-of-payments deficits, led to direct arrangements between the United States and the individual European countries that by-passed the International Monetary Fund.[7] The Fund's resources have been supplemented by the General Arrangements to Borrow, an institutional development which has made international monetary adjustments effectively a matter of negotiation between the United States and the leading European countries.

Evolution of Trading Arrangements

In the field of international trading arrangements, GATT has developed into an institution substantially different from the abortive International Trade Organization (ITO).[8] In part this has been due to the nonaccession or exclusion of the communist countries (state-trading countries were intended to participate in the ITO) and to the fact that the General Agreement did not include some important chapters of the ITO charter, notably those concerned with commodity agreements, certain aspects of agricultural trade, and protection of private foreign investment, which the ITO was intended to regulate.[9] Mostly, however, it has been the result of the policies of the major contracting parties, especially of the United States, in GATT negotiations. The rules of GATT apply equally to trade in agricultural and in industrial products; but the foreign agricultural competition attracted by its high support prices led the United States in the early 1950's to insist on a waiver allowing it to apply quantitative restrictions on a wide range of agricultural imports—an unarguable precedent for the agricultural policy subsequently adopted by the Common Market. Later, its growing problem of agricultural surpluses led the United States to oppose stubbornly the inclusion of agricultural trade and commodity agreements

[7] The problems of the pound as a reserve currency have led to similar direct arrangements between the United Kingdom and the major European countries, the United States and Canada; but those have typically been temporary arrangements for short-term finance, soon repaid by resort to drawings on the International Monetary Fund.

[8] For a detailed analytical account of the evolution of GATT, see Gerard Curzon, *Multilateral Commercial Diplomacy: The General Agreement on Tariffs and Trade and Its Impact on National Commercial Policies and Techniques* (London: Michael Joseph Limited, 1965).

[9] International commodity agreements, of which several have been established, are thus outside GATT; while in a sense they too are international institutions, they are not so treated here.

within the GATT framework, until the threat of the Common Market's agricultural policies led it to reverse its position in self-defense. The concentration of GATT negotiations on industrial products and the differential treatment of agricultural and industrial protectionism in GATT are a major focus of less developed countries' criticisms of both GATT and the policies of the developed countries.

Again the concern of the United States with the political, military, and economic advantages of European integration led it to support the formation of the European Common Market and in so doing to oppose the British scheme for a broader and more outward-looking European Free Trade Area (which has been implemented in a fragmentary form in the European Free Trade Association). In particular, the United States supported within GATT the acceptance of two features of the Common Market Treaty—the common market in agricultural products, involving support prices above the world level coupled with variable levies on imports, and the preferential arrangements accorded to the former African colonies of the members—neither of which was consistent with the basic philosophy of GATT. The first involved a further increase in agricultural protectionism in the world economy, disadvantageous both to the United States and to certain of the less developed countries. The second, besides introducing new preferences in contravention of GATT rules, established a new precedent of preferential entry to the markets of developed countries for politically preferred less developed countries.

More generally, the establishment of the Common Market brought into the center of GATT a conflict of views on how the economy of the Western world should be organized: the British-American view, embodied in the General Agreement, which emphasizes the principle of nondiscrimination in international trade, and the French view, supported by the Common Market collectively, which emphasizes exactly the converse principle. And while the establishment of the Common Market has been responsible for the revitalization of GATT, by motivating President Kennedy to seek the new and vastly enlarged authority to negotiate reciprocal tariff reductions embodied in the Trade Expansion Act of 1962, the "Kennedy Round" of GATT negotiations must frankly be regarded as primarily a struggle by the United States to contain the protectionist and regionally divisive forces of the Common Market. The conflict of views and the struggle, moreover, have virtually precluded serious action within GATT to satisfy the complaints of the less developed countries about the obstacles to the expansion of their export earnings imposed by the policies of the developed countries.

Underlying the conflict, of course, is the fundamental political struggle precipitated by General de Gaulle's ambition to aggrandize France through the Common Market and to diminish the international power and influence of the United States. These ambitions are frequently interpreted by Americans as a personal idiosyncrasy of the General's; but the substantial withdrawals of gold from the United States by all the central banks of the Common Market countries in 1964-65, and the consequent threat to the stability of the dollar-based international monetary system, is evidence that at least the second of the General's objectives commands wide support in the Common Market.

Functions of GATT

Although the General Agreement on Tariffs and Trade is the established institution through which reductions in trade barriers are negotiated and in which disagreements on international trade matters are arbitrated, its nature and functions are not generally well understood.[10] GATT is both a multilateral agreement establishing a set of rules governing the conduct of trade policy among the contracting parties and an institution performing a variety of functions related to the conduct of trade negotiations among its members. There are sixty-two full contracting parties to GATT, six that have provisionally acceded, two participating under special arrangements, and five new nations maintaining a de facto application of GATT—in all, seventy-five countries, accounting for more than 80 percent of world trade. Of the contracting parties, over two-thirds are less developed countries—an important point inasmuch as a two-thirds majority is sufficient to relieve a contracting party of its obligations under GATT, as might be required to implement the new proposals for preferential trading arrangements for less developed countries within GATT.

The provisions of GATT are based on the following four central principles:

Member countries should grant one another treatment at least as favourable as they grant any other country (the "most-favoured-nation" principle),

---

[10] An excellent short account of GATT may be found in Richard N. Gardner, *In Pursuit of World Order* (Frederick A. Praeger, 1964), Chap 6; for full details, see Curzon, *op. cit.*

subject to the right, provided certain conditions are met, to form free-trade areas or customs unions;

Protection should be afforded to domestic industries exclusively through the customs tariff and not through other commercial measures (such as quantitative restrictions), and the general level of tariff protection should be progressively reduced through successive tariff negotiations;

Contracting parties should use the procedure of consultation, directly with other contracting parties or with the CONTRACTING PARTIES collectively, in cases of dispute and to avoid damage to one another's trading interests;

Contracting parties should take such joint action—which may include the drawing up and implementation of programmes such as the Trade Expansion Programme described later in this paper—as is necessary to further the objectives of the Agreement.[11]

The first and most of the second of these principles embody the two basic general rules for the conduct of international trade under GATT: nondiscrimination among fellow members (except by members of free trade areas and customs unions) and protection only by tariffs. The remainder define the functions of the institution and prescribe the behavior of members within it.

The general rules are expressed in a long list of specific rules, often exceedingly complex. One important rule, a logical corollary of the principle of nondiscrimination, prohibits the establishment of new preferences. Another important set of rules prohibits quantitative restrictions except where these are essential to cope with a balance-of-payments problem, to implement the development program of a less developed country, or to enforce domestic governmental measures to restrict production or overcome a glut of agricultural products;[12] in these cases the principle of nondiscrimination still applies. Under these rules, GATT negotiations over the years (and also negotiations within the OEEC in conformity with GATT principles) have reduced quantitative restrictions to a hard core of "residual" restrictions maintained for protectionist purposes. Yet another rule, which concerns the for-

[11] *The Role of GATT in Relation to Trade and Development* (Geneva: The Contracting Parties to the General Agreement on Tariffs and Trade, March 1964), p. 6.

[12] Gardner (*op. cit.*, p. 153) is somewhat misleading in stating that an exception is allowed "where essential to safeguard . . . domestic programs of agricultural price support." This statement describes the de facto position; the original rule required the presence of restrictions on domestic agricultural output; it was from this rule that the United States obtained the waiver allowing restrictions on agricultural imports (see Curzon, *op. cit.*, pp. 167-68).

mation of customs unions and free trade areas, requires that the participants eliminate restrictions on substantially all trade among themselves and that in a customs union the external tariffs and other trade restrictions should not on balance be higher or more restrictive than the previous national barriers to trade. The arrangements for the association of the overseas territories with the Common Market conflicted with both the enjoinder on new preferences and the requirement that substantially all trade be freed, since it applied only to exports from and not to imports into the territories.

As an institution for the conduct of trade negotiations among its members, GATT performs three main functions. First, it provides a forum for the multilateral negotiation of reductions in tariffs and other trade barriers. The basic principle of these negotiations is reciprocity, the exchange of trade concessions of equal value to the negotiating countries. This function, in the current Kennedy Round of GATT negotiations, has included the difficult problem of devising procedures for bargaining on the new basis of across-the-board tariff reductions instead of the old item-by-item method. Secondly, GATT provides machinery for the discussion and settlement of disputes over the commercial policy measures of one member which another considers harmful to its interests. If consultation between the members affected does not produce satisfaction, the contracting parties as a group arbitrate the dispute, arranging either for the member inflicting damage to offer compensation through other trade concessions or for the damaged member to retaliate by withdrawing trade concessions previously given. This procedure has gradually built a body of "case law" around the GATT rules for trade policy. Thirdly, GATT studies trends in international trade and commercial policy problems with a view to devising new trade policies. This activity, initiated relatively recently and largely carried on by the Secretariat, has been concerned mostly with the problems of the less developed countries.

Shortcomings of GATT

The combination of the principle of nondiscrimination with the principle of reciprocity in the tariff negotiation process entails certain inherent problems and biases.[13] In the first place, reciprocity requires

[13] For a theoretical discussion of these problems, see Harry G. Johnson, "An Economic Theory of Protectionism, Tariff Bargaining, and the Formation of Customs Unions," *Journal of Political Economy*, Vol. 73 (June 1965), pp. 256-83.

that there be more than one nation willing to bargain. To be willing and able to bargain on a nondiscriminatory basis, a country must have both a good competitive position in the world market (so that it has something to gain from bargaining or possibly lose if it does not bargain) and an attractive but significantly protected domestic market (so that it has something worthwhile to offer the other party). Thus, in effect, progress in tariff reduction depends on the willingness of one of the major trading countries to forego full reciprocity (as with the United States in the early postwar rounds of GATT) or on the matching of moods of export-mindedness among the major trading countries (as was assumed to be the case in the preparation of the Trade Expansion Act).

Secondly, in combination with the reciprocity principle, the principle of nondiscrimination, applying as it does to individual commodities traded and not to the overall interests of trading partners, tends to focus bargaining on commodities of special interest to the countries in a position to bargain and hence indirectly to discriminate in favor of their trade with each other as against third parties. This was the usual result under the item-by-item method of bargaining and was the explicit intention of the "dominant supplier" authority of the Trade Expansion Act, which permitted elimination of tariffs altogether on commodities in which the United States and the Common Market countries together conducted 80 percent or more of world trade. (This authority has become empty in consequence of the rejection of Britain's application to join the Common Market.) This bias, however, is greatly reduced in the new approach of bargaining for linear tariff reductions, which will presumably provide larger spillovers for third parties, though that approach raises problems of its own (such as the tariff-disparities issue and "exceptions" to the bargaining).

A further consequence of the combination of the two principles is that the spillover of the benefits of tariff concessions to third parties resulting from most-favored-nation treatment sets limits to the range of mutually beneficial bilateral bargaining. These limits were particularly evident in the slow progress of trade liberalization under the Reciprocal Trade Agreements Acts of the 1930's-1950's, which combined the unconditional most-favored-nation clause with a bilateral bargaining procedure. In this respect the GATT procedure of multilateral bargaining is vastly superior to bilateral bargaining. Within limits set by the technical feasibility of multilateral negotiation it is free of the limitations of bilateral bargaining, since it enables countries giving concessions to claim concessions from third parties enjoying such spill-overs, thus increasing the incentive to bargain for tariff reductions, and also permits the smaller countries to obtain some leverage with the concessions they can offer. In addition, the fact that adherence to GATT confers the right to most-favored-nation treatment from all other members provides a powerful incentive to members to abide by bargains once they have been entered into; in contrast, under the pre-vious system of bilateral treaties, abrogation of an agreement exposed a country to retaliation only from the other party to the treaty. This multilateral reinforcement of tariff agreements provides some further advantage to the smaller countries.[14]

All in all, however, while multilateral bargaining does give the smaller countries more effective participation in the negotiation of tariff reductions, the reciprocity principle in particular ensures that the bargaining will be dominated by the larger developed countries. This is one point of criticism of GATT by the less developed countries. The criticism has, however, been acknowledged by GATT and in the preparations for the Kennedy Round it has been explicitly agreed that the developed countries will make a special effort to negotiate reduc-tions of barriers to the exports of less developed countries, but that they cannot expect to receive reciprocity from the less developed countries.

INTERNATIONAL INSTITUTIONS AND THE LESS DEVELOPED COUNTRIES

Just as the nature and functions of international institutions have been modified in response to the changing political and economic relations among the major Western nations, so have these institutions been evolving in response to the growing and changing needs of the less de-veloped countries. They have done so to such an extent as to make some of the contemporary criticism of their roles in facilitating de-velopment anachronistic or misinformed.

Functions of International Institutions

Ever since the establishment of the International Monetary Fund there have been strong forces—associated first with the dollar shortage and subsequently with the dollar glut—working to displace it from the cen-

[14] These points are elaborated in Curzon, *op. cit.*

tral position it was intended to occupy in monetary affairs. The field has been dominated instead by politically motivated and oriented direct relationships between the United States and the major European countries. Partly for this reason, partly because less developed countries have a stronger propensity than developed countries to get into balance-of-payments difficulties through inflation and to resort to multiple-exchange-rate practices to deal with them—and also because their exchange rates are not regarded as sacrosanct in the same way as those of the large developed countries—the ordinary operations of the Fund have become increasingly concerned with the monetary problems of less developed countries, particularly in Latin America. The Fund has developed the technique of stand-by credits and waivers of the quota limitations on borrowings and has also evolved standards to be imposed on countries receiving its help in exchange-rate reform. These requirements, which insist on monetary stability and the halting of inflationary financing, are naturally rarely popular in the countries obliged to attempt to conform to them; in some cases the consequences of conformity have, at least superficially, been the reverse of gratifying. A more significant innovation, designed specifically to meet the balance-of-payments problems of less developed countries, has been the establishment of a Fund scheme for the short-to-medium-term compensatory financing of deficits arising from declines in the export earnings of such countries through circumstances beyond their control.

The International Bank, in contrast to the Fund, was designed to facilitate the economic development of the less developed countries. While it remains a lender of capital on quasi-commercial terms, its approach has broadened considerably; its country work includes, among other things, reports that perform the useful function of pre-investment surveys, and it has taken an active part in arranging aid consortia for India and Pakistan and consultative groups for other less developed countries. The establishment of the International Development Association (IDA), an agency for lending on very soft terms (three-quarters of 1 percent with fifty-year maturities) which the Bank manages, now enables it to supplement lending on more or less commercial terms by financing that is virtually indistinguishable from development aid; recently the Bank has begun transferring funds to IDA from its own surplus.

Another agency, the Development Assistance Committee (DAC) of the OECD, established on the initiative of the United States, coordi-

B

nates and reviews the bilateral aid policies of its fifteen members (which account for over 95 percent of free world bilateral aid). Through DAC, the United States has been working to increase the flow of aid from other Western countries, to establish easier terms of lending, and to broaden the geographical distribution of aid from European countries beyond their former overseas dependencies.

The international instrument concerned with international trade, the General Agreement on Tariffs and Trade, incorporates a recognition that its principles of protection must be modified to allow for the development needs of the less developed countries. Specifically, it recognizes that these countries need more "flexibility" in their tariff structures for development and revenue needs, that tariffs may be inadequate and quantitative restrictions necessary to assist developing industries, and that the high demand for imports associated with the development process may require greater resort to quantitative restrictions under the balance-of-payments exception. These more lax standards have been applied in setting the terms of membership in GATT for less developed countries and also in determining the concessions required of the less developed countries in return for the tariff concessions agreed on by the developed countries in tariff bargaining under GATT.

Apart from according less developed countries this somewhat favored position, GATT has been taking an increasing interest in their trade problems since the middle 1950's. That interest has taken the form of the collection of information on trade trends and problems through intensive committee and Secretariat work, the accumulation of information leading to understanding and documentation of the problems and to pressure on the membership to take action regarding them.

An important investigation commissioned by GATT, the "Haberler Report"[15] on trends in international trade, revealed the failure of the exports of less developed countries to grow as rapidly as those of the developed countries and assigned an important part of the cause to tariffs and other barriers erected by the developed countries against imports of products in which the less developed countries had a particular exporting interest. In consequence, the problem of expanding the exports of less developed countries was assigned an important place in

[15] *Trends in International Trade,* A Report by a Panel of Experts (Geneva: General Agreement on Tariffs and Trade, 1958).

the program for trade expansion inaugurated in 1958, one of three committees being assigned to it. The committee made a commodity-by-commodity study of products important to the less developed countries, identifying barriers to trade and making recommendations about them; pressure was subsequently brought to bear (with moderate success) on members to implement the recommendations. This process resulted in the 1961 Declaration on Promotion of the Trade of Less Developed Countries and subsequently in the 1963 Programme of Action. Meanwhile, the committee's activities have broadened to include study of the development plans of particular countries, aimed at identifying export potential. The committee has also been instrumental in securing the establishment of a trade information and trade promotion center in GATT, which among other things is intended to train the trade officials of less developed countries in export promotion techniques.

The GATT Action Program

The Programme of Action, endorsed with reservations by the contracting parties to GATT on May 21, 1963, contained the following eight points:

Standstill provision. No new tariff or non-tariff barriers should be erected by industrialized countries against the export trade of any less-developed country in the products identified as of particular interest to the less-developed countries. In this connexion the less-developed countries would particularly mention barriers of a discriminatory nature.

Elimination of quantitative restrictions. Quantitative restrictions on imports from less-developed countries which are inconsistent with the provisions of the GATT shall be eliminated within a period of one year. Where, on consultation between the industrialized and the less-developed countries concerned, it is established that there are special problems which prevent action being taken within this period, the restriction on such items would be progressively reduced and eliminated by 31 December 1965.

Duty-free entry for tropical products. Duty-free entry into the industrialized countries shall be granted to tropical products by 31 December 1963.

Elimination of tariffs on primary products. Industrialized countries shall agree to the elimination of customs tariffs on the primary products important in the trade of less developed countries.

Reduction and elimination of tariff barriers to exports of semi-processed products from less-developed countries. Industrialized countries should also prepare urgently a schedule for the reduction and elimination of tariff barriers to exports of semiprocessed and processed products from less-developed countries, providing for a reduction of at least 50 percent of the present duties over the next three years.

Progressive reduction of internal fiscal charges and revenue duties. Industrialized countries shall progressively reduce internal charges and revenue duties on products wholly or mainly produced in less-developed countries with a view to their elimination by 31 December 1965.

Reporting procedures. Industrialized countries maintaining the above-mentioned barriers shall report to the GATT secretariat in July of each year on the steps taken by them during the preceding year to implement these decisions and on the measures which they propose to take over the next twelve months to provide larger access for the products of less-developed countries.

Other measures. Contracting parties should also give urgent consideration to the adoption of other appropriate measures which would facilitate the efforts of less-developed countries to diversify their economies, strengthen their export capacity, and increase their earnings from overseas sales.[16]

Little of substance has resulted from the Programme of Action. The endorsement of it was in fact a formal gesture masking deep divisions within the membership, particularly between the Common Market countries and the other industrialized countries. The latter agreed to the Programme, subject to reservations safeguarding their other obligations and their rights in GATT. The Common Market countries, on the other hand, while endorsing in principle the objectives of the Programme, criticized the first seven points as being concerned only with the removal of trade barriers and argued that positive measures for increasing the export earnings of the less developed countries as a whole were required. To this end they recommended: (a) an effort to organize international trade in products of interest to the less developed countries, taking account of the differences in competitive ability among such countries; (b) an effort to ensure increasing exports at "remunerative, equitable and stable prices" for the less developed countries producing primary products, together with selective measures for expanding exports of processed and semiprocessed products. The division between the two groups of countries reflected the conflict between the nondiscriminatory GATT approach and the discriminatory Common Market approach, a conflict which was to reappear in UNCTAD and which prevented the 1963 meeting of GATT from coming to any agreement on the question of free access to the markets of industrialized countries for tropical products (with the minor exceptions of tea and tropical hardwoods). For their part, the less developed countries regarded the first seven points of the Programme as minimal,

---

[16] *The Role of GATT in Relation to Trade and Development,* pp. 34-35.

pinning their hopes on the eighth, and were mostly concerned to preserve their freedom of tariff action from the standstill provision.

In connection with the eighth point, a working party was set up to study two specific proposals: the granting of preferences on selected products by industrialized countries to less developed countries as a whole; and the granting of preferences on selected products by less developed countries to all other less developed countries. These proposals obviously represent a sharp departure from the basic principles of GATT, and the willingness at least to study them represents a substantial response by GATT to the demands of the less developed countries.

The Cotton Textiles Arrangement

One further GATT activity, the Long-Term Arrangement on Cotton Textiles, effective for the five-year period beginning October 1, 1962, was the outgrowth of the "disruption" of the cotton textile markets in a number of developed countries, particularly the United States, Canada, and the United Kingdom, by competition from less developed producers. Rapid growth of low-priced exports from a number of Asian countries (Japan, India, Pakistan, Hong Kong) was concentrated on these markets because of lower trade barriers than existed in other markets (specifically those of the European countries), and especially the absence of quantitative import restrictions. The resulting difficulties for domestic producers had prompted these countries to resort to putting pressure on the exporting countries to exercise "voluntary" export restriction, a practice clearly adverse to the economic development and balance-of-payments objectives of those countries. The Long-Term Arrangement, initiated by the United States, was designed to relieve the situation by multilateralizing the problem and preventing disruption of markets while allowing a steady expansion of textile exports by the less developed countries. It provides that no country may introduce new import restrictions, that existing restrictions must be progressively relaxed and eliminated as soon as possible, and that quotas maintained be expanded at an agreed percentage rate, as far as possible leading to their disappearance within five years.

On the other hand, it allows importing countries, if they can prove market disruption or the threat of disruption—and this situation is carefully defined by the Arrangement, not left to the discretion of the individual country—to ask for export restraints at a level not lower than the previous twelve months' imports. Each extension of export restraints automatically raises the restrained level of imports by 5 percent. The Arrangement thus embodies a compromise between the exporting countries' growing need for markets and capacity to supply them competitively, and the importing countries' concern to avoid the difficulties and dislocations occasioned by rapid growth of competition for their domestic producers. The compromise is obviously superior to the unilateral use of protection and political power to prevent trade from reflecting changes in comparative advantage. The developed countries in GATT have, however, declined to consider similar arrangements for other products where the same problems have arisen.[17] In practice, largely owing to the strength of protectionist forces in the United States, the Arrangement has not worked in the trade-expansionary way intended, much to the dissatisfaction of the less developed participants in it.

GATT Chapter on Trade and Development

On February 8, 1965, the contracting parties to GATT formally signified their growing concern for the trade problems of less developed countries by adding a new chapter (Part IV) on trade and development to the General Agreement. The chapter contains three articles. Article XXXVI, on principles and objectives, states the need for a rapid and sustained expansion of export earnings by these countries and for positive efforts to ensure them an appropriate share in the growth of world trade; the need to provide better conditions of access to world markets for primary products "and wherever appropriate to devise measures designed to stabilize and improve conditions of world markets in these products, including in particular measures designed to attain stable, equitable and remunerative prices"; the need for increased access to markets for processed and manufactured products of particular current or potential interest to less developed countries; and the principle that developed countries do not expect reciprocity for commitments to reduce barriers to the trade of less developed countries. Article XXXVII, on commitments, pledges the developed contracting parties to accord high priority to the reduction and elimination of barriers to products of particular export interest to the less de-

---

[17] See Curzon, op. cit., pp. 254-58, where toys, transistors, and typewriters are mentioned as having been specifically excluded from consideration.

veloped contracting parties, including barriers that differentiate unreasonably between such products in their primary and in their processed form; to refrain from increasing barriers against such products; and to refrain from increasing, and give high priority to reducing, fiscal measures hindering the growth of consumption of primary products wholly or mainly produced in less developed contracting parties. Article XXXVIII, on joint action, provides for collaboration in implementing the objectives.

FINANCIAL AID AND TECHNICAL ASSISTANCE

Financial aid and technical assistance are the main media through which the developed countries have so far sought to promote the economic development of the less developed countries.[18] Both are supplied in two ways: bilaterally (directly from the nation providing the resources to the nation receiving them) and multilaterally (through international institutions which deal directly with the recipient nation). Technical assistance takes two main forms: technical assistance proper —the supplying of technical experts from outside, and the training of nationals of the less developed country in required skills—and preinvestment programs—surveys of investment prospects, feasibility studies, and the establishment of training institutions. Financial aid takes three main forms: grants, loans, and the transfer of resources through sales for the recipient countries' currency (almost exclusively U.S. contributions of surplus agricultural commodities under P.L. 480).

Technical assistance is an integral part of the bilateral aid program of each of the developed countries. Substantial technical assistance is also provided by the United Nations, in four major ways: through technical assistance proper (a) provided by the United Nations and financed from its own budget, (b) provided by the specialized agencies of the United Nations and financed by their own budgets, (c) provided by the specialized agencies and financed from voluntary contributions from member nations channeled through the Expanded Program of Technical Assistance; and (d) through preinvestment activities financed and executed by the United Nations Special Fund. This variety of U.N. effort is alleged to be untidy and inefficient; the United States pressed for, and the Economic and Social Council of the U.N.

---

[18] For a fuller account of existing development assistance programs, related to the concept of the "Development Decade," see Gardner, *op. cit.*, Chap. 5.

recommended, the merger of the latter two programs into a single United Nations Development Program, which came into being on January 1, 1966.

The gross total of foreign aid provided to the less developed countries is currently running (in very broad figures) around $10 billion a year.[19] Of this total the United States provides nearly half: about $3 billion in financial assistance, mostly in the form of long-term low-interest loans, and about $1.5 billion in commodities through the Food for Peace Program (P.L. 480). Other noncommunist developed countries provide $3 billion, and the communist countries a little under $1 billion. About $1 billion a year is provided through the International Bank (a specialized agency of the United Nations) and its affiliate the International Development Association, and about $0.5 billion through regional development agencies (the Inter-American Development Bank and the European Development Fund). Thus bilateral aid predominates by far over multilateral aid.

From the points of view of efficiency of staffing and administration of aid projects, equity of distribution of aid among the less developed countries, and maintenance of harmonious relations between the countries supplying and the countries receiving aid, there is much to be said in favor of providing a substantially higher proportion of aid through multilateral channels. In the 1950's it was strongly recommended in the United Nations that this be done through establishment of a special U.N. fund for economic development. The proposal failed, however, largely as a result of strong opposition from the United States, which was averse to the possibility that American aid might thereby be channeled to communist countries, doubtful that enough donor participation would ensue to constitute a truly international operation, and skeptical that standards adequate for the successful application of external aid would be maintained.

The $10 billion of aid and its distribution by sources lump together, as is general practice, the money values of grants, loans and commodity contributions. To do this, however, is to ignore important differences among these forms of aid and to overstate the amount of real resources made available by them to the less developed countries. Specifically, grants are genuine transfers of resources, though the tying of them to purchases in the donor country may, by obliging the recipient to pay higher prices than it could obtain elsewhere, make their real

---

[19] Figures, from Gardner, *op. cit.*, are intended to give only broad orders of magnitude.

value less than the nominal amount would suggest. Commodity contributions are also genuine transfers, though for a variety of reasons the prices at which they are valued may far exceed their real cost to the country making the contribution and real value to the country receiving it.

Loans, however, are not in themselves genuine transfers of resources, since they have to be repaid. They involve an element of transfer only to the extent that the interest rates charged and the terms of repayment involve an element of subsidy, by comparison with the normal rates and terms either for similar commercial loans in the lending country or for alternative sources of finance for the borrowing country. It has been calculated that the total aid commitments of seven Western European countries, Canada and the United States in 1962, nominally amounting to $7.7 billion, were actually worth $5.3 billion when only the subsidy element in loans was counted, and that if in addition P. L. 480 exports were valued at world market instead of accounting prices, the total would have been $4.7 billion.[20] The fact that aid given in the form of loans transfers less real resources than its nominal value appears from the less developed country side of the transaction as the "burden of debt service" imposed by such aid.

One other feature of aid in the form of loans is their availability almost exclusively for the financing of specific projects, not for the general support of a country's development program as a whole; often they are available only for the foreign exchange component of the total expenditure on the project. These restrictions obviously limit the usefulness of loan availability to the less developed countries.

"TOWARDS A NEW TRADE POLICY FOR DEVELOPMENT"[21]

In 1961 the General Assembly of the United Nations, following a proposal by President Kennedy, officially designated the present decade as the United Nations Development Decade—a period in which "member

[20] Pincus, in *Review of Economics and Statistics*, p. 364, assuming loan payments discounted at each country's domestic long-term interest rate; Pincus' figures have been rounded. A rough estimate, based on Pincus' calculations, of the value of P.L. 480 shipments at prices that would have cleared the world market or induced the United States to store wheat rather than sell it indicates that the total value of aid would have been about $4.2 billion on this basis.

[21] Title of the report by Raúl Prebisch, Secretary-General of the United Nations Conference on Trade and Development (United Nations, 1964). A brief account of the report is given here.

states and their peoples will intensify their efforts to mobilize and sustain support for the measures required on the part of both developed and developing countries to accelerate progress towards self-sustaining growth."

Simultaneously, the General Assembly adopted a resolution entitled "International Trade as the Primary Instrument for Economic Development," and requested the Secretary-General of the United Nations to ascertain the advisability of holding an international conference on trade and development problems. The 1962 Cairo conference on the problems of economic development strongly recommended the early convening of such a conference, and in the same year the Economic and Social Council, at the initiative of the communist bloc and with strong support from the less developed countries, resolved to convene such a conference early in 1964. A thirty-two-nation preparatory committee was set up and a great deal of preparatory work was done by the less developed countries through the regional commissions of the United Nations. These preparations were organized by the secretary-general of the conference, Dr. Raúl Prebisch, who outlined the main issues to be discussed in the conference and suggested an integrated program of measures for dealing with them. His report is important both because it presents an unusually comprehensive, well-balanced, and philosophically coherent analysis and set of recommendations for promoting the development of the less developed countries through changes in the trade policy of the developed countries, and because it largely determined the proceedings of the conference, of which Dr. Prebisch was to an extraordinary degree the guide and mentor.[22]

Need for a New Policy

The main theme of the report is the need for a positive new trade policy for development, as contrasted with the Havana Charter and GATT's allegedly negative policy of removing restrictions to trade; that new policy must be based on a political decision by the developed ("industrialized") countries to assist the less developed ("developing") countries in conformity with the obligations of the Development Decade. The analysis is set in a three-phase historical perspective. The nine-

[22] "Dr. Prebisch was not only the Secretary-General of U.N.C.T.A.D., but its *spiritus rector*, and, above all, its *hortatory economist*, a function quite unusual for a Secretariat official. It was he who conceived the platform for the Group of Seventy-Seven developing nations in Geneva." (Henry Simon Bloch, *The Challenge of the World Trade Conference* [School of International Affairs, Columbia University; one of a series of Occasional Papers, 1964-65], p. 9.)

teenth century pattern of development, centered on a resource-scarce and consequently free-trading United Kingdom, involved the export of manufactures from the center in exchange for foodstuffs and raw materials from the periphery which resulted in the development (though limited) of the periphery. This pattern broke down with the emergence as center country of the resource-rich and protectionist United States, the rise of agricultural protectionism in Europe, and the constriction of trade and collapse of commodity prices in the Great Depression, which set the developing countries off on the path of "inward-looking industrialization" based on import-substitution. The contemporary phase comprises the reconstruction of the international economic order in the postwar period with the modernization of Europe, and the emergence of new problems for trade policy associated with the needs for exports of the less developed countries.

The needs of the less developed countries, the report asserts, are the result of a "persistent trend towards external imbalance" inherent in the development process and can be countered only within limits by import-substitution policies. Development based on import-substitution becomes increasingly difficult as it progresses, due to the size limitations of national markets, and also generates new demands for imports of capital goods and, as income rises, for imports of consumer durables. Attention is deliberately concentrated on the problems of the more developed "developing" countries (and particularly the Latin American countries with which Dr. Prebisch is most familiar), which are argued to typify the problems that other less developed countries will eventually encounter.

The problem, as the report presents it, is to bridge the prospective "trade gap" implicit in the difference between the growth of imports (and of debt service payments) required to implement the Development Decade target of a 5 percent growth rate and the prospective slower growth of export earnings. The U.N. Secretariat has projected a trade gap of $20 billion by 1970, to be compared with the $10 billion of foreign aid now being provided; this figure is probably a substantial overestimate—Dr. Bela Balassa, on the basis of a much more elaborate statistical analysis, reaches alternative estimates in the neighborhood of $9.4-$12.0 billion[23]—and should be regarded primarily as a dramatizing statistic.

The solutions recommended for bridging the trade gap are derived

[23] Bela A. Balassa, *Trade Prospects for Developing Countries* (Richard D. Irwin, Inc., 1964), pp. 104-05.

from an economic analysis of the export and industrialization problems of the less developed countries that is original with Dr. Prebisch and from a philosophy of international economic policy that might be described as the internationalization of protectionism for less developed countries, or the inversion of protection in developed countries in favor of the less developed countries. The analysis is concerned with two major problems, the relatively slow growth of earnings from exports of primary products and the need for industrializing countries to export manufactures.

The explanation for the slow growth of earnings from exports of primary products is familiar from Dr. Prebisch's previous writings. It involves the influence of technical progress in developed countries in providing synthetic substitutes for natural primary products and reducing the raw material content of manufactures, the influence of the relatively lower income-elasticity of demand for primary products as compared with manufactures, and the influence of technical progress in the agriculture of the developed countries in increasing domestic supplies. These "structural" factors are aggravated by the policies of price supports, restriction of market access, subsidized export of agricultural surpluses, and heavy taxation of imports substitutable for domestic products applied to maintain the incomes of domestic producers, policies which are directly harmful in various ways to the competing exports of less developed countries. Dr. Prebisch's central proposition, however, is that even in the absence of protectionist policies in the developed countries, there is a long-run tendency for the relative prices of primary products to deteriorate in relative terms, thus reducing the export earnings of countries dependent on the export of primary products below what they would otherwise be.

The alleged long-run tendency of the terms of trade to move against primary products is not consistent with the empirical evidence, which shows a succession of upward and downward short- and medium-term trends with no clear long-term movement in either direction; nor are the theoretical explanations presented to support it logically satisfactory.[24] Nor, again, is there any sound theoretical reason for attaching welfare significance to the terms of trade between products, when population and relative productivities are changing. Nevertheless, the alleged adverse trend of the terms of trade of primary products

[24] See Appendix A for a more detailed discussion of Prebisch's empirical and theoretical views on the trend of the terms of trade of less developed countries.

is the basis of the recommendations for trade policy in this field. It is asserted that the worsening of these terms of trade represents an income transfer from producers in the less developed countries to consumers in the developed countries; that the developed countries attempt to eliminate such transfers within their own economies by price-support policies; and that they should recognize a political obligation to transfer back the income accruing to them from the worsening of the primary exporting countries' terms of trade. The industrialized countries, in short, should take a political decision in favor of parity prices for the primary products exported by the developing countries.

This decision, it is recommended, should be implemented by two complementary methods. The first is the extended use of international commodity agreements, designed to guarantee fair terms of market access and equitable prices to the exporting countries. It is pointed out that prices could be raised to the exporter without being raised to the consumer by eliminating existing tariffs and excise taxes, and that overproduction in response to these prices could be avoided by intensifying present practices of paying producers in the less developed countries less than the world market price. The second method, which would be employed where the maintenance of equitable prices would constrain consumption, is compensatory finance—the payment of sums adequate to compensate less developed countries for the losses incurred, not merely in export proceeds but for their development programs as a whole, as a result of worsening terms of trade. This part of the Prebisch program therefore entails extending to primary-producing less developed countries the types of protection that developed countries extend to their own primary producers, with the significant difference that the subsidies involved would go to the governments and not the individual producers of those countries.[25]

---

[25] This feature removes the apparent conflict that some commentators have noticed between the objective of industrialization of the less developed countries and the demand for broader market access for their exports of primary products, since it would channel the increased export earnings into industrialization while dampening the incentives to producers to expand primary production.

A knotty problem for commodity policy is raised by surplus commodity disposal, which benefits net-importing and damages net-exporting less developed countries. The report walks the fence on this issue, stressing the relatively small volume of such disposal (which, however, does not make its influence on prices negligible) and the prospect that in time the problem will be removed by the world's growing need for food (this prospect is inconsistent with the asserted long-run adverse trend of primary product prices).

Need for Industrial Exports

The second theme of the analysis is the developing countries' need to export manufactured products. This is partly a need for export earnings and partly a requirement of efficient industrialization. The development of exports of manufactures ought, it is argued, to be a complement of industrialization, as it was in the nineteenth-century development of countries that fostered development by protection. But protection in the less developed countries in the 1930's and subsequently has been of a different type, described as promoting industrialization "piecemeal" and "in watertight compartments," and not conducive to industrial exporting. Latin American experience is cited to illustrate the problems: the increasing difficulty of import substitution as it progresses, and the increasing demands for complementary industrial imports that accompany it; the vicious circle of protectionism in which small domestic markets and high costs reinforce each other in creating industries unable to compete in the world market; the unplanned increase in protectionism in response to balance-of-payments problems, resulting in the heaviest protection being given to nonessentials; the increasing concentration of imports on essentials, making further compression of imports harder and increasingly injurious to growth; and the insulation of producers in the national market from healthy competition. The way out of these difficulties, it is argued, is through increased industrial exports. Serious obstacles are imposed, however, by such barriers of the industrialized countries as differential tariffs, quantitative restrictions and "voluntary" agreements to prevent disruption of domestic markets, administrative procedures, and discriminatory practices of private enterprise. The protection exercised by the developing countries against each others' industrial exports is, likewise, a serious obstacle.

In addition to a general recommendation for greater effort in export promotion, two main lines of solution are proposed. The first is a new substitution policy within the regional groupings of less developed countries, to be implemented by granting preferences to the industrial exports of other less developed countries over those of developed countries; these preferences are intended to allow scope for competition, specialization on the basis of comparative advantage, and exploitation of economies of scale. The second solution, to which more importance is attached, is the granting by the developed countries of temporary preferences on the industrial exports of the less developed countries. This proposal, which is put forward as a logical extension of the infant-industry argument,[26] envisages free entry for exports of manufactures of the less developed countries into the markets of the developed countries for a period of ten years for each product from the initiation of its export by each country, thus providing temporary protection against competition from more developed rivals. These preferences would apply to all industrial products, subject to the discretionary reservation of a certain proportion of them by each industrialized country; for the products thus reserved, preferences could be given to the least developed countries, which otherwise might be unable to compete with the more developed countries. The preferences would be subject to global quotas for each of the developed countries and also possibly to quotas for individual products; these quotas would be used as indicative targets for imports of industrial products from less developed countries.

No reciprocal concessions would be expected of the less developed countries, though it is suggested that, in the interest of domestic efficiency, they might find it advantageous to reduce their high tariffs. In this connection, Prebisch develops a sophisticated and economically meretricious distinction between "conventional" and "real" reciprocity, according to which unilateral tariff reduction by a developed country in favor of a less developed one increases the capacity of the latter

---

[26] The logic is indeed the infant-industry logic of protection—temporary protection of an industry that requires a "learning period" to become competitive—reinforced by recognition of the need for a market on a scale larger than the domestic economy can provide; but the traditional argument called for transitional support of the industry at the expense of the consumers of the developing country, whereas the argument for preferences calls for support at the expense of the consumers of the developed countries (indirectly, by foregoing tariff receipts) thereby introducing an implicit transfer of resources from the developed to the developing countries. In short, the argument for preferences asks the developed country to contribute a part of the cost of the "investment" made in the learning process. The insistence that the argument for preferences is a logical extension of the infant-industry argument is obviously aimed at exploiting the permission of infant-industry protection under Article XVIII of GATT; the connection with GATT rules is explicitly made by Raymond Vernon (*Problems and Prospects in the Export of Manufactured Goods from the Less Developed Countries* [United Nations Conference on Trade and Development, E/Conf. 46/P/2], p. 28) who, like Prebisch, fails to point out the difference between the two policies with respect to who pays the cost of protection. Note that the use of a production subsidy in place of a tariff would eliminate the problem of restricted domestic markets without imposing part of the cost of protection on the foreign consumer.

to import the former's goods and expands world trade (real reciprocity), whereas an exchange of concessions (conventional reciprocity) makes the less developed country more dependent on its primary product exports and condemns it—and world trade—to slower growth.[27] The argument implicitly assumes that relative prices are constant, unless altered by protection, and that what adjusts to demand is quantities produced, not relative prices. Export earnings of less developed countries from advanced countries are taken as a datum determined entirely by the developed countries' policies; these earnings govern the less developed countries' imports of manufactures; protection in the less developed countries determines the amount of domestic industrial production and the total industrial consumption in these countries and their industrial production is taken to measure their growth. Each of these assumptions is an oversimplification that excludes rational analysis of trade policy problems. As in the case of primary commodity policy, the recommendation of unilateral preferences for the industrial exports of the less developed countries entails an inversion of the protectionist policies of the developed countries in favor of the less developed.

The proposal of preferences for the industrial exports of the less developed countries and also the proposal for commodity agreements raise one difficult problem: the resulting losses to less developed countries enjoying discriminatory preferences in the European Common Market and (to a lesser extent) in the British preferential system. The solution proposed (rather vaguely) is that steps should be taken to compensate those countries for their losses.

Other Needs

In addition to the two major sets of proposals, the report deals with a variety of other matters. One important matter is the supply of foreign aid, where two problems are discerned. The first is the offsetting of aid by the effects of deteriorating terms of trade; here emphasis is laid on the importance of the proposed compensatory financing for effective development planning and it is made clear that compensatory financing is to be additional to the flow of aid, for which a target of 1 percent of national income in the developed countries has already been set. The second problem is the critical burden of debt service; consol-

---

[27] Prebisch, *op. cit.*, pp. 29-31.

idation of debts and extension of payment periods is recommended. Another topic is the possibility of expanding trade with the communist bloc, to which a hopeful but indecisive chapter is devoted. A third, to which some attention is given, is the cost of maritime freight and insurance and the impact of shipping conference rates, and the possibility of developing regional shipping and insurance services.

To implement its new positive policy for trade to promote development, the report calls for the requisite changes in the rules of GATT. It also suggests the establishment of a new institution, within the United Nations framework, to be concerned with trade policy problems from the specific point of view of promoting economic development. It proposes periodic reconvention of the United Nations Conference on Trade and Development and the establishment of a standing committee to act as a preparatory committee for the conferences and a general reviewing and examining body.

While the report is primarily concerned with measures to be taken in the trade field by the developed countries, it contains in addition to its strictures on "inward-looking industrialization" a strong statement of the responsibility of the less developed countries to introduce basic social changes required to allow the process of industrialization to "take off." These changes, however, are described as changes that the developed countries should support but cannot and should not insist on, especially as an alternative to taking action themselves.

THE UNITED NATIONS CONFERENCE ON TRADE AND DEVELOPMENT

The United Nations Conference on Trade and Development met in Geneva from March 23 to June 16, 1964.[28] It was the largest such conference ever held, assembling over 2,000 delegates from 120 countries and the Vatican, and its proceedings covered the whole field of trade and development problems and policy.

Following the lines of the Prebisch report, the work of the conference was organized in five committees dealing with international commodity problems, trade in semimanufactures and manufactured

---

[28] This review of the conference draws on Bloch, *op. cit.*, and on Frederick Strauss, *Report on the United Nations Conference on Trade and Development*, U.S. Department of Commerce, Bureau of International Commerce, July 1964 (mimeographed).

goods, the financing of development, continuing institutional arrangements, and expansion of international trade and its significance for
economic development (including regional arrangements and the preparation of principles governing commercial policy for development).
In fact, however, the committees proved unwieldy and the bulk of the
work was done by special working parties, drafting committees, and
conciliation groups.

The major reason for the change in procedure was that the seventy-
five less developed countries present, which possessed a clear majority
of the voting power, determined (under the inspiration of Dr. Prebisch) to present a united front. They succeeded in maintaining the
principle of presenting agreed resolutions jointly, even on issues on
which their interests were fundamentally at variance (such as surplus
food disposal and nondiscriminatory preferences in developed countries' markets). With automatic majorities assured, it quickly became
apparent that outvoting the developed countries on motions that demanded that those same countries give concessions they were unwilling
to grant would lead nowhere; and (again under the mentorship of Dr.
Prebisch) the focus of the conference turned to working out through
conciliation (frequently on a last-minute basis) forms of wording that
were limited to stating the issues and the possible lines of action in a
way that some or most of the developed countries from which concessions were demanded could accept. Even on this basis there were many
areas in which agreement, particularly the agreement of the United
States, could not be reached.

In contrast to the unity of the less developed countries, the developed countries—both Western and communist—were divided among
themselves and ill-prepared for the encounter with the united group. It
was soon evident that the communist countries, which had strongly
supported the conference, had little of real significance to offer the less
developed countries, whose attention consequently concentrated on the
trade policies of the Western countries. The Western countries differed
sharply in their responses to the demands of the less developed countries and the sympathy they appeared to evince for their problems,
with the United States appearing to be the most uncompromisingly
hostile to the new ideas put forward by the less developed countries.
Broadly speaking, the United States stood for further action along
GATT lines, but was absolutely opposed to the idea of preferences for
less developed countries in developed-country markets and was pre-

pared to conciliate only on regional cooperation to increase trade among the less developed countries and on the financial questions of increasing the supply of compensatory finance, reducing the burden of debt service, and increasing the supply of public and private capital for development (the "soft option").

The French, and supporting them the other Common Market countries, consistently advocated a cumbersome scheme for "organizing" the markets for primary products and for imports of manufactures and semimanufactures, so as to ensure remunerative prices, on a discriminatory basis taking account of the stage of economic development of each trading country. The British (and other EFTA and Commonwealth countries), besides being sympathetic on financial issues, were prepared to contemplate the generalization of Commonwealth preferences to all less developed countries; they were ambivalent, however, about international commodity agreements owing on the one hand to Britain's heavy dependence on imports of food and raw materials and on the other to the interests of leading Commonwealth countries in exports of primary products.

Sources of Disagreement

Within the committee on primary products, there was sharp disagreement over whether priority should be accorded to improved market access (the British and American view) or to "market organization" or "stabilization" (the French-led Common Market view); this issue was conciliated only by a resolution allowing a free choice of the alternatives. In the committee on trade in semimanufactures and manufactured products, the main source of disagreements was the issue of preferences, on which both less developed and developed countries were divided. The less developed countries disagreed about whether the purpose of preferences was to increase export proceeds or support infant industries; whether preferences should be temporary, permanent, or for the duration of the period of underdevelopment; whether preferences should apply equally to all less developed countries or be differentiated by degree of development; and whether existing preferences enjoyed by some countries should be retained at the expense of the rest or sacrificed in favor of general preferences for all. Nevertheless, the less developed countries managed to produce a consolidated joint recommendation.

The developed countries differed even more sharply. The United

States flatly refused to consider preferences at all, on the grounds that they would not significantly expand less developed countries' export earnings, that they would mean new discrimination and foster uneconomic production, that they would impede general tariff reduction by creating vested interests, and that they would foster undesirable political dependency. The other developed countries differed on whether preferences should be accorded generally (the British position) or selectively (the French position) to less developed countries, and whether it was a necessary precondition for all developed countries to participate in granting the preferences. Eventually, the less developed countries withdrew their consolidated resolution on preferences; the final resolution noted the disagreement among the developed countries over preferences versus the most-favored-nation principle and passed the problem on to a committee of government representatives from developed and less developed nations to be established by the Secretary-General of the United Nations.

Only the committee on financial problems found it easy to reach agreement—perhaps partly because generosity with the taxpayers' money comes more naturally than generosity in disposing of protectionist positions built up by the lobbying of vested interests and the political designs of commercial policy. The committee on the expansion of trade failed to arrive at any agreement on the principles that should govern commercial policy and trading arrangements for economic development, owing to the great differences that appeared between what the less developed countries insisted was desirable and what the developed countries were prepared to consider. This failure influenced the decisions of the committee on continuing machinery. Some of the less developed countries, and presumably the communist bloc, had envisaged a new international trade organization that would replace the Havana Charter and absorb GATT. Instead, the final resolution called for a periodic reconvening of UNCTAD; for the establishment of a trade and development board composed of representatives of fifty-five nations in which the less developed countries predominate (the standing committee recommended in the Prebisch report) and for three committees of that board to deal respectively with commodity trade, trade in manufactures, and invisibles and financing related to trade; and for the provision of a secretariat. This recommendation, however, was agreed on only after a conciliation process in which the United

States insisted on, and obtained, acceptance of the principle that the voting procedure in the board must emphasize the prior conciliation of disagreements rather than their exacerbation by use of the automatic voting majority of the less developed countries.

The fact that the less developed countries—thanks to the secretariat— were well prepared for the conference, while the developed countries were not, gave them the initiative. This had two significant consequences for the proceedings and results of the conference. In the first place, there was a marked tendency to discount the contributions of the existing international institutions, particularly GATT, to the solution of problems of trade and development and to favor new ad hoc arrangements. Secondly, and naturally enough, relatively little attention was given to reforms that the less developed countries themselves could introduce to improve their trade prospects, these being regarded somewhat disingenuously as matters of domestic policy concern only.[29]

Final Act

The manifold resolutions and recommendations of the conference were embodied in its final act[30] which contained inter alia fifteen general and thirteen special principles to govern international trade relations and trade policies conducive to development. As a consequence of conciliation, these had been considerably watered down by comparison with what the less developed nations had proposed; nevertheless, many of them were unacceptable to one or more developed countries, and they were passed over the opposition of the latter by the force majeure of the less developed countries supported (with minor exceptions) by the votes of the communist bloc. In the final voting the Common Market countries (with the exception of the Federal Republic of Germany) followed the practice of abstention, as for the most part did Japan and the members of EFTA other than the United Kingdom. As a result the United States appeared frequently as the sole opponent of a general consensus favorable to the desires of the less developed group, or as an

[29] The policies of the less developed countries that inhibit their exports are discussed in Chapters II and III. These policies are an important component in the setting of the problem raised for U.S. commercial policy by UNCTAD, but for the reason given in the text it has proved convenient to defer detailed discussion of their nature.

[30] *Final Act of the United Nations Conference on Trade and Development* (United Nations, E/Conf. 46/L.28, June 16, 1964).

opponent supported only by one or two of the senior members of the British Commonwealth.[31]

From the point of view of the less developed countries and their sympathizers, UNCTAD obviously failed, and indeed could not have hoped to succeed, in establishing a new international order for the conduct of world trade oriented toward increasing their export earnings. It was, however, successful in establishing and demonstrating their capacity to organize and conduct themselves as a cohesive political group in opposition to the developed countries (both Western and communist). It called attention to the seriousness of their trade problems and the ways in which these are aggravated by the developed countries, and brought into the open for debate the differences of attitude toward trade and development policy among the developed countries, differences on which they can hope to play in the longer run for changes in trade policies beneficial to themselves and their aspirations for development. Whether the continuing machinery of UNCTAD will prove useful in resolving differences and promoting progress or disintegrate into a mutual recrimination society is a question it is as yet too early to answer. Both the tendency of the political side of the United Nations to degenerate into a debating society and the financial and staffing problems of the organization may condemn it to ineffectiveness. Nevertheless, the first conference has impressed the developed-country participants with the reality of the problem and the necessity of doing something about it and has put into circulation some appealing proposals for fundamental change in the organization and conduct of trade between developed and less developed countries.

U.S. POLICY PROBLEMS AFTER UNCTAD

In the face of the demands of the less developed countries for drastic changes in the organization and conduct of international trade, the United States appeared at UNCTAD as the arch-defender of a system of international trade they believe to be strongly biased against their trade and development interests and the chief opponent of changes they believe essential to the foundation of a more equitable international trading order. The United States had reasons for the stance it adopted, reasons rooted in the historical evolution of its economic and

[31] See Appendix B for a summary of negative votes and abstentions on the general and special principles.

political relations with the other developed nations and with the less developed nations, in the lessons of past experience with some of the proposals refurbished by the less developed nations at Geneva, and in the logic of the basic principle of U.S. commercial policy and of GATT, the principle of nondiscrimination. To an important extent, also, the United States served as scapegoat for other developed countries, especially the European Common Market countries, carrying the burden of resistance to the demands of the less developed countries while the other countries avoided commitment through abstention from voting.

After the confrontation in Geneva, however, the United States cannot persist in maintaining this predominantly negative stance. In purely political terms it has suffered a serious defeat from the less developed countries group, and has moreover been revealed to be partially isolated from the other developed countries and less sympathetic than they to new movements of opinion among the less developed countries. The United States must regain the political initiative if it is to maintain its influence among the less developed countries. As a result of UNCTAD, too, the opportunity to do so exists, for the preparatory work and proceedings of UNCTAD have demonstrated conclusively to the less developed countries the inability of the communist bloc to offer them trade opportunities comparable in magnitude and substance to those of the developed Western countries. UNCTAD also generated increasing skepticism about the usefulness and feasibility of the Common Market proposal for a comprehensive system of organized markets.

The United States has the opportunity to develop a positive program of constructive proposals for mitigating or resolving the real problems underlying the discontents that prompted and were vented vociferously at UNCTAD, while minimizing or avoiding the new difficulties that would be created by implementation of at least some of the solutions there proposed. A positive program would serve not only the political but the humanitarian interest of the United States in the economic progress of the less developed countries, if only because of the moral superiority of development through trade over development through aid. It would also serve the enlightened self-interest of the United States. In the first place, if the demand for assistance of the less developed countries has shifted from grants, loans and technical assistance to expanded opportunities for export earnings, it is to the U.S.

economic interest to respond by shifting its emphasis from aid to trade, so as to maximize whatever returns it obtains from such assistance per unit of cost, or minimize the cost per unit of return. If the less developed countries want patronage rather than philanthropy, it is inefficient of the United States to insist on confining itself to the role of philanthropist. In addition, by adapting its trade and domestic policies to match the needs of the less developed countries as they see them, the United States may be able to exercise more influence in pressing the less developed countries to modify those of their domestic and trade policies that the United States believes are restraining their economic development.

The United Nations Conference on Trade and Development raises three major issues for U.S. policy toward less developed countries. The first concerns the "mix" of trade and aid; the other two concern the new proposals for the organization of international trade endorsed by the less developed countries in UNCTAD: broader market access and international commodity arrangements for primary commodities, and preferential arrangements for manufactures both between developed and less developed countries and among the less developed countries.

Consideration of a possible shift in emphasis from aid to trade requires an analysis of the comparative contributions of these two policy approaches to development; for though they have generally been considered as substitutes, in reality they are not so, from the point of view of either the assistance-giving or the assistance-receiving country. Concrete evaluation of the trade alternative raises some difficult economic problems, since what is in question is the offer of improved market opportunities whose real value depends on a variety of factors and is not readily comparable with aid. Further, assistance through trade encounters political-institutional problems of two sorts. The first arises from the possibility of conflict with domestic policy objectives, such as the desire to support farm incomes or to protect established producers from violent market disturbances, a conflict whose resolution requires the development of new methods of implementing these objectives. The other, and in some ways more difficult, arises from the network of institutions, principles, and practices governing commercial policy among the developed nations, and particularly from the principle of effecting tariff reductions by bargaining on a basis of reciprocity.

In order to assist the less developed countries by expanding their export opportunities, the United States may well have to choose between the principles of reciprocity and of nondiscrimination. Specifically, while the United States and other GATT members have waived the requirement of reciprocal concessions for the less developed countries in the negotiation of tariff reductions of special interest to those countries in the Kennedy Round, the result has been to establish a new principle of reciprocity—equality of tariff concessions to the less developed countries. This new principle, like the old, makes successful tariff reduction depend on the willingness of more than one major trading country to negotiate, and so may block progress along this line within the framework of GATT—as indeed it has already been doing. In this case, if the United States still wished to open trade opportunities for the less developed countries, it would have to choose between according unilateral tariff reductions to both developed and less developed countries to preserve the principle of nondiscrimination, sacrificing reciprocity from both groups, and according preferential tariff reductions only to the less developed countries, preserving the principle of reciprocity with respect to advanced countries at the sacrifice of the principle of nondiscrimination. These alternatives, however, pertain to the technical problem of enlarging trade opportunities for less developed countries within the GATT framework; the best form of trade assistance to the less developed countries is a question of a different order.

The specific question of broader market access for primary products raises the same problems of conflict with domestic policy objectives as does trade assistance in general and necessitates the consideration of similar alternative methods of resolving the conflict. The more far-reaching proposal of measures to raise and stabilize primary product prices and earnings raises questions of probable effectiveness and necessitates consideration of the choice between the broad alternatives of buffer stock and compensatory financing schemes, as well as of problems of administration and of equitable distribution of burdens and benefits.

The two related issues of trade preferences for less developed countries in developed country markets and preferential arrangements among less developed countries raise a variety of thorny issues in the theory and empirical analysis of preferences. For the first type of preference, a great variety of alternatives has been propounded, the main axes of differentiation being between temporary as against permanent preferences, preferences for unlimited quantities as compared with preferences subject to quotas, preferences for all or most products as contrasted with a selected list of products, equal preferences for all less developed countries as contrasted with differentiation among less developed countries, and preferences granted multilaterally by all developed countries as contrasted with preferences granted individually by each developed country. An important consideration in examining the differing effects of these alternatives on economic efficiency and in the promotion of development is the magnitude and elasticity of the supply potential from the less developed countries. The second type of preference, regional or other arrangements among the less developed countries, has been accepted in U.S. policy without critical examination, perhaps as a consequence of earlier acceptance of discrimination against the United States by the European countries, and of the comfortable assumption that the less developed countries are too unimportant to U.S. trade for such arrangements to cause concern. There are, nevertheless, some issues connected with trade preferences among less developed countries that should be explored.

Examination of the issues raised by the new proposals for trade assistance to the less developed countries will require some questioning and critical reexamination of the established principles and presumptions of U.S. international trade policy and domestic economic policy, which some will find discomforting and even sacrilegious. The choice is not between a perfect or easily perfectible world economy attainable by traditional policies and a world economy eternally condemned by the adoption of new economic heresies; in an imperfect world, imperfect policies intelligently applied may produce more desirable results than theoretically perfect policies applied only in fragmentary fashion. Though many of the new policies demanded at UNCTAD appear to be in sharp conflict with the traditional principles of U.S. foreign economic policy, there are precedents for the application of more of them than might appear at first thought. The international coffee agreement has already been cited. In addition, the United States has in the past given the equivalent of temporary preferences for less developed countries to its former dependencies; in the new automotive agreement with Canada it has accorded preferential entry for a single product group to a country that considers itself "developing" rather than "developed"; and in its sugar policy it has established the equivalent of a managed market providing prices above the world level to a favored group of less developed countries. These are of course minor exceptions to the austerely nondiscriminatory grand design of U.S. trade policy; but they concede the principle of discrimination that the less developed countries have been advocating for more general application.

II

International Aspects of Economic Development

The development problem of the less developed countries is one of converting a "traditional" society predominantly based on subsistence or near-subsistence agriculture and/or the bulk export of a few primary commodities, in which per capita income grows slowly or may even be declining as a result of population pressure, into a "modern" society in which growth of per capita income is internalized in the social and economic system through automatic mechanisms promoting accumulation of capital, improvement of technology, and growth of skill of the labor force. Until quite recently, such a conversion was generally considered a matter of political liberation of the society from "colonialism" and "imperialism," social reform oriented toward redistribution of property and income, and economic planning oriented toward material capital accumulation. It is now generally recognized to require far more fundamental transformations of the political and social structure.

To establish a modern society capable of self-sustaining economic growth at a reasonable rate requires, in broad cultural terms, the attainment of political stability and a reasonable impartiality of governmental administration,[1] to provide a political institutional framework within which individuals and enterprises (whether working for their own gain or within the public sector) can plan innovations with maxi-

[1] "Honest government" is an excessively stringent requirement, and in some circumstances would be an obstacle to growth, e.g., if it involved rigid enforcement of a multitude of petty regulations hampering the improvement of economic efficiency. Corruption in government may be an efficient compromise between the desire of public opinion and legislators to regulate economic activity and the needs of business to avoid punctilious compliance with each and every regulation in the interests of efficiency. Still greater efficiency, of course, could be achieved by abandoning regulatory endeavors whose chief consequence is to generate corruption.

mum certainty about the future environment. It requires the establishment of a legal system defining rights of property, person and contract sufficiently clearly, and a judiciary system permitting settlement of disputes sufficiently predictably and inexpensively, to provide a legal institutional framework within which production and accumulation can be undertaken with a minimum degree of noneconomic risk. And it requires the establishment of a social system permitting mobility of all kinds (both allowing opportunity and recognizing accomplishment), and characterized by the depersonalization of economic and social relationships, to provide maximum opportunities and incentives for individual advancement on the basis of productive economic contribution. This transformation is by no means complete in the most economically advanced countries, even after two centuries of industralization which were preceded by several centuries of manufacturing and commercial development. It encounters strong resistance from traditional values and traditional systems of social control over individual activity and aspirations, which have a strong power of survival. Given that some of the less developed countries start from a tribal level of organization, others from an elaborate and accomplished traditional culture adapted only too well to a nonindustrial way of life, and still others from a "colonial" culture derived from an eighteenth or nineteenth century European landed-aristocratic culture already anachronistic when it was implanted, it is no wonder that they have great difficulty in making the transition, let alone in accelerating it.

INDUSTRIALIZATION
OF LESS DEVELOPED COUNTRIES

In more specifically economic terms, the establishment of a modern economy requires "industrialization." By this term, however, is meant something different from the establishment of "industry" (the production of manufactured products) as distinct from and in replacement of "agriculture" (the production of commodities from the soil). Industrialization properly speaking involves the organization of production in business enterprises, characterized by specialization and division of labor both within and among themselves; this specialization is based on the application of technology and of mechanical and electrical power to supplement and replace human effort and motivated by the objectives of minimizing costs per unit and maximizing returns to the enterprise. The conscious pursuit of these objectives by enterprises in a competitive environment leads to the accumulation of capital and to the development and application of new technology, new managerial and marketing methods, and new labor skills, thereby building economic growth automatically into the functioning of the economy.[2] Growth, in turn, reinforces itself by providing expanding opportunities for specialization and division of labor, technical improvements and the exploitation of economies of scale. So conceived, industrialization is an economy-wide phenomenon, applying to agriculture and the service trades as well as to manufacturing; the essence of it is not the production of the products typically considered as "industrial" but the rational approach to the production process itself that it embodies.

Industrialization in this relevant broad sense requires far more than the investment of capital in the establishment of industrial facilities and in the "infrastructure" (roads, railways, docks, the generation and transmission of electric power, etc.) required to power them and link them to markets. Among its more obvious requirements are the development of a skilled, disciplined, and acquisitively motivated labor force and the creation of a professional managerial class able to combine disciplined teamwork with imaginative entrepreneurship; both demand a particular kind of educational system, which it is almost universally a responsibility of the government to provide. Among its less obvious requirements are the integration of markets for goods, capital and labor, necessary both for the creation of a competitive environment and for the efficiency of resource allocation and investment decisions and entailing the creation of appropriate institutions, some of which at least require governmental initiative or support. Least obvious but perhaps most important are the institutional, social and motivational changes which may demand radical changes in the system of land tenure (to initiate the transformation of agriculture into business enterprises) and in the distribution of income (to create a "middle

---

[2] "A competitive environment" is not coterminous with "a free enterprise system," nor vice versa. Evidently the communist countries have achieved a competitive system for the most part, though their dogmatic insistence on the collectivization of agriculture has prevented their attaining the same success in improving agricultural productivity (to the point of creating an embarrassing policy problem) as the Western countries; conversely, some free enterprise economies are characterized by monopolistic organization of industry and the absence of self-sustaining growth at a reasonable rate.

class" properly motivated to accumulate property through saving and to improve its own and its children's economic position by work and education), as well as abandonment of the practice of exercising close social control over economic life characteristic of traditional societies.

Thus economic development and industrialization require the transformation of the society and the economy, and the transformation must be largely an internal one. The international economic relations of a country can, however, play a crucial role in the process of transformation. First, exposure to the outside world through international trade and investment tends in a variety of ways to exert pressure for the transformation and modernization of the traditional economy. This pressure is not necessarily compelling, however; moreover, it has in the past been resisted by the traditional society or by the policies of imperialist powers governing traditional societies as colonies and it is at present impeded by policies of interference with free international economic relations pursued by both the less developed and the developed countries. The apparent limitations of participation in the international economy as a generator of economic growth are an important basis of the contemporary belief that development in the less developed countries must be fostered by conscious economic planning, including deliberate interference with the allocative functions of international competition. The limitations also provide moral support for the less developed countries' belief that the world economy is organized to their disadvantage by the developed countries who thus owe them compensation for past and present injury in the form of development assistance and arrangements for "a new international division of labor." This introduces the second aspect of the role of international economic relations in the transformation process of development, the possible contributions that the developed countries can make to the acceleration of economic growth in the less developed countries.

This chapter deals, first, with the ways in which development tends to be diffused automatically throughout the world economy and in which economic relations with the developed countries tend to transform and modernize the less developed countries, together with some inherent limitations of these processes; detailed discussion of how the diffusion of development is impeded by the policies of the two types of countries is deferred until Chapter III. The chapter concludes with a discussion of the external requirements of accelerated economic development and compares and contrasts the contributions that the developed countries can make through trade policy, foreign aid, and private foreign investment.

THE DIFFUSION OF DEVELOPMENT

The process of industrialization has a definite agglomerative and self-reinforcing quality, for once it has started in a particular country or region it tends to feed on itself. The higher incomes attained through specialization and division of labor and the exploitation of economies of scale draw capital and labor into the market region from outside, generating further economies of specialization and scale and further increases in income, and drawing in additional factors of production in a beneficent circle of economic growth. This self-reinforcing quality has been noted by a number of political economists who have emphasized the resulting tendency toward increasing disparity of incomes between centers of development and the peripheral regions and stressed the implication that a competitive development process is somehow unfair to or biased against the people of the peripheral regions.[3]

The logic of this analysis is not altogether impeccable, at least on the assumption of a world economy without barriers to capital movements and migration. Owners of capital resident in the periphery can invest in the growth of productivity at the center on the same terms as residents of the center, while those with entrepreneurial talents or labor power to sell can migrate to the center to compete for the higher incomes available there. (Massive movements of capital, entrepreneurship, and labor were in fact characteristic of the period of development before World War I.) The implication of unfairness must therefore rest on one of two grounds. The first is the existence of barriers in the center to the influx of capital and people from the outside, which would prevent the periphery from sharing fully in the prosperity of the center; an example is the highly discriminatory barriers against the immigration of people from the less developed countries maintained by the developed countries since World War I. The second is the fundamentally nationalistic assumption that the effects of growth at the center on the periphery are to be measured solely in terms of the incomes of those who continue to reside (and to invest or work) in the

[3] See, for example, the numerous writings of Gunnar Myrdal.

peripheral regions, and that these people have a moral claim to increases in income commensurate with those in the center even though they do not participate directly in the growth process that produces those increases. This is a value judgment respecting equity between the populations of politically delineated pieces of land, not a proposition in scientific economics; it is no more valid to critize the economic system for failing to provide equal income to people no matter where they live than to criticize nature for failing to endow all parts of the earth's crust with an identical climate and soil fertility.

More important than the ethics of disparate growth, however, is the "cumulative circle of causation" which generates economic pressures tending to diffuse the development process to the periphery. Of special importance is the growing pressure of demand on the center economy's natural resources and supplies of foodstuffs and raw materials, particularly minerals and other exhaustible resources. The resulting tendency toward rising prices prompts a search for cheaper supplies in the periphery and an outflow of capital and skilled labor to develop peripheral sources of supply. Through the opportunities thus created, the residents of the periphery become linked to the specialization and division of labor of the center and participate in the rising incomes generated at the center, this participation being reflected in a rising flow of imports. Rising incomes, in their turn, gradually make it profitable to establish in the peripheral regions facilities for producing or fabricating imported goods subject to heavy transport costs and not subject to severe diseconomies of small scale; the growth of these eventually gives rise to an export trade with neighboring peripheral regions and ultimately with the center region.

This was the predominant mechanism of the development of the periphery in the period up to World War I. It has been claimed by Prebisch and others, first, that the peripheral development so achieved was limited (in some unspecified sense), and second, that the mechanism no longer operates, owing to the emergence of a new phase of industrialization in which technical progress applied to the processing of raw materials and the production of agricultural products reduces the growth of demand for primary products while increasing the supplies in the developed countries relatively faster than the demand. Insofar as the biasing effects alleged to be the product of technical progress exist, they are associated with the practice of protectionism toward domestic

D

primary producers by the developed countries, and specifically the use of price supports and import quotas; these measures create an incentive for output-increasing innovations in the developed countries that would not pay in the less developed producing countries and may also bias industrial innovation toward materials-saving methods.[4] The practice of protectionism toward industry and taxation and other restrictions on agricultural exports by the less developed countries create a parallel bias against innovations in primary production in their economies. In the absence of restrictions on international trade, there would seem to be no reason why technical progress in primary products would hamper the operation of this aspect of the diffusion mechanism.

The second important aspect of the automatic diffusion mechanism is associated with the relative international immobility of labor, as compared with capital and technology, and with the general tendency of technical progress to raise real wages, if the supply of labor is not governed by the Malthusian population principle. Technical progress at the center would gradually raise real wages there, by comparison with the periphery, because labor would not move readily from the periphery in response to the growing demand for workers in the center. This would make it increasingly profitable to establish production facilities in the periphery, employing capital and technology from the center along with the cheap labor of the periphery. Such facilities would be designed initially to service markets in the periphery formerly supplied from the center, and later, once the cost advantage outweighed the transport costs back to the center, to export to the center itself. An important element in this mechanism is the fact that real wages, in the form of foregone earnings, are an important element in the cost of training labor, so that the relative rise of real wages at the center would give the periphery an increasing comparative advantage in training labor for the production of labor-intensive goods. The mechanism would operate most strongly on the labor-intensive lines of production, especially those employing relatively unskilled labor and not strongly subject to economies of scale and specialization; such industries would tend steadily to shift toward the periphery, the center

[4] W. P. Travis, *The Theory of Trade and Protection* (Harvard University Press, 1964), Chap. 6, finds that the French input-output matrix is biased toward materials-intensity by comparison with the U.S., British, and German matrices, a bias he associates with (and predicts from) the greater bias of the French tariff structure in favor of imported materials and the postwar French inflation.

meanwhile concentrating on the industries most subject to economies of scale and specialization and requiring the most highly trained and finely specialized grades of skill.

The operation of these two mechanisms for transmitting the development process to the periphery is, however, dependent on a favorable local environment, which may be lacking or precluded by deliberate policy. The first mechanism, in which the transmission depends on the growth of export income, may be restrained or nullified by demographic developments: the growth of population in response to export opportunities, in the face of diminishing returns to land, can easily prevent the growth of income per capita on which the development of local industry may depend. In the case of capital-intensive extractive industries, like mining, the local employment and income provided may be too small to create an adequate market for further development. Furthermore, traditional social organization, especially if its preservation has been the objective of a colonial power, may prevent agriculture from becoming a dynamic sector, by failing to provide the educational and agricultural extension services on which the development of a progressive "industrial" agriculture depends.

Similarly, with respect to the mechanism of industrialization based on a comparative advantage in labor, the traditional society or the colonial power might not provide the requisite training facilities or might prefer to support educational establishments designed to turn out an educated class more suited to the cultured landed life or to politics and professional and administrative employment than to industrial activity. In addition, both traditional societies and colonial administrations typically display a certain antipathy to the exercise of entrepreneurship, especially by members of minority or immigrant groups.

In short, the social environment may be unreceptive or actively hostile to the automatic pressures for the transmission of the development process. Apart from this (as will be discussed in Chapter III) even limited transmission of development under the pressure of free international competition may be positively impeded by barriers to these competitive pressures imposed by both the developed and the less developed countries.

Finally, two characteristics inherent in the operation of the automatic market pressures for the transmission of the development process and the diffusion of industrialization almost inevitably prove objectionable to the political and economic authorities of the less developed countries, particularly the more nationalistic countries. First, since the pressures are a consequence of the disparity in development between the less developed periphery and the developed center, their operation implies both the continuance of that disparity and the setting of the pace of development in the periphery by the pace of development at the center. The resulting condition of dependency and relative impotence is bound to be affronting to the sense of national pride and the belief that the essence of political power is the ability to change the environment by positive policy actions. Second, the dependence of economic development along the lines of natural economic evolution upon integration of the peripheral economies into the economic system of the center gives most of them an economic function both highly specialized, and therefore in sharp contrast to the possession of general industrial competence that is assumed to characterize a modern nation, and extremely vulnerable to economic, political and military disturbances to trade emanating from the developed countries of the center.

It is therefore politically understandable that the less developed countries should be anxious to accelerate their economic development by deliberate policy; that their policies should be aimed at establishing industrial structures similar to the exemplars provided by the developed countries and marked by a desire for greater self-sufficiency; and that their new-found desire for industrialization based on exporting should be hedged by demands on the developed countries for special privileges in international competition.

EXTERNAL ASSISTANCE IN ACCELERATING DEVELOPMENT

The developed countries, which have long since accepted an obligation to assist the less developed countries in their endeavors to increase their rates of economic growth, have provided significant amounts of assistance in the postwar period, primarily in the form of financial aid and technical assistance. Meanwhile, the less developed countries have increasingly been demanding both more foreign aid on substantially easier terms and new opportunities for expanded export earnings to be opened by changes in the international trade policies of the developed countries, specifically by international commodity agreements and new preferential trading arrangements. It is therefore helpful to examine in general terms the nature of the needs of the less developed countries for external assistance, the contribution that various forms of assistance make or can make and the economic effects of giving assistance in these various forms on the country supplying it.

For this purpose, it is useful to distinguish conceptually between two major aspects of the acceleration of economic development, the macro-dynamic and the microdynamic. The former comprises the aggregative aspects of planned economic development—the saving-investment and balance-of-payments aspects. The latter comprises the general process of raising the level of efficiency in individual segments of the economy and of establishing automatic mechanisms promoting the steady improvement of technology, skill, and managerial efficiency in those segments, so as to make the progress of the economy self-sustaining and self-reinforcing. It is also realistic to assume that a less developed country engaged in the planned acceleration of its economic growth typically is producing domestically a wide range of goods at prices substantially above the prices at which they could be imported at the existing exchange rate. This is the consequence both of exchange controls and restrictions introduced for balance-of-payments reasons and of development planning based on a policy of import substitution.

The common practice in economic analyses of the macroeconomic aspects of development and the potential contributions of aid and trade to it is to separate the analysis—usually in the context of projecting the foreign assistance requirements of a target rate of growth over a period of years ahead—into two distinct parts, one concerned with the relation between investment requirements and prospective domestic saving, the other with the relation between prospective import requirements and debt service obligations on the one hand and prospective export sales and aid receipts on the other. This approach tends to obscure the facts that an investment-saving relationship is implicit in the balance of payments and that this relationship must be consistent with the overall income-expenditure relationship. The excess of imports over exports is necessarily equal to the excess of resources used by the economy over resources supplied by it, or the excess of investment over saving. Treatment of the balance-of-payments problems of an economy in isolation from its saving-investment problem fosters the fallacious notion that trade and aid (and reduced debt service) are perfectly interchangeable means of remedying a prospective balance-of-payments deficit, since they are all expressible in terms of foreign exchange supplied. In fact (apart from certain direct or indirect resource gains achievable through trade) foreign aid can close a prospective balance-of-payments gap without any extra saving effort by the country concerned, whereas to close the same gap by trade requires not only that the country supply the goods but that it increase its domestic saving to the extent of the additional export proceeds. To avoid the dangers of fallacious reasoning inherent in concentration on the balance-of-payments aspect of the development problem, it is necessary to employ a general-equilibrium approach and to integrate the domestic and foreign aspects of development finance.[5]

Viewed in these terms, the problem of accelerating economic development initially appears as one of increasing the rate of saving so as to free more resources for development and investing those resources in expanding the productive capacity of the economy at a greater rate than would otherwise occur. Given the dependence of less developed countries on the developed countries for the supply of the greater part of the equipment they require (and the technical expertise involved in the investment decision and the installation of the equipment), the increased rate of saving and investment entails a shift of aggregate demand from domestic to foreign resources. This shift of demand creates a problem which from the theoretical point of view may be thought of either as a potential excess of domestic supply over demand for domestic output, or as a potential excess of demand for imports over prospective export earnings. On either view, the country must restore equilibrium by taking measures to shift demand back to domestic supplies, or (what is the same thing) to equilibrate import demand with export earnings; in essence, it must convert domestic resources into foreign resources either by selling domestic resources in foreign markets or by substituting domestic resources for existing imports, either of which yields foreign exchange that may be converted into foreign resources.

Such measures may consist of devaluation, which (assuming that the country is too small to influence the prices of its imports) will turn the country's terms of trade against it unless the demand for its exports is perfectly elastic. Alternatively, restrictions may be imposed on imports, which will force resort to higher-cost domestic substitutes. In both

---

[5] Failure to consider the implicit saving-investment relationship is characteristic of present techniques of balance-of-payments projection; on this point, see Harry G. Johnson, "The International Competitive Position of the United States and the Balance of Payments Prospect for 1968," *Review of Economics and Statistics*, Vol. 66 (February 1964), pp. 14-32.

cases, the method of international equilibration involves either a decrease in the real consumption of the population or a reduction in the real quantum of investment purchasable with the savings extracted by the development plan, by comparison with what they would be if domestic resources could be converted into foreign resources in unlimited quantities at constant terms. Typically, less developed countries are averse to the use of devaluation and rely primarily on import restrictions. The theory of the optimum tariff indicates that import restriction is preferable to devaluation (in its effects on real income) until the degree of restriction becomes equal to the degree of monopoly power the country's exports command in world markets; thereafter devaluation is preferable to further restriction. It appears reasonable to assume that the degree of import restriction characteristic of less developed countries significantly exceeds what could be justified by the optimum tariff argument.

Either the difficulty of extracting enough domestic resources, or the loss involved in transforming domestic into foreign resources, or (generally) the two together may and almost universally do prevent the country from achieving a growth rate adequate to its political and economic objectives. From this situation derive the potential macroeconomic contributions respectively of foreign aid and trade assistance.

Trade and Aid

Conceptually trade assistance involves flows whereas foreign aid consists of stock transactions, generally involving a sequence of payment of a capital sum to the less developed country followed by payments of interest and amortization by it to the developed country or international institution providing the aid. To render the two comparable, it is simplest to conceive of aid as providing a continuous flow of foreign resources free to the less developed country. This simplification abstracts from problems associated with the time-profile of transfers of resources to and from the less developed country involved in aid, and from the complication that the net transfer of resources to the less developed country implicit in most foreign aid programs is substantially less than the gross capital sums furnished.

As a first approximation, foreign aid serves two functions in the development process. First, it provides real resources additional to what can be extracted from the domestic economy, increasing the total available for investment; second, since the resources are foreign, it averts the real income losses to the country involved in transforming domestic into foreign resources.

The opening of additional opportunities to trade differs from the provision of additional aid in that, again as a first approximation, it does not provide additional real resources for investment. Instead, it provides the opportunity to convert additional domestic resources into foreign resources without the losses that would ensue on the country's own efforts to effect this transformation. The contribution of resources is obviously to be measured, not by the value of the additional trade, but by the losses the opportunity permits the country to avoid. Where the alternative is to lower the prices of exports in order to sell more of them, the contribution is measured by the difference between the marginal revenue from selling the goods in the absence of the opportunity and the aggregate price at which the opportunity permits them to be sold. Where the alternative is additional substitution for imports, the value of the opportunity is measured by the proportional excess of the cost of producing import substitutes over their price in the world market, multiplied by the value of the additional exports allowed by the opportunity. This is in practice the most relevant alternative. By the assumptions made earlier, expanded export opportunities for less developed countries are likely to afford them substantial resource gains by increasing the efficiency with which domestic resources are converted into foreign resources.[6]

Strictly speaking, the foregoing analysis of the contribution of trade assistance to less developed countries applies only to the opening of opportunities to sell more at the same prices, such as might be effected by a general reduction of tariff barriers to or quantitative restrictions on trade by the developed countries. Trade assistance that raised the prices paid by developed countries for exports of less developed countries (such as international commodity agreements to raise primary product prices or preferential arrangements that enabled the less developed countries to charge the ruling internal market prices for their industrial products in the markets of developed countries) would involve an explicit net contribution of foreign resources to the less developed countries. This contribution would be a direct transfer from the consumers or indirect transfer from the taxpayers of the developed

---

[6] A third alternative may be for the resources that could be used to produce the additional exports to remain in the subsistence sector, in which case the value of the opportunity is the difference between the values of the export and the subsistence outputs these resources would produce.

countries to the governments or the individual producers of the less developed countries, the amount depending on the amount of the price increase and the trade volume to which it applied.[7]

One further point should be noted. The attractiveness to the less developed country of external assistance, in both trade and aid, as compared with reliance on domestic saving, increases with the degree of import restriction it practices (measured by the proportional excess cost of production of import substitutes over world prices). The higher the excess cost of producing import substitutes, the greater is the release of resources through importing rather than domestic production made possible by additional exports; and the higher the excess cost, the lower is the relative real value of domestic resources as compared with foreign aid resources of the same nominal value at the country's exchange rate. The relative attractiveness of trade as compared with aid, however, increases with the degree of import restriction (though of course trade can never provide as large a flow of resources as foreign financial aid of the same real value).[8] This is probably one of the reasons why countries developing themselves through import substitution and encountering its increasing costs (rising proportional excess cost of import-substitute production) have become increasingly interested in export opportunities.

Trade Opportunities and Investment Returns

The foregoing analysis of the respective potential macroeconomic contributions of trade and aid is confined to their roles in providing resources for investment in the development process. The pace of development that can be achieved, however, depends not only on the

---

[7] Commodity agreements would transfer resources from developed-country consumers to less-developed-country producers or governments, depending on how they were operated; compensatory finance on Prebisch lines would involve a transfer from developed-country taxpayers to less-developed-country governments. Preferences that allowed price increases would involve consumers paying the full domestic price to the less developed producers, instead of paying part of it to themselves as beneficiaries of tariff receipts, so that the transfer would be an indirect one from the taxpayers of the developed to the producers of the less developed countries.

[8] Let c be the proportional excess cost of marginal import substitutes, X be the foreign exchange value of the opportunity to sell a certain additional quantity of existing exports, and A be the value of a quantity of foreign financial aid. X releases domestic resources equal to cX; A provides the equivalent of $(1 + c)A$ additional domestic resources; the relative attractiveness of X as compared to A is $(c/1 + c)(X/A)$, which increases with c between the limits of zero and X/A. If X and A are equal, the limits are zero and unity.

amount of resources available for investment, but also on the increase in future income that can be obtained per unit of resources invested. In this connection another significant difference between trade and aid emerges. As the development process typically evolves in practice, the rate of return (in terms of additional output) to investment in production for the home market progressively falls relatively to the rate of return that could be obtained from investment in production for export. This difference becomes increasingly important as the development process progresses and underlies the growing demands of the less developed countries for freer market access and (especially) preferential market entry for their industrial products.

This feature of the development process, and the resulting crucial role of export opportunities controlled by the developed countries, is not a consequence of the operation of economic law. On the contrary, it is the result of specific policies commonly followed by the less developed countries in their general economic management and development planning—in particular of their attachment to fixed exchange rates and unwillingness to devalue, their dislike of their traditional export industries and unwillingness to invest in them, and their pursuit of industrialization through import substitution policies—in conjunction with the rising cost of import substitution as it is progressively extended.

Rigidity of exchange rates—especially when combined with the domestic inflationary pressures generated by weak government, lax fiscal policy, and overambitious development planning—tends to restrict the growth of exports and produce chronic balance-of-payments difficulties that can only be corrected (given the aversion to devaluation) by import restrictions. The chronic balance-of-payments difficulties reinforce the other motives for development through import substitution. The progressive extension of the policy of import substitution encounters rising costs, as substitution extends to goods whose efficient production depends on a large market demand or on producing domestically the specialized parts and services that only a large diversified economy can produce efficiently. The rising costs of import substitution increase the attractiveness of both foreign aid and trade opportunities relative to domestic saving and also increase the attractiveness of trade relative to aid.

More important in the present context, the rising cost of import substitution means a falling yield (in terms of increased income) from the investment of foreign aid in production for the domestic market. Eventually, this yield must fall substantially below the yield that would be available from investment in the production for export of additional traditional exports or (more appealingly) of the import-substitute products with the lower excess costs, if foreign markets for these could be found.[*] In this situation trade opportunities have the advantage over aid of offering a greater contribution to the growth of income, even though they provide less foreign resources than would aid. To put the same point another way, given the typical pattern of planned development, foreign aid involves the gift of a series of successively lower-yielding investments, whereas trade opportunities make available the possibility of a higher-yielding investment.

It is important to notice, however, that this advantage of trade over aid is created by the specific policies of the less developed countries. Except in a world in which the developed countries deliberately blocked all possibility of expansion of less-developed-country exports through price competition by countervailing tariffs and restrictions—and while they do behave to some extent in this manner toward some products important to the less developed countries, the result is more to impede than to nullify price competition—the less developed countries could avoid the rising cost of import-substitution. They could do so by investing in producing for export either more of their traditional export products or those of their relatively lower-cost import-substituting industries, obtaining the foreign markets for the output by devaluing their currencies. The main reasons for their aversion to this policy, apart from the universal fetishism that surrounds exchange rates in the present international monetary system, appear to be, first, their dislike of the increased dependence on their traditional exports, and the increased incomes for producers thereof, that would result from devaluation, and second, loss of the monopoly power that overvaluation enables them to exploit in the markets for their traditional exports. The first difficulty could be handled by imposing an export tax at a rate calculated to offset the effect of devaluation in raising producer prices and incomes. As to the second, monopoly power would be more efficiently exploited by levying an appropriate export tax than by main-

[*] The excess of the costs of these goods above world market prices provides a motivation for demanding preferences in the markets of the developed countries rather than a nondiscriminatory lowering of barriers to trade.

taining an overvalued currency. Devaluation would not, of course, yield the income transfers that could be gained from preferences in developed-country markets.[10]

Technical Assistance

The microdynamics of development—defined earlier to comprise effects on the efficiency of, and the automaticity of progress in, individual segments of the economy—are as relevant as the macrodynamics to the evaluation of the potential contributions of the various forms of foreign assistance. They are by definition almost the special concern of technical assistance in all its various forms. The contribution that externally provided expert personnel can make both to improving the efficiency of development planning and raising the technical level of the less developed economy and to propagating the philosophy of a rational scientific approach to problems of economic and social organization is obvious. What require more discussion are the probabilities that trade opportunities can contribute more than aid to building into the developing economy the automatic mechanisms of self-sustaining growth and that private foreign investment can contribute more than governmental foreign aid to the process of modernization of the less developed economy.

The central consideration in trade versus aid is the benefit derived from competition, particularly in industrial production, with producers in other countries. Competition may serve as a powerful agent for inculcating the concern for productive and managerial efficiency and stimulating the constant effort to improve product quality and reduce costs that are characteristic of industry in a developed economy in ways that could not be duplicated by any amount of investment planning

---

[10] On these points, see Raúl Prebisch, *Towards a New Trade Policy for Development* (United Nations, 1964), pp. 74-75, where the alternative of subsidizing industrial exports is also considered. Prebisch's point, however, is exceedingly obscure. He argues correctly that there may be no single exchange rate that will permit a less developed country to export manufactures as well as primary products, but then goes on to refer to alternative levels of the exchange rate as "over valued" or "undervalued" with respect to one or the other product group. Besides being a misuse of terms (since the test of overvaluation or undervaluation is the balance of payments, not the pattern of production) this would logically imply the desirability of establishing a dual rate system; but instead he asserts that devaluation would be a "possible solution." Multiple exchange rates are of course simply an alternative to a system of trade taxes and subsidies.

and manpower training for production for a protected domestic market. In a small protected national market, competitive pressures for increasing efficiency may operate very weakly and may even be suppressed by the monopolistic practices that protection permits. Expanded trade opportunities could enlist the forces of competition more positively in the development process both directly, through their effects on the industries benefiting from the trade opportunities, and indirectly, by reducing the incentives to push import substitution into high-excess-cost industries and allowing more scope for foreign competition in the markets of less developed countries. In addition, the industries given enlarged opportunities to export would probably become increasingly aware of the extent to which they were handicapped by the high costs of other industries enjoying a protected position in the domestic market, and increasingly able to exercise effective pressure for the reduction of such protection.

Private Foreign Investment

Private foreign investment comprises both portfolio investment and direct investment. Private portfolio investment has the possible advantage over government investment of being more efficient in selecting projects to finance, since its choices are not subject to the political pressures that the government of a less developed country can bring to bear on the government of a developed country in favor of projects it favors for political reasons. Private direct investment has the great advantage of bringing to the less developed country in one package capital, modern technology, managerial skills, and improvement-mindedness. Direct investment by international corporations through the establishment of affiliates and branch plants has the further advantage of having at its command the technological and managerial innovations of the parent company and its affiliates, so that automatic progress is built into its local operations in a relatively inexpensive way. In addition, private foreign investment offers the recipient country, as a result of double-taxation arrangements, the considerable advantage of being able to tax profits on foreign capital at the direct expense of the government of the country from which the capital comes.[11]

On the other hand, direct private foreign investment may be a source of problems in the development process, especially if it is at-

[11] On the advantages of private direct investment by foreigners, see Harry G. Johnson, *The Canadian Quandary* (Toronto: McGraw-Hill, 1963), Introduction.

tracted to the less developed country by import substitution policies implemented by tariffs or import prohibitions. In these cases the motivation of the investing company is obviously to maximize its profits while minimizing its commitment to the country invested in; and it may well be able to contrive to exploit the protection it receives by producing with an obsolete technology or a modern one inappropriate to the labor-abundant and capital-scarce conditions of the country. These problems are of course the consequence of protection rather than of the foreign ownership of the investment; but the foreign ownership means that the excess profits that may be created by protection are not purely internal redistributions of income, but are international redistributions of income away from the less developed country. The burden of such transfers tends to be enhanced by the maintenance of overvalued exchange rates.

More important—especially in considering whether it should be encouraged by the developed countries—direct private investment, particularly by large international corporations, is a potent generator of political ill will and suspicion in the less developed countries. Most of these reactions are irrational, based on a misunderstanding of the economics of modern industry and especially a failure to appreciate the economic value of superior technology and the high professional skill required of industrial management; they are nonetheless real. The sources of resentment are familiar. Majority or complete foreign ownership and control arouses envy and distrust, though it may be only through ownership of its local production facilities that a foreign firm can maintain its technological and managerial superiority and ensure itself a fair return on its past investments in research and development. The employment in top positions of foreigners rather than nationals is regarded as unfair discrimination, though nationals may lack the necessary professional qualifications or dedication to the organization. High profits are regarded as evidence of monopolistic exploitation, though they may reflect superior efficiency or constitute a necessary return on past investments in technology and organization. Foreign corporations are often identified, mistakenly, as agents for the execution of the political objectives of the governments of their countries. These political irritations must be weighed against the economic contribution private direct foreign investment may make to the development process.

Effects on Donor Country

Foreign assistance to the economic development of the less developed countries also affects the developed countries providing the assistance. Broadly speaking, foreign aid involves a transfer of real resources from the developed to the less developed country, at a sacrifice to the developed country. The sacrifice is measured by the net transfer involved in the aid transaction—the nominal amount of capital transferred less the present (discounted) value of interest and amortization payments— not by the gross amount of the capital transferred under the title of aid. Where the recipient country would in the absence of aid have had to reduce its export prices to convert domestic into foreign resources, the donor (or possibly third countries) incurs an additional element of cost, the loss of benefits from the lower prices; conversely, where the aid permits the donor country to sell its exports at higher prices than they would otherwise have fetched, the donor receives some offset to the sacrifice involved in the aid transfer. That offset, however, can obviously never be great enough to turn the sacrifice into a net benefit.

The contribution by the developed country involved in opening a trade opportunity to a less developed country (or less developed countries in general) depends both on the nature of the opportunity and on the point of view adopted in assessing the economic welfare effects of trade policy changes. These problems are discussed in greater detail in Chapter VI. Broadly speaking, if the welfare of individual consumers is taken as the standard, and the short-run problems of reallocation of factors of production are ignored, there is a broad presumption that the developed country will gain and not lose from nondiscriminatory reduction of its barriers to international trade. This presumption is firmest for the reduction of exceptionally high barriers to trade and weakest for the reduction of exceptionally low barriers to trade. For discriminatory reduction of trade barriers, such as the granting of preferences to less developed countries as a group or selectively, the developed country may either gain or lose, a loss becoming a certainty if the preferences are designed solely to transfer trade from existing suppliers to the preferred suppliers. If, however, a protectionist standard of welfare is adopted, the opening of a trade opportunity without reciprocity must involve a loss—though a protectionist might be persuaded to the contrary by Prebisch's argument that unilateral concessions to less developed countries would involve "implicit" reciprocity because they would automatically spend their additional export earnings on additional imports of industrial goods from the developed countries.[12]

In private foreign investment the developed country under double taxation agreements forgoes corporate tax revenue that it would otherwise receive. Special tax incentives to foreign investment in less developed countries would add to this potential loss.

Finally, the provision of technical assistance involves the cost of the salaries and work-associated expenses of the personnel. Not all of this may be a true cost, however, since the salaries necessary to induce people to serve in such capacities may exceed the value of their expected contribution at home, and their experience may increase their future contribution to their country beyond what it otherwise would have been.

[12] Prebisch, *op. cit.*, pp. 29-31.

III

Policy Obstacles to Development

There are a number of policy measures that the United States might take, alone or in concert with the other developed countries, to promote the economic development of the less developed countries, especially through changes in trade policies designed to increase those countries' export earnings. Concentration on the barriers to development through trade inherent in the trade policies of the developed countries and removable by changes in those policies, however, courts certain obvious dangers of bias and exaggeration.

In the first place, the temptation is particularly strong for the less developed countries to attach too much importance to the trade and other policies of the developed countries as determining factors in the development of the less developed countries. Fundamentally, the process of initiating self-sustaining economic growth is a process of effecting internal social and economic changes. The external trading environment may be influential in determining the relative difficulty of the process, but it is not crucial. While the policies of the developed countries impede international trade in a variety of ways, the impediments are not absolute; they are surmountable by competition and they have not prevented either the rapid growth of world trade or the emergence of new industrial powers on the world market. It is, moreover, a safe generalization that the big differences observable between the per capita incomes of different countries are attributable to differences in technological levels, accumulated capital, educational levels, economies of scale and specialization and division of labor—the traditional causes of the wealth of nations—only a small fraction being assignable to differences in the gains derived from international trade.

E

Secondly, emphasis on the denial of trade opportunities tends to divert attention from the equally important question of ability to take advantage of trade opportunities and to generate the mistaken belief that trade policy changes by developed countries offer a magic new route to painless development. The main obstacle to development through trade is very likely to be the condition of underdevelopment itself, which inherently imposes countless impediments to the establishment of profitable trade.

Thirdly, concentration on the trade policies of the developed countries obscures the fact that in many ways the policies of the less developed countries themselves impede, either deliberately or incidentally, the exploitation of existing opportunities to trade, and would impede the exploitation of new trade opportunities that might be opened up by policy changes in the developed countries.

These counterconsiderations indicate the need for caution in assessing the potential contribution of expanded trade opportunities for the less developed countries to their development. It is easily possible, however, to convert them into skepticism about the capacity of trade policy changes to do anything to further the development of the less developed countries. This tendency is reinforced by the common belief that the barriers to international trade, in manufactures if not in important primary products, are already low and will become virtually insignificant after the Kennedy Round of GATT negotiations. That belief is not justified by the facts, especially if attention is concentrated on industrial products of special interest to the less developed countries and the degree of protectiveness of the tariffs of the advanced countries is evaluated in a more fundamental way than by merely considering the tariff rates levied on commodities.

While the effects of opening new opportunities for export earnings for the less developed countries on their economic growth would necessarily depend heavily on their success in effecting the socioeconomic changes involved in the initiation of a self-sustaining growth process, an exploration of these problems would lead far afield from the central concerns of this study. The impediments that the policies of the less developed countries themselves place in the way of their development through trade are, however, directly relevant, for they influence the kinds of trade policy changes that the less developed countries would most like the developed countries to make. Furthermore, if the developed countries do introduce major changes in their trade policies designed to promote the growth of the less developed countries, they legitimately may—and should—press the latter to modify or eliminate those domestic policies that prevent them from exploiting as effectively as possible the trading opportunities offered. This chapter therefore surveys the obstacles to efficient development, and particularly to development through trade, created by economic policies in both types of countries. It must be emphasized, however, that the less developed countries constitute a large and extremely heterogeneous group, both in their development and trade problems and in the economic policies they follow; therefore, the policies discussed are to be understood as typical of less developed countries, but not necessarily followed by all such countries or practiced to the same degree in all of them.

POLICIES OF LESS DEVELOPED COUNTRIES

The promotion of economic development by deliberate economic policy has throughout modern history been associated with the political objective of building a nation-state or strengthening a nation-state in rivalry with others; this is almost universally the case with the less developed countries of the present time. The nationalist objective, with its overtones of possible military conflict, provides the motivation for bearing the costs of establishing a "modern" national economy and polity, and may well be the only force capable of mobilizing a society for economic development. On the other hand, nationalist motivations inevitably lead to economic policies that waste economic resources and inhibit the economic development they aim to stimulate.[1]

The main reasons for this are, first, that nationalism generally derives its economic objectives by imitation and emulation of the economic structure of established nation-states, and second that it envisages economic development as consisting in the ownership and control by nationals (individually or collectively) of desirable types of "modern" property—industrial factories, professional and managerial jobs—rather than as consisting in the development of a system of economic organization that efficiently exploits the country's available human and material resources and improves its own efficiency. Nationalism, in short, sees development as the accumulation of property rather than

[1] For a fuller and more theoretical discussion, see Harry G. Johnson, "A Theoretical Model of Economic Nationalism in New and Developing States," *Political Science Quarterly*, Vol. 80 (June 1965), pp. 169-85.

the raising of income. This approach is fostered by the fact that the propagation of nationalism is the peculiar province of the intellectuals, for whom it provides a sheltered market, and who are prone to think about economics in terms of the visible symbols of economic power rather than the invisible processes of economic competence and improvement.

Nationalism inevitably places great emphasis on economic self-sufficiency, for reasons both of obtaining control over the country's "economic destiny" and of rivalry with and imitation of the established nation-states, the most important of which are economically large and diversified enough to be approximately self-sufficient. The obvious and appealing route to self-sufficiency is through import substitution, particularly as it offers the opportunity to prove national competence by replacing foreign with national producers. In addition, nationalism tends to emphasize investment in visible symbols of development—large irrigation projects rather than individual wells, large new modern factories rather than improvements to old factories—in preference to less visible but frequently more socially profitable types of investment. Finally, the imitation of more developed countries extends beyond the imitation of economic structure to the imitation of economic and social institutions—especially labor union and social security legislation—which impede development by raising the private cost of labor above its social opportunity cost.[2]

In addition to nationalism, the urge for development is conditioned by a variety of political and social ideas, absorbed in large part from the Western Christian cultural tradition, that support policies inimical to efficient economic development. One such is the notion, deeply implanted by the Great Depression of the 1930's and its consequences, of the moral superiority of "socialism" over "capitalism," and the associated belief that economic planning is essential to overcome or hold in check the deficiencies of competitive economic organization. Another, in which the urban-centered political philosophical tradition of Western civilization meshes with the feudal-aristocratic social values of many less developed countries, is the notion of the inherent inferiority of those who work the land, a notion that prompts and supports the

[2] For a relevant empirical study of the extent to which a rising minimum legal wage rate has restricted the growth of industrial employment in Puerto Rico, see L. G. Reynolds, "Wages and Employment in a Labor-Surplus Economy," *American Economic Review*, Vol. 55 (March 1965), pp. 19-39.

exploitation of the rural primary-producing sector for the benefit of the urban industrial sector.

Economic Planning and Controls

Economic planning, implemented by controls of all kinds over the allocation of investment resources, commodities, and foreign exchange, is characteristic of less developed countries. It is a consequence of both their own political preferences and various pressures exercised by the developed countries from which they obtain foreign aid and technical assistance. The principle of planning the investment of scarce resources in the development program and the allocation of production in an economy of scarcity is difficult to quarrel with; but in practice economic planning and controls over private economic activity give rise to all sorts of inefficiencies and wastes of resources. The planning process— which is ultimately a political process governed by legislators dependent on their constituents for political support if not in some cases for election—involves the taking of economic decisions on other than economic grounds and incorporates its own biases in terms of preferred types and locations of investment projects. Moreover, the system of control over private enterprise by permits and licenses imposes costs on private enterprise which may be substantial and entails rigidities which militate against competition and the improvement of efficiency. Licensing systems inevitably favor the established enterprise against the new competitor and hamper the ability of the more efficient firm to enlarge its share of the market at the expense of the less efficient. The obtaining of licenses may be an expensive business in terms of time and travel expense—not to speak of the bribery that license controls encourage—creating an artificial incentive to locate enterprises in administrative centers rather than in market or supply centers. Fair distribution of scarce licenses may impose the necessity of producing far below capacity, entailing heavy excess costs; discriminatory distribution of licenses may protect the inefficient producer at the expense of the efficient. The main impediment to efficient development imposed by licensing, however, is its displacement of the market mechanism of allocating scarce resources by price. Licensing substitutes the administrative mechanism of detailed quantitative decisions by civil servants, who generally lack the economic training that would be necessary to make these decisions as efficiently as the market could, who may have a financial interest of their own in the outcome of the decisions and whose employment may represent an essentially unproductive use of an important fraction of an extremely limited supply of talent. The resulting inefficiencies and instabilities of production obviously impede economic development; they are likely to constitute a particularly serious obstacle to development through exporting, by making it difficult for the producer in the less developed country to compete with the producer in the developed country in terms of assured steady flow of supplies and unvarying standards of quality.

Agriculture and Traditional Exports

The policies of less developed countries with respect to agriculture—both agriculture producing for the domestic market and agriculture producing staple primary products for export to the world market—typically impede development in a variety of ways.

Domestic agricultural production, whether a subsistence sector or a producer of marketable surpluses for the domestic market, is generally the largest sector of the less developed economy, and a sector therefore in which modest improvements in productivity could effect significant increases in real income per capita. Yet development plans typically steer a disproportionate share of the available investable resources toward industry and other nonagricultural sectors, tending to starve the agricultural sector (relatively) of capital for development. Further, development policy typically depresses the incentives to agricultural producers to improve productivity. First, development policy based on import substitution tends to raise the prices of industrial inputs for agriculture (and also to limit their supply), thereby retarding the industrialization of agriculture required to improve its efficiency. Secondly, development policy generally attempts to hold down the prices received by agricultural producers for the benefit of the urban dwellers and industrial workers, frequently under the guise of preventing the inflationary effect on industrial wages and prices of increases in food prices, by far the largest item in the urban cost of living. These policies are made easier and are frequently justified by reference to the availability of surplus food from the United States. It is questionable, however, whether it is wise policy to rely on politically determined supplies of surplus food—which may not remain in surplus for many years, given the growth of world population and demand—in order to permit neglect of the development needs of the domestic agricultural sector in favor of industrial investment.

In less developed countries that have traditionally produced an exported surplus of agricultural products, it is generally deliberate policy to tax their producers heavily to provide resources for development, thereby discouraging production for the market. While optimum tariff considerations and fiscal expediency can be adduced in defense of such policies, it is extremely doubtful that the degree of taxation generally imposed could be justified by these arguments. Countries that traditionally produce export surpluses of foodstuffs generally restrict these exports so as to maintain or increase the real consumption of their urban dwellers and industrial workers at the expense of their farmers. On the other hand, countries that traditionally produce nonfood staple exports and import foodstuffs frequently seek to divert agricultural resources from exports to increase their self-sufficiency in food. The consequence of these policies is to reduce the export earnings the country derives from its world market opportunities, and to induce shifts in demand away from its export goods (including induction of technical changes reducing the amount of goods required) and to encourage the development of alternative supplies from elsewhere (including synthetic substitutes).

A notable example of these effects was the failure of supplies of natural rubber to grow as rapidly as the demand in the postwar period; this was in part due to political disturbances and policies of promoting self-sufficiency in food in the Southeast Asian producing countries. It undoubtedly helped to foster the growth of synthetic rubber production. The development of soluble coffee, partly in response to the high prices of coffee resulting from supply restriction, is another example. That innovation both reduced the amount of coffee needed per cup and shifted demand from the higher-grade South American coffees to the lower-grade African coffees. The degree to which these policies of restricting agricultural exports have been pushed by many of the less developed countries does not appear to be justifiable by any of the usual arguments advanced in their defense, but instead seems to involve serious losses of allocative efficiency and impediments to the growth of the agricultural sector.

Industrialization by Import Substitution

The defects of the policy of industrialization based on import substitution have been well summarized by Dr. Prebisch as follows:

(a) The simple and relatively easy phase of import substitution has reached, or is reaching, its limit in the countries where industrialization has made most progress. As this happens, the need arises for technically complex and difficult substitution activities, which usually require great capital intensity and very large markets if a reasonable degree of economic viability is to be attained. Thus there are limits to import substitution in the developing countries which cannot be exceeded without a frequent and considerable waste of capital.

Moreover, the extension of import substitution to a wider range of goods generates or increases demand for other imports, whether of raw materials and intermediate goods to manufacture products in respect of which such substitution is taking place, or of new lines of capital goods or consumer goods that technology is constantly creating.

(b) The relative smallness of national markets, in addition to other adverse factors, has often made the cost of industries excessive and necessitated recourse to very high protective tariffs; the latter in turn has had unfavourable effects on the industrial structure because it has encouraged the establishment of small uneconomical plants, weakened the incentive to introduce modern techniques, and slowed down the rise in productivity. Thus a real vicious circle has been created as regards exports of manufactured goods. These exports encounter great difficulties because internal costs are high, and internal costs are high because, among other reasons, the exports which would enlarge the markets are lacking. Had it been possible to develop industrial exports, the process of industrialization would have been more economical, for it would have made possible the international division of labour in manufacturing.

(c) Usually industrialization has not been the result of a programme but has been dictated by adverse external circumstances which made it necessary to restrict or ban imports; these measures have been applied especially to non-essential imports that can be dispensed with or postponed. Thus home production of these goods has been encouraged, absorbing scarce production resources, often regardless of cost. A more rational policy would have given priority to import substitution in respect of goods which could be produced under more favourable conditions than others, not only consumer goods, as has generally been the case, but also raw materials and intermediate and capital goods.

(d) This substitution in respect of non-essential or not urgently needed goods has led those developing countries which are most advanced in the process of industrialization to concentrate, so far as their imports are concerned, on essential goods, particularly those required by productive activities. Hence, any sizable drop in the earnings of primary exports cannot be offset as easily as in former times by compressing imports, because nowadays the margin of such imports that can be eliminated without slowing the pace of internal economic activity and employment is much narrower.

(e) Finally, excessive protectionism has generally insulated national markets from external competition, weakening and even destroying the incentive necessary for improving the quality of output and lowering costs under the private-enterprise system. It has thus tended to stifle the initiative of enterprises as regards both the internal market and exports.[3]

The most important points of this indictment relevant to development through exports are the effects of import substitution in raising the cost of production above world market costs and the effects on competition and efficiency of protected production for a small market. Prebisch blames this situation on the unwillingness of the developed countries to open their markets to industrial producers in less developed countries, instead of on the maintenance of overvalued exchange rates by protectionist import-substitution policies. The solution he recommends is preferential entry, whose high costs would be borne by the consumers of the developed countries, instead of a combination

[3] Raúl Prebisch, *Towards a New Trade Policy for Development* (United Nations, 1964), pp. 21-22. While the reference is primarily to Latin America, the same problems have arisen in the economic development of India and Pakistan. Compare, for example, G. M. Radhu, "The Rate Structure of Indirect Taxes in Pakistan," *Pakistan Development Review*, Vol. 4 (Autumn 1964), pp. 527-51, especially Table 6 and the author's comments therein. The table shows that in 1962-63 the average rate of duty on imported consumption goods rose from 55 percent for essentials through 111 percent for semiluxuries to 140 percent for luxuries; for raw materials for consumption goods the average rate was 27 percent (unprocessed) and 48 percent (processed); for raw materials for capital goods 28 percent (unprocessed) and 39 percent (processed); for machinery and equipment 17 percent, and for consumer durables 85 percent. The author points out that the high rates on imported consumer goods and low rates on capital goods and materials encourage the use of imported materials; stimulate substitution of domestically produced for imported consumer goods, thereby promoting an "automatic decontrol of consumption" and decrease in saving; and, by confining industrialization to the growth of the domestic market, ensure an ultimate deceleration of industrial growth. Like Prebisch he recommends the extension of import substitution to intermediate and capital goods. The force of his findings is strengthened by the fact that the escalation of tariff rates implies a much steeper escalation of effective rates of protection of value added in producing the higher-tariff goods and may imply negative effective protection of producers' capital goods production.

Soligo and Stern have subsequently calculated for forty-eight industries in Pakistan the rates of protection of value added (more correctly, the rates of subsidy to value added) implicit in the Pakistan tariff schedule. For no less than twenty-three of the forty-eight, the implicit rate of subsidy is over 100 percent. That is, the net subsidy received through tariff protection exceeds the total value added, and the operation of these industries subtracts from instead of adding to national product. (Ronald Soligo and Joseph J. Stern, "Tariff Protection, Import Substitution and Investment Efficiency," *The Pakistan Development Review*, Vol. 5 [Summer 1965], pp. 249-70.)

of exchange-rate adjustment and import liberalization by the less developed countries.

It is particularly necessary to stress the importance of the input-output relations in a modern industrial structure and the effects of protection of inputs in raising the cost of production of the user industries, rendering them unable to compete in the world market. If a "new international division of labor" is to be established, a necessary condition for its success would seem to be a change in the policies of the less developed countries, and specifically the abandonment of the effort to achieve self-sufficiency in favor of specialization on a few processes or products, allowing the producers to take full advantage of the availability of materials, components, and equipment in the world market.

Monetary, Fiscal, and Exchange-Rate Policies

The pursuit of industrialization through import substitution and the problems of inefficiency and noncompetitiveness to which it gives rise are intimately associated with the pursuit of inflationary monetary and fiscal policies in combination with unwillingness to devalue the currency.[4] Inflationary policies lead to balance-of-payments deficits, and unwillingness to alter the exchange rate leads to resort to import substitution. Moreover, the choice of imports to be sacrificed under import substitution policies initiated by this route is guided by political expediency and particularly by the priority accorded to investment goods and materials over consumer goods (especially "luxuries") so that the resulting protectionist system is extremely inefficient. The continuation of inflationary monetary and fiscal policies creates a vicious circle in which further import substitution becomes both necessary and increasingly painful, because both inflation and import substitution (through its cost effects) increase the difficulties of exporting and the incentives to import. Typically, at some stage the policy-makers of the afflicted country resort to partial devaluation, by means of export subsidies, multiple exchange rates which favor some exports, or export bonus schemes giving exporters allocations of scarce foreign exchange. Typically, also, these devices favor the exports of "new" industry over the traditional export sectors, thereby introducing further distortions into the allocation of resources.

[4] On this and related problems of development finance, see Harry G. Johnson, "Fiscal Policy and the Balance of Payments in a Growing Economy," *Malayan Economic Review*, Vol. 9 (April 1964), pp. 1-13.

As contrasted with a forthright devaluation, these devices have the great disadvantages of tying up a great deal of resources—both governmental and private—in the working of the control system and of creating wide divergences of private from social opportunity costs which governmental policy then has to correct for. Yet the alternative of devaluation is almost invariably strongly resisted, for various alleged social reasons or as a result of financial conservatism, and sometimes as a result of belief that devaluation combined with trade liberalization would have adverse effects on the terms of trade. It would seem evident that if less developed countries are to obtain the full benefit of any new trade opportunities opened by changes in the policies of the developed countries, they must be willing to make appropriate adjustments of their exchange rates, rather than defend them tenaciously by import-substitution policies that reduce their ability to compete in the world market.[5]

Apart from their effects in obliging governments averse to devaluation to resort to import-substitution policies of a peculiarly mischievous kind, inflationary fiscal and monetary policies have a variety of deleterious effects on economic development and efficiency. The most serious are, first, the distortions in the economy caused by the effort to protect certain segments of the population from the effects of inflation, for example by holding down the domestic price of food or of urban transport to shield the industrial worker, or by holding down interest

[5] As a matter of pure theory, and possibly with some relevance to reality, it is not necessarily true that a country pursuing a heavily protectionist policy would have to devalue its currency if it removed its protectionist barriers. Protection, because of the input-output relationships among production processes, may have a stronger effect in inhibiting exports than it does inhibiting imports. For a demonstration of the possibility, see Harry G. Johnson, "A Model of Protection and the Exchange Rate," *The Review of Economic Studies*, Vol. 33 (April 1966), pp. 159-63.

As an indication of the extent to which policy may go in maintaining an overvalued exchange rate, M. L. Pal ("The Determinants of the Domestic Prices of Imports," *Pakistan Development Review*, Vol. 4 [Winter 1964], pp. 597-622) has estimated the average profit margin on imports in Pakistan at about 60 percent of the landed cost for all types of goods. Deducting 10-15 percent for the normal mark-up and distribution cost, he arrives at a crude measure of the extent of overvaluation of the currency of 45-50 percent. The landed cost, however, includes duty and excise tax; the estimated mark-up on cost and freight value is typically over 100 percent, frequently over 200 percent; thus, deducting the 10-15 percent normal mark-up and the normal 15 percent excise tax, it would appear that quantitative restrictions and import duties together support an overvaluation of the Pakistani rupee in the range of 100-125 percent by comparison with what the rate would be under relatively free trade. Both estimates are, of course, extremely crude.

rates to channel real income to manufacturing firms;[6] and second, the disturbance of the normal processes of investment decision by extreme uncertainty about the short-run rate of inflation to be expected.[7] These effects of inflation are harmful both to economic development in general and to the possibility of basing development on industrial exporting in particular. It must be recognized, however, that the reason for endemic inflation in a less developed country is almost invariably political inability to agree either on the taxation required to finance the development program or, more generally, on the division of the national income among the claimants to it. Inflationary financing represents the only available way of bridging deep political divisions. The insistence of outside advisers on conservative monetary and fiscal policies in these circumstances amounts in reality to a demand for political stabilization and generally a demand for resolution of political conflict in favor of one of the disputants.[8]

Attitudes toward Private Foreign Investment

The strength of economic nationalism in the modern world, and the irrationality of which it is capable, is nowhere more evident than in the extreme hostility and suspicion with which private direct foreign investment is generally regarded by the "host" country. This is true not merely in less developed countries with a colonial past and present political weakness, but in the developed countries of Europe and the British Commonwealth. The deepest hostility appears to be aroused by the large international corporations engaged in the extractive industries—mining and petroleum—and the mass-production, technically-most-advanced manufacturing industries—vehicle manufacturing, chemicals and petroleum refining. Yet these are the industries where the large-scale mobilization of risk capital for exploration or research and development and the possession of the most advanced production technology and managerial and marketing techniques are of crucial

[6] Such policies frequently produce a vicious circle of necessary inflation, for example when the policy of holding down fares produces deficits on government-owned urban transport enterprises which can only be financed by money creation.

[7] And related uncertainties about exchange rates and import restrictions.

[8] For a fuller discussion of the limited theoretical potentialities and practical disadvantages of inflationary development finance, see Harry G. Johnson, "Is Inflation the Inevitable Price of Rapid Development or a Retarding Factor in Economic Growth?", paper for the August 1965 Rehovoth Conference on Fiscal and Monetary Problems in Developing States, published in *The Malayan Economic Review*, Vol. 11 (April 1966), pp. 20-28.

importance for competitive economic production, and where consequently the established international corporations can offer the greatest contribution to the modernization and acceleration of growth of the less developed economies.

Nevertheless, the less developed countries regard the operations of such corporations within their borders with great suspicion and generally attempt to dictate stringent and restrictive conditions on which the companies may incorporate, invest, and repatriate profits, and also the manner in which they must organize their production and distribution. In particular, minority or even majority resident participation in the ownership and management of such enterprises is frequently demanded and local production or purchase of components and supplies required.

While the political and cultural motivation of these restrictions is understandable, their effect is frequently to reduce seriously the company's organizational efficiency and to prevent it from utilizing the methods of specialization and division of labor among its various departments and divisions that account for its competitive efficiency in its headquarters country. In particular, its local use of the technological knowledge available within its international complex may be conditional on its ability to maintain the secrecy of its methods, which would be jeopardized by having outsiders it may have no reason to trust forced into its board rooms and executive positions. Moreover, its efficiency in its operations in developed economies may, and in a modern industrial economy is very likely to, depend on its ability to mobilize supplies of hundreds or even thousands of component parts from suppliers each of whom is specialized in producing a few needed parts, does so efficiently as a result of specialized experience, and can be relied on to meet exacting standards of product quality and regularity and reliability of delivery. The attempt to force the company to reproduce this system within a less developed economy incapable of the same economic sophistication tends to raise costs and reduce product quality, making the local operation uncompetitive in spite of the advantage of low labor cost by comparison with the developed countries.[9]

[9] Jack Baranson ("Technical Adjustment in a Developing Economy: A Study in the Transfer of Technology by an International Corporation," [Doctoral thesis, Indiana University, 1965]), has found that the chief difficulty in the transplantation of corporate operations to such countries is not the commonly discussed problem of training labor, but the problem of developing local supply sources as required by the characteristic emphasis on self-sufficiency, together with the problem of the longer "pay-off period" for the operation to become profitable.

These considerations suggest that less developed countries might be well advised to change their policies toward direct investment by international corporations in order to maximize the contribution to their development those investments might make. First, they should accept corporate ways of doing business as a part of the price of the corporations' assistance in development and seek (where possible) to control the influence and profits of these corporations by policies encouraging more competition from domestic rivals and imports rather than by attempting to impose political control over and participation in their managements. Second, they should abandon the effort to force policies of local self-sufficiency and import substitution in favor of integration of the local operation in the worldwide operations of the parent company—specifically, they should encourage the local operation to specialize on production for export of a few components or parts in which local comparative advantage exists or can be established, in return for free imports of other components and parts from the company's operations in other countries.[10]

POLICIES OF DEVELOPED COUNTRIES

Economic policies of the less developed countries that have the direct or indirect effect of reducing their efficiency and impeding their economic growth, and especially their growth through participation in world trade, are of course adopted largely for domestic economic and political reasons, and not with the object of impeding economic growth. The same is true of developed-country policies that operate to impede the development of the less developed countries. They too have been adopted largely for domestic economic and political reasons and not with the object of hampering the development of the less developed countries. Moreover, these policies have been motivated primarily by, and directed against, competition from developed rather than less developed countries. The leading developed countries have also in significant respects arranged their policies to favor producers in some groups of less developed countries over producers in other developed countries (as well as over producers in other less developed

---

[10] This is the policy change Baranson's researches lead him to recommend. It is also the policy change that the Canadian government is seeking to implement for the Canadian automotive industry through the 1965 Canadian-United States Automotive Products Agreement.

countries), notably through the British Commonwealth preference system, the association of overseas territories with the Common Market, and certain U.S. quota arrangements for commodities. Nevertheless, in an important sense the trade policies of the developed countries may be said to discriminate against the less developed countries. While they generally do not discriminate against those countries in the form proscribed by the most-favored-nation principle, i.e., by imposing differential barriers to the importation of the same specific good from different countries, their policies are in effect discriminatory in that the most serious barriers are erected against goods which the less developed countries typically have a comparative advantage in producing—agricultural commodities in raw or processed form, and labor-intensive, technologically unsophisticated consumer goods.[11]

The policies in question are essentially protectionist policies, justified by the same type of nationalistic philosophy as those in the less developed countries. The difference is that whereas nationalism in less developed countries justifies protection as a means of establishing new industries at the apparent expense of the foreigner and actual expense of the consumer, nationalism in developed countries justifies protection as a means of preserving old industries at the expense of both the consumer and the foreigner, particularly the poor foreigner, who could supply the product cheaper. The asymmetry arises because the difficulties of producers in the developed countries that motivate protectionism are directly or indirectly the consequence of the steady rise in average labor income that marks the condition of development and that would in a well-functioning competitive system allow transfer of the lines of production that could not afford rising wages to lower-wage producers in less developed countries. Instead of facilitating the transfer of resources out of low-income-yielding industries, however, developed countries seek to offset the relative decline in incomes in such industries by protectionist policies—price-support policies coupled with supporting import barriers for farmers, the maintenance of relatively high tariffs and other trade barriers for industrial producers suffering from lower-wage competition.

In surveying these barriers to the export earnings of the less de-

[11] See Chapter I for related comments on the principle of nondiscrimination in GATT. On the theoretical difficulties inherent in the concept of nondiscrimination, see J. E. Meade, *The Theory of International Economic Policy. Vol. I: The Balance of Payments* (London: Oxford University Press, 1951), Chap. 28.

veloped countries, especially as a background for consideration of the remedial measures proposed at the United Nations Conference on Trade and Development, it is most convenient to follow the UNC-TAD procedure of treating trade in primary commodities and trade in manufactures separately. As a prelude to consideration of trade barriers, however, it is appropriate to consider some of the inefficiencies (with respect to the promotion of development) inherent in the present system of foreign assistance, since these are related to trade barriers through the influence on aid policy of nationalism and protectionism. It is also appropriate to review migration policy—barriers to the movement of people—since its relevance is frequently overlooked.

Inefficiencies in Aid Policy

Quite apart from any question of the adequacy and prospective rate of growth of foreign aid, the provision of aid in its present predominantly bilateral and project-tied form involves certain inefficiencies that reduce its effectiveness and usefulness to the recipients by reducing the real value of the resources it transfers and restricting the uses to which it may be put.

One group of problems arises from the preference—dictated in the United States by congressional attitudes, elsewhere by commercial calculation—for giving aid in the form of "soft" loans[12] rather than outright grants. As pointed out in Chapter I, reckoning the face value of these loans as aid overstates the real amount of resources transferred by the lender and received by the borrower, and this may give rise to unwarranted complacency about the magnitude of the real assistance being given and received.[13] This, however, is a question of magnitude rather than efficiency. The use of loans rather than grants does generate inefficiency to the extent that the borrowers are induced to underestimate the economic burden of their commitments to future repayment or to overestimate the rate of growth either of their export earnings or of fresh supplies of aid from which the repayment must be made, and consequently find the repayment burden difficult or impossible to shoulder when the time comes. This is the "problem of debt service,"

---

[12] That is, loans at lower interest rates and more favorable repayment terms than the commercial market offers, at times also with interest and capital payments specified in the borrower's currency.

[13] The difference between the actual and nominal value of concessionary loans to both lenders and borrowers is discussed in Appendix C.

which has increased in seriousness in recent years in consequence of the relatively slow growth of both aid and export earnings and to which considerable attention was devoted at UNCTAD; most of the proposals there advanced for still further softening of loans were implicitly recommendations to increase the quantity of aid.

Another and apparently more serious set of problems arises from the interaction of a number of elements in the present system of supplying aid: the predominance of bilateral aid, the predominance of project over program aid, and the practice of tying aid to purchases in the donor country, a practice other countries have always followed (evidently from protectionist motives) and the United States has increasingly adopted for balance-of-payments reasons. The chief sources of inefficiency resulting from this interaction are as follows.

First, less developed countries may be able to obtain aid for projects of a "display" or "monument" type because some country likes to finance that type of project, but not for other projects that have more developmental value because no donor is interested. This source of inefficiency would be reduced by competition in aid giving if more total aid were provided by more countries and each of the donors scattered its favors among a larger number of less developed countries, or if relatively more program aid were supplied, or (probably) if more aid were supplied multilaterally so that the assessment of projects were divorced from national fads.

Second, less developed countries may have to pay substantially more than the competitive world market price for equipment used in aid-financed projects. Consequently an element of inefficiency (artificially high capital costs) and uncompetitiveness is built into the project unless the excess cost is written off. Moreover (except in the rare case of grant finance) the repayment of the loan will involve returning more real value than was received, and this may far more than offset any elements of "softness" in the loan[14] These excess costs are associated with

---

[14] For example, suppose that the tying of aid involves a 50 percent excess cost of the project over world market prices, so that the real resources provided are worth only two-thirds of their money price. This would more than cancel out the transfer involved in a ten-year interest-free loan payable in full at maturity where the alternative cost of capital was 4 percent, or a fifteen-year interest-free installment loan at an alternative opportunity cost of capital of 5 percent (see table in Appendix C). This is presumably one reason why the less developed countries have suggested that, where possible, repayments should be made in the goods produced by the project.

F

the combination of project aid and country tying of purchases and may result from either of two economic influences. First, the project may require equipment which the donor country is not the most efficient in producing. Second, the two types of tying may require the recipient country to purchase equipment from a single national producer, or a small group of producers, who can extort a noncompetitive price. This source of inefficiency, again, would be mitigated by more competition among countries in aid giving, or by more program aid, either of which would permit recipient countries to shop more efficiently for the lowest-price suppliers among or within the aid-giving nations.[15] However, one potentially serious inefficiency due to aid tying would remain: the inability of aid-receiving less developed countries to use aid money to purchase investment goods from each other, though such purchases might procure both cheaper and technologically more suitable goods and at the same time promote the development of the supplying country.[16]

A related source of inefficiency, associated with country tying of aid and the absence of stronger competition in aid giving, is that less developed countries may have to be content with less expert advisers than are available in the world market and, perhaps more important, accept a technology that is not well adapted to their economic conditions and especially their relative factor-scarcities.

A final source of inefficiency is the practice of the United States, as the largest aid donor, of requiring 50 percent of aid shipments to travel in American bottoms, at a cost greatly in excess of world shipping costs. Though countries can in exceptional cases obtain waivers from this requirement, they can only save costs by so doing if they have foreign exchange resources or nontied (multilateral) aid to finance the shipments. This requirement, an overt manifestation of protectionism, clearly has the same adverse effects on the real value of U.S. aid as do excesses of U.S. prices of aid goods above world market prices.

The seriousness of these inefficiencies depends on the extent to which aid recipients can take advantage of competition among aid do-

[15] The deleterious effect of the double tying of aid on supplier competition and its consequence in excessively high prices have been strongly emphasized by John P. Lewis, *Quiet Crisis in India* (Brookings Institution, 1962), pp. 284-85. It is probable that European producers are worse offenders than American producers in this respect.

[16] The demand of the less developed countries at UNCTAD for preferential arrangements for trade in manufactured goods among themselves reflects the importance they attach to this means of development.

nors to avoid paying excessive prices for development equipment purchased with tied aid. Several experts have expressed strongly the view that competition among aid donors is now keen and pervasive enough to prevent aid tying from producing serious inefficiencies. A very recent quantitative study by Dr. Mahbub ul Haq, of the Pakistan Planning Commission, provides evidence sharply at variance with this complacent view.[17] In an item-by-item comparison of the lowest quotation from the tied source with the lowest quotation on international competitive bidding in a sample of twenty development projects financed by six different countries, the weighted average price came out to be 51 percent higher from the tied source than on the international bids. Dr. Haq comments that the worst offenders were Japan, France, Italy and the Netherlands, and that if more credit had been available from West Germany and the United Kingdom it would have facilitated switching the projects to the cheapest procurement source. Another comparison, for commodities procured from the United States under nonproject assistance, shows that U.S. prices were 40-50 percent higher than international prices for most iron and steel products and that Japan would have been a much cheaper source but happens to offer negligible nonproject assistance to Pakistan.[18] A third set of data shows freight charges on U.S. flag ships under tied credits running 43-113 percent above the lowest quotation on international bidding.

Dr. Haq offers a rough estimate that, if the $500 million Pakistan was likely to receive in 1965 were untied, the country could save $60 million by procuring supplies in the international market; thus tying raises the average price of procurement by more than 13½ percent ($60 million ÷ $440 million). The apparent relative lowness of this estimate is accounted for by the availability of untied aid and of tied aid from competitive suppliers.[19] But the estimate still indicates a substantial loss

[17] Mahbub ul Haq, "Tied Credits—A Quantitative Analysis," paper for the International Economic Association Round Table on Capital Movements and Economic Development, July 21-31, 1965, Washington, D.C., pages 1-11 and data tables.

[18] Dr. Haq cites several instances of price quotations being substantially higher (40-50 percent) when the suppliers knew that the credit was tied than when bargaining was on a cash or untied credit basis, thus confirming the observations of Lewis, op. cit.

[19] Dr. Haq discusses the various ways in which the recipient country can keep costs down by adroit use of the alternatives of financing from export earnings, untied loans, and tied loans available from different donors; but his empirical results and general discussion indicate that Pakistan has not yet acquired the administrative sophistication required to do this efficiently. It would probably be at

of real value of aid due to tying. Moreover, the loss should properly be related not to total aid but to the proportion of it that is tied; on the basis of Dr. Haq's rough figures for the relative amounts of tied and untied aid, the increase in the average price of procurement due to tying would be about 20 percent.

Dr. Haq's findings demonstrate conclusively that the various inefficiencies associated with aid tying cannot be dismissed as negligible. Many commentators on aid nevertheless argue that the ability to tie aid leads the aid-giving countries to be substantially more generous than they otherwise would be. However, no quantitative comparisons are available of the increase in aid induced by the attractions of tying as opposed to the resources wasted through inefficiencies associated with tying, presumably because of the difficulty of devising a scientifically satisfactory way of estimating what the value of aid would have been in the absence of tying. In any case, the question is irrelevant to the assessment of the economic effects of aid as presently provided; the argument that raises it belongs to the politics rather than the economics of development assistance.

Barriers to Commodity Trade[20]

Exports of primary commodities account for some 85 percent of the export earnings of the less developed countries; hence the barriers to trade in these commodities imposed by developed countries are of great importance.[21] These barriers are of many kinds, including tariffs, quantitative restrictions, excise taxes and other devices such as mixing regulations and discrimination by state trading monopolies; they vary

---

least as difficult for most other less developed countries since Pakistan is probably more fortunate both in alternative sources for financing development imports and in the quality of its development planning staff.

[20] A convenient summary of barriers to commodity trade imposed by the developed countries is provided in *International Commodity Problems* (United Nations Conference on Trade and Development, E/Conf. 46/PC/17).

[21] In 1962 the total exports of the underdeveloped regions amounted to $28,890 million, including $8,360 million in food, beverages and tobacco products, $7,370 million in crude materials excluding fuels, $8,750 million in mineral fuels, etc., $345 million in chemical products, $265 million in machinery and transport equipment, $3,600 million in other manufactured goods (about a quarter of this represents base metals) and $200 million in miscellaneous transactions and commodities. Of the total, $20,760 million went to developed countries and $6,300 million to underdeveloped areas (the remainder being unclassifiable); $5,790 million went to the United States and $11,930 million to Europe ($6,870 million to the EEC and $4,380 million to the EFTA, of which $3,550 million went to the United Kingdom). Source: *United Nations Statistical Yearbook 1963*, Tables 159 and 160.

considerably in complexity and severity with the nature of the commodity. All of them tend to restrict the export volumes and lower the prices received by foreign suppliers. In addition quotas and other quantitative restrictions, by transferring some of the burden of adjustment to changing conditions from domestic producers to the world market, increase the instability of prices in that market and hence aggravate the instability of export earnings from primary production. The potential export earnings of producers of primary raw materials are further restricted by the practice of imposing higher tariffs on processed than on raw products, which encourages the importing of such products in raw rather than processed form. A final problem is U.S. disposal of surplus commodities, which compete directly or indirectly with the exports of certain less developed countries, even though they benefit other less developed countries that receive them as gifts.

In order to assess the quantitative significance of these various barriers to trade in primary products, and particularly barriers imposed by the United States, it is convenient to divide primary products exported by less developed countries into three groups: those that compete with products produced in the developed countries (mainly temperate agricultural products and a few metals), those that do not compete with products produced in the developed countries (mainly tropical fruits and beverage crops), and products that compete as substitutes for products produced in the developed countries (for ease of exposition, certain minerals produced in developed countries are treated under this class).

RESTRICTIONS ON COMPETITIVE PRODUCTS. Temperate agricultural products (cereals, sugar, dairy products, meat) are subject to the most complex and generally severe restrictions, involving quantitative control over imports (quotas) as well as tariffs or equivalent price-raising charges. The trade policies of the developed countries with respect to these products are an adjunct of their policies of providing price supports for their domestic producers.[22] Price supports in turn have been prompted by the tendency of agricultural prices to fall in consequence of rapid technical progress in agriculture, the price- and income-inelasticities of demand for such products, and the difficulty of moving agri-

---

[22] An exception is the United Kingdom, which has used deficiency payments but has been shifting toward price supports combined with quotas on the model of other developed countries. On theoretical grounds, deficiency payments constitute the superior method since they do not prevent consumers from benefiting from the low cost of external supplies.

cultural labor off the land. These policies damage the exporting countries both by curtailing demand and by stimulating domestic supply, while the use of quotas to control imports aggravates the instability of the world market.

A detailed assessment of the effects of these protective agricultural policies on international trade, and in particular on the export earnings and gains from trade of the less developed countries, is impossible owing to the complexity of the individual national policies and the lack of information on the relevant demand and supply elasticities. A rough idea of the extent of agricultural protectionism in the developed countries may however be gained from Table 1, taken from D. Gale Johnson's Presidential Address to the 1964 Meetings of the American

TABLE 1

Percentage Excess of Value of Output Measured at Prices Received by Farmers Over Value of Output at Import Prices of Same Year, Leading Countries, 1955-56 and 1961-62[a]

Country	1955–56	1961–62
France	24	17
West Germany	22	39
United Kingdom	33	29
Italy	19	25
Sweden	26	41
Norway	20	43
Belgium	6	13
Denmark	3	0
United States	[b]	16

Source: D. Gale Johnson, *op. cit.,* pp. 922-23.
[a] U.S. figure excludes direct payments to farmers, approximately 6 percent; similar payments (except U.K. deficiency payments) excluded for other countries.
[b] Not available.

Farm Economic Association, which was devoted to calling attention to the problems such protectionism creates for the less developed countries.[22] Johnson calls particular attention to the sharp increase in agricultural protectionism in most countries, which he holds partly responsible for the retardation of the growth of exports by the less developed countries in the latter 1950's. With respect to its effect on the less developed countries, he reasons as follows:

[22] D. Gale Johnson, "Agriculture and Foreign Economic Policy," *Journal of Farm Economics,* Vol. 46 (December 1964), pp. 922-23.

The protection given agriculture in the industrial countries restricts exports from the less developed countries [LDC's] in one or both of two ways—increasing output and reducing consumption. Only in the United Kingdom have the consumption effects been largely eliminated through the use of deficiency payments. If the increase in prices received by producers averages 20 to 25 percent and if the increase in prices paid by consumers averages 15 to 20 percent, even very low elasticities of supply and demand will result in substantial contraction in the demand for exports of the less developed regions. If supply elasticities are as low as 0.15 and demand elasticities 0.2, the effect on the value of agricultural imports of the industrial countries would be as much as $3.5-4.5 billion. Some of the increased import demand [that would result from eliminating this protection] would be met by developed countries such as Canada and Australia. But if the increase in LDC exports were to be only half that indicated or about $2 billion, the importance is very great when compared with total LDC exports of agricultural products of approximately $12 billion.[24]

For one commodity, however—sugar—more detailed estimation is possible. In a study of the effects of protection in the world sugar industry,[25] R. H. Snape estimates that if existing protective systems in the noncommunist countries were replaced by deficiency payments designed to maintain domestic output at existing levels, the increase in consumption would have been 30 percent of total net international demand and more than 70 percent of net free-market trade in 1959. This, together with the half-cent-a-pound increase in export price Snape suggests might have followed the change, would have increased the export proceeds of the (less developed) free-market producers by $357 million; if the communist countries had increased their consumption in the same proportion, the increase in export proceeds would have been $440 million.

This estimate, sizeable as it is, refers only to the effect of shifting to a more efficient system of sugar protection. It is possible, however, to use Snape's figures (and some bold assumptions) to estimate the effect of completely free trade in sugar and the net amount of additional resources that would accrue to the less-developed sugar producers through increased export earnings or could be made available to them from the savings that free trade would yield to consumers in the protectionist countries, for the seven leading Western sugar-protecting

[24] *Ibid.*, pp. 926-27.

[25] R. H. Snape, "Some Effects of Protection in the World Sugar Industry," *Economica*, Vol. 30 (February 1963), pp. 63-73. A summary and further findings based on Snape's article are presented in Appendix D.

countries. This exercise is presented in Appendix D as an example of the kind of work that needs to be done (and done better) in this field. The main findings are that free trade would have led to a minimum increase of $897 million in the value of sugar imports into these countries and would have permitted the release of $482 million of resources that could have been used for development purposes.

RESTRICTIONS ON NONCOMPETITIVE PRODUCTS. For tropical agricultural products the main barriers to the exports of the less developed countries are the heavy excise taxes imposed by the Continental European countries on consumption of coffee, cocoa and bananas. The Food and Agriculture Organization of the United Nations has estimated, for twelve European countries in 1962, that complete abolition of excise taxes and customs duties would have increased imports of coffee by 11 percent, cocoa by 8 percent and bananas by 5 percent.[26] A related GATT study estimates the effects of the same changes to be increases of 4 to 6 percent of 1961 world exports of cocoa (40,000 to 60,000 tons, with an f.o.b. value of $18 to $27 million), 4 or possibly 5 percent of world exports of coffee (70,000 to 80,000, or possibly 100,000, tons), and somewhat over 5 percent of world exports of bananas (200,000 tons).[27] Applying these last percentages to the values of world trade in 1961[28] yields estimates of increases in export earnings of $19.5 to $29.2 million for cocoa, $74.4 or possibly $93 million for coffee, and $16.6 million for bananas, a range in total from $110.5 million to $128.8 million.

RESTRICTIONS ON SEMICOMPETITIVE PRODUCTS. Among the semicompetitive products, there are significant barriers to trade in tobacco in the form of state monopolies, quantitative controls, tariffs, and bilateral agreements (including those between the United States and the Philippines and Turkey), and similar barriers to trade in vegetable oil seeds and oils, which in the case of the United States involve virtually prohibitive specific duties on imports of domestically produced commodities like peanuts and flaxseed. U.S. policy imposes the main barriers to

[26] "Europe's Demand for Tropical Agricultural Products" (ERC/62[6]), quoted in *International Commodity Problems* (E/Conf. 46/PC/17).

[27] *GATT Program for Expansion of Trade in Tropical Products* (Geneva: The Contracting Parties to the General Agreement on Tariffs and Trade, 1963), pp. 30, 47, 76.

[28] Food and Agriculture Organization of the United Nations, *Trade Yearbook, 1964*, Tables 42, 60, 61; if 1963 trade values were used the totals would be about $8-10 million smaller.

trade in cotton and wool; cotton is subject both to specific duties and to quotas (which confine imports to approximately 0.2 percent of domestic short-staple production, 17 percent of long-staple production and 1 percent of domestic output overall), while domestic producers of wool are subsidized from the proceeds of high duties on imports of raw wool and wool manufactures. Of the nonferrous metals, tin and copper move freely in world trade, the United States being the only important country that imposes duties on imports of them; aluminum, lead and zinc are subject to much more serious barriers in the form of tariffs and, until October 1965, U.S. quotas on lead and zinc confined imports to the average rates of 1953-57.[29] It has been estimated by the Department of Commerce that the removal of U.S. quotas on lead and zinc would increase imports by $45 million.[30]

The United States was also until 1966 the only developed country that imposed quotas on crude petroleum; the others impose no restrictions on it (not being important producers of it), though coal-producing countries generally levy duties and taxes on petroleum products competing with coal. The general practice of taxing gasoline heavily for revenue purposes also tends to depress consumption. The U.S. quotas, which were removed in March 1966 as an anti-inflationary measure, limited the import of crude petroleum into the area east of the Rockies each half-year to 12.2 percent of the output of crude petroleum and gas oil in the area in the corresponding part of the preceding year (there was a low import duty but no quota west of the Rockies); since the limits on imports from Canada and Mexico were only informal, the burden of the restriction fell mainly on the other suppliers, especially Venezuela and the Middle East. These quotas constituted a major restriction on trade important to some less developed countries. John H. Lichtblau, Research Director of the Petroleum Industry Research Foundation, has estimated that if they had been removed imports would have risen in 1963 by 1.35 million barrels a day; at the average f.o.b. price of imports of $2.25 a barrel he quotes, this would im-

[29] U.S. tariff rates run up to 9 percent on tin and to 27 percent on copper ore, while on copper they are 7-8 percent; they are 0-10 percent on aluminum, 6-10 percent on lead, 7 percent on lead ore, 7-19 percent on zinc and 13 percent on zinc ore.

[30] Mordechai Kreinin, "Effects of An Atlantic Free Trade Area on the American Economy," paper for the Council on Foreign Relations; Kreinin does not indicate the source within the Department of Commerce. Only part of the increase would be likely to accrue to less developed countries.

ply an increase in the exports of producing countries of $1,109 million a year.[31]

PROTECTION OF PROCESSING. The fact that most primary products used as raw materials for other products are subject to low or zero tariffs on entry into the developed countries appears on the surface to imply that those countries are allowing the less developed countries to maximize their potential export earnings from these products. This, however, is not the case, for the developed countries typically protect the processing of these products; in these circumstances free entry of the raw product increases the protective effect of the tariff on the processed product above what it would be if the raw product were subject to the same tariff rate. Export earnings are thus reduced below what they would be if the primary producers performed the processing, as would in many cases obviously be the most economical division of labor in the absence of protection. The economic point involved here is that the protective effect of a tariff structure is measured not by the tariff rates on the individual commodities, but by the effective rate of protection of value added in production processes. A tariff on the input into such a process is a tax on it, as contrasted with the subsidy provided by a tariff on the output, and free or low-tariff entry of inputs reduces the tax and increases the net subsidy.[32]

The effective protection afforded to processing of raw products in the developed countries by the combination of a tariff on the processed

---

[31] John H. Lichtblau, "The Economics and Politics of U.S. Oil Imports," talk given at the London School of Economics, June 25, 1964, unpublished, cited in Kreinin, *op. cit.* Of course, much of the money would accrue as oil company profits, rather than as royalties and other earnings for the less developed countries; but even if profits are put at 25 percent of the f.o.b. price, the increase would be around $825 million.

Lichtblau also estimated that the "consumer cost" of the oil restrictions was $2 billion, a more conservative figure than the $3.5 billion estimate of President Kennedy's Special Petroleum Study Committee of 1962. The increase in price to the consumer, however, is not the economic measure of the loss of resources involved. From his estimates that imports would increase 16 percent and were already 14 percent of domestic production, one can estimate the cost saving from contraction of high-cost domestic production at $1/2 \times 16/114 \times 2 billion = $140 million approximately; to this should be added the loss of consumers' surplus due to higher domestic prices.

[32] See Harry G. Johnson, "The Theory of Tariff Structure, With Special Reference to World Trade and Development," in Harry G. Johnson and Peter B. Kenen, *Trade and Development* (Geneva: Librairie Droz, 1965), pp. 9-29.

POLICY OBSTACLES TO DEVELOPMENT 91

product with free entry of the raw material may be very high indeed, because the cost of processing may be small by comparison with the cost of the raw material. The point is illustrated by the following calculations made by the GATT Secretariat: for copper wire, tariff rates of 10 percent in the United Kingdom and the EEC and 3 percent in Sweden provided effective rates of protection to processing of 77 percent and 23 percent respectively; for shelled groundnuts and the processed product of crude oil and cake the effective rate of protection of the processing industry was 80 percent for the United Kingdom and

TABLE 2

Nominal and Effective Protection of Processing of Agricultural Products, United States and European Economic Community
(Percent)

Processing Industry	U. S. Protection Rates		EEC Protection Rates	
	Nominal	Effective	Nominal	Effective
Coconut oil (refined)	5.7	57.5	15.0	150.0
Jute fabrics	3.1	5.3	23.0	39.6
Cigarettes	47.2	89.0	a	a
Hard fiber manufactures (cordage)	15.1	38.0	a	a

Source: Unpublished computations by Padma Mallampally from scattered data on processing costs.
a Not available.

140 percent for the EEC.[33] The calculation of effective protection rates on processing is difficult, because it requires data on the composition of costs, and no comprehensive detailed study of the extent to which industries processing primary products are protected by the developed countries has been made. Table 2 shows nominal and effective rates of protection of processing for four agricultural products. It may be remarked that the structure of the common tariff of the EEC provides very substantial protection of processing industries.

[33] Cited in Gerard Curzon, *Multilateral Commercial Diplomacy: The General Agreement on Tariffs and Trade and Its Impact on National Commercial Policies and Techniques* (London: Michael Joseph Limited, 1965). Calculations by D. Gale Johnson cited in Johnson and Kenen, *op. cit.*, show that European tariffs of 10 percent on the processing of cottonseed and of soybeans would entail effective protection rates of 34 and 160 percent.

SURPLUS COMMODITY DISPOSAL. Another policy of the developed countries that restricts the primary commodity exports of the less developed countries is the surplus commodity disposal program of the United States. On this subject, D. Gale Johnson comments as follows:

During the 50's the annual rate of growth of the quantity of exports from the less developed countries was 3.6 percent compared to 6.9 percent for the industrial countries. But what is even more important is that much of the growth in exports occurred by 1956. In value terms the exports from the nonindustrial countries to the industrial countries increased by 33 percent between 1950 and 1956; from 1956 through 1962 the increase was only 14 percent.

Some of the reduction in import growth of the industrial countries of the products of the underdeveloped countries may have been due to a decline in the rate of national income growth during the 50's and to overcoming the effects of World War II on agricultural production in Western Europe. But some role must surely be assigned to the rising tide of agricultural protectionism in Western Europe after the end of the Korean War and the large increase in surplus disposal by the United States, especially under P.L. 480 beginning in 1954 and increasing in later years.

The significance of the increase in surplus disposal resulting from P.L. 480 can be seen by comparing it with the change in the value of world exports of the main agricultural products among the major regions between 1952-53 and 1960-62. The increase in the interregional trade in agricultural products was $3,283 million during the period. This increase may be partitioned as follows: (1) the increase in the exports of the less developed countries was only $815 million; (2) the increase in commercial exports of the industrial countries was $1,097 million; and (3) the increase in the value of products made available as economic aid or surplus disposal by the United States was $1,371 million. Thus the increase in the value of shipments by the U.S. under programs such as P.L. 480 was much greater than the increase in exports of agricultural products from the less developed regions and somewhat greater than the increase in commercial sales by industrial countries, even though a substantial fraction of the latter increase was due to the use of export subsidies. How much substitution there has been between P.L. 480 shipments and commercial exports of all countries, including the U.S., is subject to dispute, but it is highly probable that there has been a significant degree of substitution.[34]

About Johnson's last point, that surplus disposal does substitute for the products of the less developed countries, there can be no real argu-

[34] D. Gale Johnson, *op. cit.*, p. 926. Johnson does not mention the relevant fact that receipt of P.L. 480 aid is generally conditional on the recipient's undertaking to restrict its exports of commodities competitive with those in surplus supply in the United States.

ment, though it suits the convenience of U.S. agricultural policy to maintain that surplus disposal does not, or can be managed so as not to, reduce the demand for commercial supplies, or that any damage falls only on other developed-country producers. If half of the increase in surplus disposal replaced less-developed-country exports, that would mean lost earnings of $685 million annually—over two-thirds of a billion dollars—and this figure makes no allowance for the effects of surplus disposal in depressing world prices for other producers.

The more interesting question is whether the damage to the export earnings of the less developed countries affected by surplus disposal is greater or less than the benefit of the gift element in surplus disposal to the countries receiving the aid; unfortunately, no study of this question is available. The gift element is, however, substantially less than the value at which the surpluses are accounted by the United States, because (a) commodity grants under Titles II and III of P.L. 480 are valued at Commodity Credit Corporation (CCC) costs, which are substantially above world market prices, (b) part of the revenue from sales for local currency is earmarked for local U.S. expenditure and a further part is provided to the recipient country as a loan rather than a grant, (c) recipient countries have to pay for shipment of half the goods in American bottoms, which involves costs substantially above world transport charges.[35]

Not all the protectionist policies of the developed countries are necessarily harmful to the export earnings of the less developed countries. For one thing, some of the less developed countries are included in the protective systems of the developed countries; the effect of this, however, is very likely a gain for the favored few at the expense of a net loss

[35] John A. Pincus ("The Cost of Foreign Aid," *Review of Economics and Statistics*, Vol. 45 [November 1963], pp. 360-67) values P.L. 480 aid shipments in 1961 at world market prices and arrives at a figure of $1,131 million, $477 million less than the figure at which the United States reports the value of this aid to the Development Assistance Committee (DAC) of the OECD. The difference is mostly due to reporting of the local currency proceeds of sales and the valuation of grants at CCC prices, each of which accounts for nearly $200 million. Pincus estimates that at market-clearing values the shipments would be worth $908 million, $700 million less than the value reported to DAC.

A much earlier study by T. W. Schultz ("Value of U.S. Farm Surpluses to Underdeveloped Countries," *Journal of Farm Economics*, Vol. 62 [December 1960], pp. 1019-30) estimated that the value of P.L. 480 products to the recipient countries was about 37 percent of the CCC costs of those products and that, given the farm program, the opportunity cost of the products to the United States could be reckoned at zero.

for the group as a whole. For another, as Gale Johnson points out,[36] agricultural policies that restrict output and accumulate stocks to maintain prices raise prices for and stimulate production by rival producers in other countries; this has been the effect in the past quarter-century of U.S. cotton and tobacco policy. But the United States is the only major developed country that has actually tried to restrict production, and it is extremely doubtful that it has had any real success in so doing.

The various estimates of the effects on the annual export earnings of the less developed countries of the barriers to trade in primary commodities are summarized below. The estimates overlap and cannot be added together.

Agricultural protectionism in developed countries	$2,000 million
Sugar protection by existing methods as contrasted with protection by deficiency payments	$357-525 million
European duties and excises on coffee, cocoa and bananas	$110-125 million
U.S. lead and zinc quotas (no longer applied)	part of $45 million
U.S. petroleum quotas (no longer applied)	$1,109 million
U.S. surplus disposal	$ 685 million

Tariff Barriers to Trade in Manufactures

Exports of manufactures from the less developed countries are as yet relatively small; roughly, they account for under 10 percent of these countries' total exports and about 4 percent of world trade in manufactures.[37] Somewhat over half of these exports (about $1.5 billion worth) go to markets in the developed countries, the vast bulk of them to the United States and United Kingdom. The supply of these manufactures is heavily concentrated in a few less developed countries and the exports themselves are heavily concentrated on a narrow range of goods, four-fifths of them being textiles and miscellaneous (light) manufactured goods.[38]

[36] Op. cit., p. 924.
[37] Excluding processed foodstuffs and base metals from "manufactures."
[38] In 1962, the total c.i.f. import value of developed-country imports of manufactures from less developed countries was $1,643 million (this is about 10 percent higher than f.o.b. values). The leading exporting countries were Hong Kong ($400 million), India ($370 million), Israel and Mexico (about $100 million each), Iran and the Philippines ($110 million together), Pakistan, Taiwan, Argentina and Brazil (about $130 million altogether), these ten accounting for three-quarters of the total and no other country providing more than $5 million. Four product classes (clothing, cotton fabrics, other textile fabrics, and pearls and precious and semiprecious stones) accounted for two-fifths of the total, and ten product classes

These facts have led many observers to conclude that tariffs and other barriers to trade in manufactured goods imposed by the developed countries are not an important impediment to the development of the less developed countries—and particularly will not be so after they have been reduced to the extent expected from the Kennedy Round—and consequently that special action to reduce or remove them on products in which the less developed countries are specially interested would do little to increase their export earnings and promote their growth.[39] The characteristics of the manufacturing exports of the less developed countries, however, may just as well reflect the presence and strength of barriers to these exports as inability to supply them competitively; and the actual strength of these barriers cannot be established by simple inference from United States propaganda about the intentions of the Kennedy Round. It is, moreover, somewhat inconsistent to maintain that less developed countries could not take advantage of improved trade opportunities when their demonstrated ability to sell rapidly increasing quantities of cotton textiles in spite of relatively high barriers to imports in the major markets has prompted the importing countries to resort to quota limitations.

Barriers to exports of manufactures by less developed countries, like barriers to exports of primary commodities, include both tariffs and nontariff barriers. In analyzing barriers to exports of manufactures it is convenient to treat tariff and nontariff barriers separately. A survey of existing barriers, however, does not fully account for the impediments to trade, for it omits the separate influence of uncertainty about the future magnitude of those barriers—associated with the freedom of

---

for nearly two-thirds of the total. (Exports of processed foodstuffs from less developed to developed countries, excluded along with base metals from these figures, had a c.i.f. value of $329 million in 1961.) The data are taken from *Measures for the Expansion of Markets of the Developed Countries for Exports of Manufactures and Semi-Manufactures of the Developing Countries* (United Nations Conference on Trade and Development, E/Conf. 46/6, February 14, 1964).

[39] One writer, for example, argues strongly that the less developed countries should concentrate for the present on barriers to primary commodity trade and not lose goodwill by complaining about barriers to trade in manufactures, which he believes will not be an important issue until the tenth meeting of UNCTAD, or possibly the fifth (thirty or possibly fifteen years hence), and that before they can make a sensible case for reduction of such barriers they must transform themselves into industrial economies. This argument is comparable to telling Negroes that they can demand an end to discrimination only after they have proved that they can do as well as white men in spite of discrimination.

countries to raise barriers or impose new ones if their industries suffer increased import competition—in deterring investment in production for export markets.

The impression that barriers to exports of manufactures by less developed countries are now quite low is derived from the fact that as a result of successive rounds of GATT negotiations quantitative restrictions on manufactured imports have been steadily removed and average tariff rates on manufactures have been steadily reduced to a range somewhere between 10 and 20 percent, depending on the type of average used.[40] However, the impression is misleading because the tariff averages ignore the dispersion of individual tariff rates about the average and conceal the fact that tariff rates on manufactures in which the less developed countries are particularly interested are relatively high, running from 20 up to 40 percent or more; furthermore, the tariffs on such items frequently have been excluded from the GATT negotiations.[41]

EFFECTIVE RATE OF PROTECTION OF VALUE ADDED. Tariff rates on commodities, however, are not the appropriate basis for assessing the restrictive effect of a tariff structure on trade. What is relevant is the effective rate of protection of production processes, i.e. of "value added" in those processes.

This concept is important because the tariff structures of the developed countries (and, for that matter, of the less developed countries) are typically escalated by stage of production, rates of duty rising from raw materials to semimanufactures and from semimanufactures to finished goods, and are generally set lower on capital goods than on consumer goods. Escalation thus gives effective protection at rising rates—and at rates higher than the nominal tariff rates on the goods—to goods at successive stages of the production process; it also gives greater effective protection—at rates higher than the nominal tariff rates on the goods—to consumer goods than to capital goods. These tariff structures consequently impose especially heavy barriers to the goods that the less developed countries are most likely to be able to produce for export, namely consumer goods that are relatively labor intensive and employ a relatively unsophisticated technology.

[40] None of the commonly used methods of calculating average tariff rates is satisfactory, even on purely statistical index-number grounds, let alone as an approximation to the economic concept of degree of restriction of trade.

[41] Detailed evidence is provided in *International Commodity Problems* (E/Conf. 46/PC/17), especially Appendix Table 1.

The concept of the effective rate of protection of value added as a measure of barriers to trade is not universally accepted. It has been argued, in particular, that where effective rates are high relative to nominal rates, value added is small relative to materials costs, so that a reduction in barriers that transferred the production of value added to the suppliers of the materials would add relatively little to the value of their exports. This observation is generally correct, so far as it goes; but its point is fully taken into account in a proper analysis of the response of trade to a reduction of barriers. Moreover, the objection implicitly assumes, in the tradition of international trade theory, that the restrictive effect of trade barriers is directly correlated with their height; it might instead be the case that the influence of trade barriers on the location of economic activity operates discontinuously, high barriers serving to preserve the bulk of the market to local producers and low barriers having a negligible effect in distorting competition. Finally, in view of the emphasis placed by the less developed countries on the importance of establishing industrial activities within their territories, the true height of the trade barriers to industrial exports is a matter of interest independent of their effects on actual trade volumes.

From the point of view of assessing the impediment created by the tariff structures of the developed countries to the export of manufactures from the less developed countries, it is arguable that a still more relevant concept is the effective rate of protection of value added by labor. The argument is that in the long run it can be assumed that capital and technology are internationally mobile, so that the international location of production will be determined primarily by the interaction of tariffs and relative labor costs; the rate of effective protection of value added by labor measures the extent to which the tariff permits labor cost in the country's industry to exceed the value of labor's contribution at world market prices.

While the documents prepared for UNCTAD explicitly mentioned the effect of escalation of tariff rates by stage of production and presented evidence on it, no use was made of the two concepts of effective protection. Subsequently, however, two sets of estimates of effective protection rates have become available; one, by Giorgio Basevi,[42] estimates the two sets of effective tariff rates implicit in the United States

---

[42] "The United States Tariff Structure: Estimates of Effective Rates of Protection of United States Industries and Industrial Labor," *Review of Economics and Statistics,* Vol. 48 (May 1966), pp. 147-60.

G

tariff structure for a large number of manufacturing industries; the other, by Bela A. Balassa,[43] presents a comparative estimate of effective rates of protection of value added for thirty-six industries in the United States, the United Kingdom, the Common Market, Sweden and Japan as part of a more comprehensive study of these tariff structures and their effects on trade.

The results of these calculations conform reasonably well with one

TABLE 3

*Averages of Effective and Nominal Rates of Duties
for Four Commodity Categories, 1962*

(*Percent*)

Category	United States		United Kingdom		Common Market		Sweden		Japan	
	Nom-inal	Effec-tive	Nom-inal	Effec-tive	Nom-inal	Effec-tive	Nom-inal	Effec-tive	Nom-inal	Effec-tive
Intermediate Products I[a]	8.8	17.6	11.1	23.1	7.6	12.0	3.0	5.3	11.4	23.8
Intermediate Products II[b]	15.2	28.6	17.2	34.3	13.3	28.3	8.5	20.8	16.6	34.5
Consumer goods	17.5	25.9	23.8	40.4	17.8	30.9	12.4	23.9	27.5	50.5
Investment goods	10.3	13.9	17.0	23.0	11.7	15.0	8.5	12.1	17.1	22.0
All commodities	11.6	20.0	15.5	27.8	11.9	18.6	6.8	12.5	16.2	29.5

Source: Balassa, *op. cit.*, Table 5, p. 591.
[a] Manufactures whose main inputs are natural raw materials.
[b] Intermediate goods at higher levels of fabrication.

another and support the predictions of theoretical analysis, providing evidence that the tariffs of the developed countries do impose especially heavy barriers to the manufactured exports of the less developed countries. In the first place the average effective rate of protection of value added is substantially higher than the average nominal tariff rate; Balassa, using the composition of total trade to weight each country's tariffs, obtains the following average effective tariff rates (average nominal rates in parentheses): United States 20.0 (11.6), United Kingdom 27.8 (15.5), Common Market 18.6 (11.9), Sweden 12.5 (6.8), Japan

[43] "Tariff Protection in Industrial Countries: An Evaluation," *Journal of Political Economy*, Vol. 73 (December 1965), pp. 573-94.

29.5 (16.2). Secondly, effective rates of protection on goods escalate by stages of production, with the minor exception of effective rates of protection of consumer goods in the United States; this is verified in Table 3. Thirdly, effective rates of protection of value added tend to be especially high on manufactured goods in which the less developed countries have a special interest, as demonstrated in Tables 4 and 5, which match the products of special interest to the less developed countries with effective rates of protection on them.

RESTRICTIVENESS OF TARIFF BARRIERS. The figures assembled in these tables demonstrate that the tariffs of the developed countries do impose

TABLE 4

Estimated Effective Rates of Protection of Value Added in Industrial Products of Special Interest to Less Developed Countries in Four Major Markets, 1962

(*Percent*)

Product	United States	United Kingdom	Common Market	Japan
Thread and yarn	31.8	27.9	3.6	1.4
Textile fabrics	50.6	42.2	44.4	48.8
Hosiery	48.7	49.7	41.3	60.8
Clothing	35.9	40.5	25.1	42.4
Other textile articles	22.7	42.4	38.8	13.0
Shoes	25.3	36.2	33.0	45.1
Wood products including furniture	26.4	25.5	28.6	33.9
Leather	25.7	34.3	18.3	59.0
Leather goods other than shoes	24.5	26.4	24.3	33.6
Rubber goods	16.1	43.9	33.6	23.6
Plastic articles	27.0	30.1	30.0	35.5
Synthetic materials	33.5	17.1	17.6	32.1
Other chemical materials	26.6	39.2	20.5	22.6
Chemical products	15.6	16.7	13.1	22.9
Ingots and other primary steel forms	106.7	98.9	28.9	58.9
Metal manufactures	28.5	35.9	25.6	27.7
Nonelectrical machinery	16.1	21.2	12.2	21.4
Electrical machinery	18.1	30.0	21.5	25.3
Bicycles and motorcycles	26.1	39.2	39.7	45.0
Precision instruments	32.2	44.2	24.2	38.5
Sports goods, toys, jewelry, etc.	41.8	35.6	26.6	31.2

Source: Balassa, *op. cit.*, Table 1. Products selected from Balassa's table are those included in the interim report of the UNCTAD Secretariat on *Measures for Expansion of Markets in Developed Countries for the Exports of Manufactures and Semi-Manufactures of Developing Countries* (United Nations Conference on Trade and Development, E. Conf. 46/PC/20, 6 May 1963).

TABLE 5

Nominal U.S. Tariff Rates and Effective Rates of Protection of Value Added and of Value Added by Labor for Industrial Products of Special Interest to Less Developed Countries, 1958-60[a]

(Percent)

Product	Industrial Classification	Nominal Tariff Rate	Effective Rate of Protection	
			Value Added	Value Added by Labor
Bicycles	Motorcycles, bicycles and parts	17.5	34.3	67.4
Cutlery	Cutlery	35.4	50.8	417.6
	Edge tools	19.1	27.3	67.4
Electric motors	Motors and generators	13.0	16.1	29.9
Electric fans	Electric housewares and fans	16.0	23.2	78.8
Glass and glassware	Float glass	14.9	19.1	46.2
	Glass containers	23.9	37.5	126.7
	Other pressed and blown glass	15.0	18.7	40.3
	Products of purchased glass	32.1	51.2	300.0
Internal combustion engines	Internal combustion engines	10.0	13.1	26.4
Iron and steel, semi-processed goods	Gray iron foundries	8.0	9.7	15.6
	Malleable iron foundries	18.2	29.4	40.5
	Blast furnaces and steel mills	6.1	8.5	17.5
	Steel wire drawing	10.0	8.7	16.7
	Steel foundries	9.0	11.4	18.3
	Iron and steel forgings	13.1	27.3	45.1
	Metal stampings	16.0	25.7	49.7
Leather footwear	Footwear cut stock	11.0	14.9	27.9
	Footwear, except rubber	12.4	14.4	26.1
	House slippers	16.2	30.2	59.7
Leather goods	Leather gloves	33.3	68.6	195.2
	Luggage	20.0	30.4	69.8
	Handbags and purses	20.8	34.1	70.5
	Other leather goods	12.0	15.3	30.6
Linoleum	Hard surface floor coverings	14.0	19.2	55.7
Machine tools	Metal-cutting machine tools	15.3	19.8	30.2
	Metal-forming machine tools	14.5	20.1	28.6
	Special dies and tools	26.7	35.8	62.1
	Machine tool accessories	26.7	36.6	70.0
	Other metalworking machinery	15.3	21.9	48.3

TABLE 5. *Continued*

Product	Industrial Classification	Nominal Tariff Rate	Effective Rate of Protection	
			Value Added	Value Added by Labor
Metal manufactures	Secondary nonferrous metals	7.0	23.7	59.4
	Copper rolling and drawing	8.8	7.5	16.2
	Aluminum rolling and drawing	10.5	22.2	56.0
	Other rolling and drawing	16.7	32.7	83.3
	Nonferrous wire drawing, etc.	14.3	21.2	50.6
	Brass, bronze, copper castings	10.0	12.8	21.5
Plywood	Veneer and plywood plants	16.8	37.9	80.4
Pulp, paper, paperboard	Pulp mills	0.0	−2.2	−5.6
	Paper mills, except building	0.3	−6.9	−13.4
	Paperboard mills	9.0	14.9	51.4
	Pressed and molded pulp goods	9.5	11.8	32.8
	Other paper and board products	4.4	7.6	18.1
	Building paper and board mills	7.8	6.9	15.5
Radio receivers	Radio and television receiving sets	12.5	20.2	51.9
Rubber manufactures	Tires and inner tubes	8.9	7.7	19.2
	Rubber footwear	15.8	19.7	40.3
Rugs and carpets	Woven carpets and rugs	20.1	17.8	35.3
	Tufted carpets and rugs	20.1	28.3	195.4
	Other carpets and rugs	20.4	33.2	85.0
Sewing machines	Sewing machines	10.9	13.3	17.7
Soap	Soap and other detergents	8.6	9.9	73.7
Steel furniture	Metal household furniture	17.8	30.0	67.5
	Metal office furniture	18.0	25.3	69.0
	Public building furniture	18.0	28.5	56.6
Wood furniture	Wood furniture, not upholstered	14.3	21.6	39.6
	Wood furniture, upholstered	14.3	14.7	27.3
	Wood office furniture	18.0	27.7	54.8

Source: Basevi, *op. cit.* The estimated effective rates of protection used are the lower of Basevi's two alternative sets of estimates.

a Products selected are those included on the list of semimanufactures and manufactures of importance in the export trade of less developed countries examined by GATT, Committee III, printed as Appendix Table II to *Measures for the Expansion of Markets of the Developed Countries for Exports of Manufactures and Semi-Manufactures of Developing Countries* (E/Conf. 46/6). Unfortunately some important items in the list could not be matched with Basevi's estimates.

substantial barriers to imports of manufactured products which the less developed (and especially the "developing") countries are particularly likely to be capable of exporting. The really difficult probem, however, is to assess the extent to which these barriers actually restrict the exports of the less developed countries. The answer obviously depends in part on the relative elasticities of supply of products now being exported in the less developed countries as compared with their rivals in the developed countries, and on the extent to which the elimination of these barriers (especially an assured permanent elimination) would lead to the development of new export products from the less developed countries. This last factor is extremely important, given the magnitudes of the effective rates of protection of value added—and especially of value added by labor—on some products, the large differences in income and wage levels between the developed and the less developed countries, and the international mobility of capital and technological knowledge, which would increase greatly in a world economy of genuine free trade.

Apart from these supply factors, the effects would depend on the extent to which free trade would increase the demand of the developed countries for manufactured imports from the less developed countries. Most economists, probably, would guess that the absolute effect would be relatively small, reasoning from the apparently low average levels of nominal tariff rates and small volumes of existing industrial exports of the less developed countries and the general impression, supported by past econometric work, that the elasticities of demand in international trade are low.[44] This, however, is not a correct approach; the proper theoretical formulation requires that demand elasticities in the im-

---

[44] This is the procedure of G. L. Reuber, the only author who appears to have attempted an estimate of the effects of alternate trade policy changes on the exports of less developed countries (Grant L. Reuber, *Canada's Interest in the Trade Problems of Less-Developed Countries* [Montreal: The Canadian Trade Committee of the Private Planning Association of Canada, May 1964]). Reuber assumes (p. 26) an average tariff rate of 12 percent and a demand elasticity of 2, for the case in which tariffs are assumed to be eliminated by all countries on their industrial imports from less developed countries only, and arrives at an estimated long-term increase in the latter's exports of 25 percent, with a dollar value of about $250 million. This figure excludes textile yarns and fabrics, on the assumption of continuation of existing quantitative controls on imports. Reuber estimates that the effect of removing tariffs on commodities as well, while maintaining quantitative restrictions, would be at most an increase of $600 million in exports, while if quantitative restrictions were also removed the maximum increase would be $1½ billion.

porting country be weighted by the ratio of consumption to imports and multiplied by the nominal tariff rates, and the supply elasticities (in the individual processes) in the importing country be weighted by the ratios of value added in the country to imports and multiplied by the effective rates of protection of value added.[45] Using this approach and reasonable assumed values of the relevant elasticities and ratios, together with the nominal and effective rates of protection shown in Table 3, Balassa has calculated that the elimination of duties on manufactured goods would lead to the following relative increases in imports of manufactured goods: Japan 39.9 percent, United States 38.2 percent, United Kingdom 30.9 percent, European Common Market 28.2 percent, and Sweden 14.0 percent; if the elasticity of supply in the United States is assumed to be one-half higher than in other countries, as might be reasonable, the relative increase in U.S. imports would be 54.1 percent.

These figures may be regarded as estimates of the degrees of trade restriction these countries impose on industrial products through tariffs. Similar calculations could be used to compute the expansion of demand for imports of manufactures from the less developed countries that might result from the adoption of free trade by these countries, on the assumption that the expansion would be divided between other developed countries and the less developed countries in the same ratio as present trade.[46] An extremely rough calculation of this kind made by applying the estimated percentage increases to 1961 manufactured exports by less developed countries, using the U.S. percentage for North America, the U.K. percentage for the European Free Trade Association, and the Japanese percentage for all other developed countries, yields a total estimated increase of 34 percent ($445 million on $1,310 million). This is probably a substantial underestimate, because the effective protection rates on less-developed-country exports are higher than the average, and the expansion of demand for these products should therefore be greater than the average (the dollar amounts are also too low owing to the exclusion of processed foodstuffs and base metals from the concept of manufactures employed; the increase would be $500 million on the $1.5 billion of exports to developed countries in 1962).

[45] Balassa, *op. cit.;* formula developed by Harry G. Johnson and Bela Balassa.
[46] An adjustment would of course have to be made for the effects of the Cotton Textiles Arrangement on imports of textiles from the less developed countries.

In addition to the tariff structures of the developed countries themselves, certain features of tariffs and their administration assertedly impede the manufactured exports of less developed countries especially severely. These include the use of specific rather than ad valorem duties, mostly by the United States and the United Kingdom, which weigh heavily on lower-quality and cheaper products; the use of assumed norms or domestic retail prices in valuing goods for duty (such as the American selling price applied to items like rubber boots and knitted gloves); and the administration of antidumping laws which may be called into operation, at least to the extent of initiating an investigation, by the fact that prices are low, even though no dumping is actually involved. The last two of these are more properly classed as nontariff barriers.

Nontariff Barriers to Trade in Manufactures

As tariffs have been reduced in successive GATT negotiations, international trade negotiators and experts have become increasingly concerned about nontariff barriers to trade. This subject is an extremely complex one, both the existence of such barriers and their restrictive effects being almost impossible to obtain information on.[47] The UNCTAD Secretariat prepared the following list of barriers, grouped by types:[48]

Foreign trade policies
　Licensing requirements
　Quota restrictions
　Negotiated export limitations
　Foreign exchange restrictions
　State trading
　Procurement policies favoring domestic products
　Antidumping and similar regulations
　Subsidies to exports

Administrative practices
　Classification of goods for customs purposes
　Documentary, marking and packaging requirements
　Incomplete or delayed publication of customs information

---

[47] For a discussion of such barriers and the difficulty of removing them, see Mark S. Massel, "Non-Tariff Barriers as an Obstacle to World Trade," *The Expansion of World Trade: Legal Problems and Techniques*, Dennis Thompson, ed. (The British Institute of International and Comparative Law, 1965; Brookings Institution Reprint 97).

[48] *Measures for the Expansion of Markets* (E/Conf. 46/6).

Internal economic policies affecting imports
   Internal taxes for revenue purposes
   Taxes applied to imports to compensate for indirect taxes borne by comparable domestic goods
   Pricing policies and price control regulations
   Restrictions on advertising of goods

Internal health and safety regulations affecting imports
   Sanitary regulations
   Technical specification requirements
   Regulations applied for national security reasons

To these governmental practices should be added a variety of private business practices that may particularly impede the manufactured exports of less developed countries, such as market allocation among the affiliates of international corporations and the setting of ocean shipping rates by shipping conferences.

The most frequently used form of nontariff barrier is import restrictions coupled with licensing requirements, most common in the Continental European countries and Japan. How far these discriminate against the less developed countries is difficult to gauge; there is reason to think that Germany in particular uses its quantitative restrictions in this way. Table 6 shows the import restrictions applying in 1963 to manufactures of special interest to less developed countries. As mentioned, the general trend in GATT has been to reduce the number of, and liberalize, such restrictions. The exception, of course, is the Cotton Textiles Arrangement which legitimizes "voluntary" export restraint by less developed countries and has operated mainly to restrain Japanese exports to the United States. Kreinin[49] has estimated, by comparing rates of growth of controlled and uncontrolled products in the period 1957-62, that voluntary restraints applied by Japan in cotton textiles and twenty-eight other products excluded from the United States market $193 million of potential imports, of which $102 million were textiles. No estimates are available of the effects of the voluntary restraints and in some cases quotas on cotton textile exports from Pakistan, India and Hong Kong to the United Kingdom; it should also be noted that the United Kingdom maintains a state import monopoly in jute goods to protect its processing industry.

Among the other forms of nontariff barriers are customs administration practices, discussed earlier. Government procurement practices,

[49] *Op. cit.*

TABLE 6

Nontariff Import Restrictions on Manufactures and Semimanufactures of Importance in the Export Trade of Less Developed Countries, October 1963ᵃ

Country	Canned Fish	Tobacco Manufactures	Leather	Leather Goods	Cotton Textiles	Jute Manufactures	Coir Manufactures	Internal Combustion Engines[b]	Sewing Machines	Electric Motors	Electric Fans	Bicycles	Steel Furniture	Leather Footwear	Sporting Goods
Australia	—	—	—	—	—	—	—	—	—	—	—	—	—	—	—
Austria	—	S	—	—	Q*	Q	Q*	—	—	Q*	—	Q*	—	Q	—
Benelux	—	—	—	—	•	—	—	—	—	—	—	—	—	—	—
Canada	—	—	—	—	—	—	—	—	—	—	—	—	—	—	—
Denmark	—	—	—	—	•	R*	R*	—	—	—	—	—	—	—	—
Finlandᵈ	Q*	—	Q*	Q*	Q*	Q*	q*	Q	—	Q*	—	Q	—	Q	—
France	q*	S	—	q*	q*	Q*	q*	Q	—	Q*	—	Q	—	—	q*
Germany (Federal Republic)	—	—	—	—	—	—	—	—	r*	—	—	—	—	—	—
Italy	R*	S	q*	—	q*	q*	—	R*	—	—	—	—	—	—	—
Japan	Q	S	R*	R	q*	—	—	R*	—	—	—	—	—	R	—
New Zealand	Q	R	Q	R	Q*	Q*	Q*	Q	L	Q	R	Q	—	R	Q
Norway	—	—	—	—	•	—	—	—	—	—	—	—	—	—	—
Sweden	—	—	—	—	—	—	—	—	—	—	—	—	—	—	—
Switzerland	—	—	—	—	—	S*	—	—	—	—	—	—	—	—	—
United Kingdom	—	—	—	—	q	S*	—	—	—	—	—	—	—	—	—
United States	—	—	—	—	qᶠ	—	—	—	—	—	—	—	—	—	—

(Symbols indicate quantitative restriction as follows: Q = global quota; q = bilateral quota; L = licensing requirement; R = import restriction, unspecified, on imports from all sources; r = import restriction, unspecified, on imports from some sources only; S = state trading or trading by an authorized monopoly; * = restriction on part of item only.) Source: *Measures for the Expansion of Markets* (E/Conf. 46/6); their data from "Quantitative Restrictions Affecting Exports of Less Developed Countries" (GATT documents COM. III/72, 12 April 1962, 1 April 1962, 1 July 1963, and COM. III/116, 17 October 1963) and official national sources. ᵃ Table refers to trade between GATT contracting parties and associated countries; products are among those examined by GATT, Committee III. ᵇ Engines under 50 horsepower only. ᶜ Quota restrictions on imports from Japan. ᵈ Import permit required for most imports from countries not on the "multilateral treatment list"; list includes all GATT countries except Cuba, Czechoslovakia, Greece, Israel, Poland, Turkey and the United Arab Republic. ᵉ Various items restricted from Czechoslovakia, Poland, and Japan. ᶠ Restraints applied in accordance with Long-Term Arrangement on Cotton Textiles.

which include the tying of aid and discrimination in defense expenditure, are obviously potentially important nontariff barriers to trade but are unlikely to discriminate against potential exports of less developed countries.

Immigration Policy

In several important senses the immigration policies of the developed countries, which generally discriminate severely against immigrants from the less developed countries, especially the poorly trained and educated, may be said to lie at the core of the development problem. In political terms these policies are a manifestation of discrimination by the white people of the world against the colored, the reaction against and imitation of which is responsible for much of the violent nationalism or ethnism that motivates certain inefficient economic policies in the less developed countries. In economic terms, these policies are largely responsible for the form that the problem of assisting development now takes—the problem of transferring modern industrial society and technology to backward peoples in the geographical setting in which they have been born and raised, through foreign aid and technical assistance. From a strictly economic point of view, the easiest method of modernizing the members of a nonindustrial culture and raising their incomes is to transplant them to a rich industrial economy and let their willingness to work for low wages bring about their integration into that economy; the share of their wages they can afford to send home to their families may well exceed their total potential earnings in their home environment. This proposition is well confirmed by the mass migrations of the nineteenth century, and by those that have been allowed to occur in the post-World War II period (for example, West Indian and other immigration into the United Kingdom, migration of southern European labor to the Common Market countries).

The relative numbers and the procreative propensities of the less developed peoples obviously make development through freer immigration into developed countries an impractical policy proposal (though a policy of bringing in substantial numbers of young men and women from less developed countries to work in American small businesses for a limited period of years might be far more effective in modernizing their societies than the Peace Corps can hope to be). Nevertheless, it is important to appreciate that the preference of the people of the developed countries for avoiding social contact with and competition from the people of the less developed countries necessitates promoting development in the politically and economically most difficult way, and is therefore ultimately responsible for much of the inefficiency and frustration felt about the aid program. The developed countries prevent the people of the less developed countries from personal participation in their opulence through immigration and at the same time impede them from absentee participation in it through international trade; in this set of circumstances, foreign aid on a massive scale appears less like generosity than like compensation for injury.

Apart from the general exclusiveness of immigration policy, immigration laws invariably discriminate less severely against, and in the case of some countries positively encourage, the immigration of educated and professionally trained people. This is a possible source of special damage to the less developed countries. From the point of view of strictly private economic welfare, of course, such immigration prima facie involves a net economic gain, since it raises the real incomes of the immigrants; it may, however, involve an economic loss to the country of origin, in the form of educational costs borne by the government. From the nationalist point of view it may well involve a serious loss to the less developed country since thousands of poor people may derive enough psychic satisfaction from the scientific achievements or cultural contribution of one educated person of their own race or nationality to compensate for a great deal of material privation, satisfaction that would not be matched by the satisfaction of having one of themselves make good in some unknown way in some far-off rich country plus the satisfaction to residents of that country of adding one more foreigner to its elite. There may be, and often is, also a real economic loss if the migrant could have been employed in his country of origin to do work which instead has to be undertaken by technical experts sent out at vastly greater cost from a developed country or by domestic researchers in the developed country who have to be paid the higher salaries of that country. This kind of loss is the consequence of nationalism in the provision of technical assistance and research money, which confines the high salaries and facilities to citizens and residents of the country providing these forms of aid.

It can, of course, be argued that any losses imposed on the less developed countries through emigration of talented people are more than offset by the contributions of the developed countries to the education of students who return home after training. This, however, is not all that clear from the evidence, at least for the United States, since about 10-15 percent of students from foreign countries remain in the United States. Research by H. G. Grubel and A. D. Scott into the economics of the international flow of students, which attempts to compute the U.S. balance on student exchange by considering the capital values of nonreturning students, as well as the cost of foreign and U.S. contributions to the education of foreign students, indicates that the United States in 1962-63 contributed to the rest of the world resources valued at $146 million gross, which came to only $16 million net after deduction of the capital value of nonreturning students and some other adjustments.[50] These data are for all foreign students; since a larger proportion of European students than of students from less developed countries return home on completion of their training, it is likely that the United States derives a net positive gain with respect to students from the less developed countries. This, however, is a subject on which more research is needed. The situation does not necessarily imply that the United States should force students from less developed countries to return home after training, for some of them stay to avoid political trouble at home rather than for economic reasons. Instead, the United States might consider paying, or obliging the immigrant to pay, an annuity or capital sum to the government of the country of origin; and, in the interests of economy as well as avoiding damage to the less developed countries, it might consider the use of technical assistance funds to improve the wages and working conditions of educated nationals of the less developed countries in their own countries.

This chapter has surveyed the obstacles to the development of the less developed countries through expanding trade that have been imposed by the commercial and other policies of both these countries and the developed countries. It is clear that much of the difficulty the less developed countries encounter in increasing their exports is of their own making. Their nationalistic orientation to economic policy, their preference for centralized economic planning, their exploitative attitude toward traditional agriculture, their commitment to import substitution, their policies of inflation and currency overvaluation, and their hostility to private investment in their industry by foreigners can

[50] Herbert Grubel, "Nonreturning Foreign Students and the Cost of Student Exchange," *International Educational and Cultural Exchange* (U.S. Advisory Commission on International and Cultural Affairs, Spring 1966), pp. 20-29.

all be adduced in explanation of their export problems. But it is also clear that many facets of the aid and trade policies of the developed countries impose serious barriers to the development of the less developed countries, barriers whose reduction might contribute substantially to the promotion and diffusion of economic growth throughout the world. The next three chapters are concerned with the ways in which these barriers might be reduced, or alternatively with the ways in which their adverse effects on the less developed countries might be mitigated or compensated for.

IV

Action Within the Existing Framework

The United Nations Conference on Trade and Development served as a forum for the less developed countries' denunciation of the trade and aid policies of the developed countries and of the present institutional framework governing international economic relations. It provided a platform from which they voiced demands for new trade and aid—especially trade—policies designed to increase the external resources made available to them from the developed countries. Much of their criticism of developed-country policy is economically valid, and the practices complained of are genuine matters for concern to everyone interested in promoting the development of the less developed countries—an objective to which the United States and the other developed countries have acknowledged their commitment. On the other hand, the trade policy changes recommended by the less developed countries involve inverting in their favor the very policies of which they complain and to which there is the strongest objection on grounds of economic inefficiency. The policies themselves violate the spirit, and often the established principles, of the existing system of international economic organization, which was instituted with the purpose of reestablishing a liberal international trading system. It is therefore natural to question whether the demands of the less developed countries for additional external resources for development, and in particular for additional opportunities for export earnings, could be met within the existing international institutional framework.

An initial problem is determining to what extent the existing framework limits the policy alternatives that might be adopted. For example, international agencies now in existence furnish a great deal of technical assistance and a limited amount of financial aid to the less developed countries; would the establishment of a large new international development assistance agency, channelling large amounts of new or previously bilaterally provided funds to the less developed countries and controlled by the United Nations or possibly by representatives of the governments contributing the funds, fall within the existing framework or constitute a major change in it? In terms of the politics of aid, both among the donors and between donors and recipients, the shift from bilateralism toward multilateralism in either form would constitute a major change. In terms of contemporary political-economic relations among the developed countries, United Nations control would represent a major change whereas control by the aid-giving nations, if confined to the noncommunist donors, would more properly represent an extension of the existing system, since these nations are accustomed to a great deal of cooperation in the monetary, trade, and aid fields. But in terms of existing institutions, neither arrangement would be a revolutionary change, since the United Nations is already an important part of the existing framework.

Again, international commodity agreements of the type demanded at UNCTAD have been established and function as part of the present institutional framework governing world trade. These arrangements are neither under the General Agreement on Tariffs and Trade nor subject to any specific principles agreed on inside GATT or outside it. Extension of such arrangements to a great many more commodities would therefore not change the existing framework in general principle, though it would transform it in practice by substituting international commodity agreements for the present maze of national tariffs, quantitative import controls, and domestic price support policies.

Finally, it is true that preferences for the industrial exports of the less developed countries would conflict with the GATT ban on new preferences, that some preference schemes would conflict with the prohibition of protection by quotas rather than customs tariffs, and that preferential tariff schemes among groups of less developed countries would not conform to the terms of the GATT exception for customs unions and free trade areas. Nevertheless, these rules have been violated in the past with the formation of the European Economic Community and (in principle, regarding quotas) the initiation of the Cotton Textiles Arrangement. Moreover, the rules of GATT can always be reinterpreted by the contracting parties to allow new trade arrangements or policies considered to be in accord with the spirit of the General Agreement. Already the principle of reciprocity has been abandoned as an obligation on less developed beneficiaries of tariff reductions negotiated by developed countries, and a GATT working party is considering the extension of trade preferences by all developed countries to all less developed countries as a group and the establishment of preferential trading arrangements among less developed countries.

For the purposes of this study it is most convenient to conclude pragmatically that the existing framework of international institutions imposes no restraint on the alternative ways of increasing the supply of external resources in the form of aid and technical assistance. However, it must be considered to exclude extension of the use of commodity agreements, since they entail replacing free international competition by cartelization of the market, and to require conformity with existing GATT principles of commercial policy, especially nondiscrimination and the prohibition of quantitative restrictions on imports. More generally it must be viewed as being based on belief in the desirability of a liberal international trading system.

PREREQUISITES OF ACTION

If the existing framework is defined in this way, it is immediately clear that virtually all the impediments that the present trade and aid policies of the developed countries place in the way of the development of the less developed countries are the consequence of the failure of the existing system to secure its announced objectives. The defects in the system of providing external resources in the form of foreign aid and technical assistance are attributable to several factors, principally the unwillingness of the developed countries to give aid on a scale adequate to the goal. Furthermore, they tend to provide aid in the form of soft loans in order both to disguise the gift element from the eyes of those who do not approve of gifts and to exaggerate its magnitude in the eyes of those who do, as either givers or receivers. They attempt to maximize the short-run political gains from aid by providing it on a bilateral basis, controlling it closely, and concentrating it on specific identifiable projects rather than supporting general programs. Finally, they wish to maximize short-run national economic gains from aid in protectionist ways, by tying it to domestic purchases or giving it in the form of surplus commodities (both of which, as contrasted with untied

H

cash aid, involve forcing the recipient to bear the costs of protectionism in the aid-giving country).

Similarly, the defects in the present system of providing opportunities to earn external resources through trade are attributable, not to the fact that that system is intended to establish a liberal international trading order, but to protectionism in the developed countries. Those countries attempt to protect their low-income domestic producers in agriculture and light industry against international competition though they exalt the competitive system as the foundation of their domestic prosperity and subscribe to it as a desirable basis for international economic organization. In particular, the defects reflect the unwillingness of the advanced industrial nations to conform to the rules of a liberal international system and their readiness to resort to additional measures if existing protectionism is not adequate.

A great deal could be done to provide the external resources required to accelerate the economic growth of the less developed countries within the existing framework simply (in principle, not in practice) by eliminating nationalist and protectionist policies and practices. Present practices prevent the system's working according to its intended fundamental principles, and indeed result in its working in important respects in direct conflict with those principles. Still more could be done by moving deliberately and rapidly toward a genuinely liberal international economic order free of impediments to trade and to the free choice of expenditure of aid receipts.

Theoretically, the best solution to the problem of providing additional external resources for the acceleration of development would be free trade, plus the provision of aid on a scale determined either by the net resources required to support rates of growth in the less developed countries endorsed by the developed countries, or by the amounts of resources agreed on by the developed countries to be necessary to fulfill their commitments to the less developed countries. This would be the best solution for the developed countries because protectionism in all its manifold varieties wastes their resources and impedes their own growth. It would be the best solution for the less developed countries because all of the solutions proposed at UNCTAD are inefficient means of supplying one of two things: more net aid from the developed countries, or improved access to developed-country markets.

All the different ways of softening loans or reducing debt service burdens, for example, implicitly involve increasing the net gift element

in loan aid. Higher prices achieved by commodity agreements or preferences in developed-country markets involve an implicit transfer from
developed-country to less-developed-country citizens or governments;
all such implicit transfers through ostensibly commercial transactions
are inefficient by comparison with transfers given in cash not tied to
specific transactions. Similarly, market access secured through international commodity agreements or tariff preferences could be secured
more efficiently through quota increases or tariff reductions. The apparent exception to this conclusion—the Prebisch extension of the infant-industry argument into a case for preferences in industrial products—could be accommodated by applying instead the economically
efficient policy for genuine infant industries. This policy calls for subsidizing infant-industry production (or whatever feature of it is responsible for the divergence of private from social cost or returns that
justifies policy intervention) as a social investment in a socially
profitable learning process. The subsidy should properly be financed
through the development program and hence enter into the reckoning
of net foreign aid requirements.

To move effectively toward providing substantial additional
resources for development along traditional lines, however, requires
fundamental concurrent changes in both public attitudes and the policies currently sanctioned. These changes are in some cases conditional
on the solution of basic international political and economic problems.
To mention the more important of the latter, the present policy of the
United States of stressing bilateral aid and adopting a cautious and
skeptical position on aid provided multilaterally through the United
Nations, while it is based on reasonable doubts about the effectiveness
of the United Nations as a distributor and manager of aid, is in large
degree a manifestation of Cold War politics, both international and
domestic.[1] Thus a cooling off of the international political situation is

---

[1] Both the desire to deny foreign aid to communist countries and the desire to
have the United States get direct credit for and exercise direct control over its aid
to the less developed countries rest on debatable premises. Historical experience
suggests that as countries become richer they may become more conservative and
tolerant, rather than more aggressive in propagating their ideologies internationally
by military means, and that insulation from international political and economic
relations is a potent breeder of disruptive international behavior; hence it is
debatable that U.S. interests are served by attempting to impose an economic
quarantine on communist or extreme socialist countries, and to retard their economic growth so far as possible. Nor is it clear that whatever improvement in
the efficiency of economic development planning is achieved by enforcing U.S.

probably a prerequisite of any major change toward a more rapid multilateralization of aid. Similarly, many of the protectionist elements of present trade and aid policies are ultimately the consequence of the inadequacy of the present international monetary system; fixed exchange rates supported by inadequate liquidity and adjustment mechanisms oblige countries to resort to aid tying and trade intervention to protect their balances of payments. Reform of the international monetary system is thus a prerequisite for eliminating the protectionism and arbitrary interventionism of those policies.

An obvious prerequisite of any move to expand external assistance for less developed countries along traditional lines is public acceptance of the desirability of so doing. This requires not mere sentimental endorsement of the objective but willingness to accept the increased tax burden implied in more aid and the adjustments in the domestic economy and traditional domestic policies implied in expanded trade opportunities.

The reduction of barriers to imports from less developed countries is in the long run not a gift made to them at the expense of the American economy, for which some compensations such as a reduction in foreign aid should be extracted. Rather, it is a change benefiting the American economy as well as the less developed countries, lowering the cost of living to American consumers and increasing the general efficiency of the American productive system through the broader exploitation of comparative advantage and the generally beneficent influence of more competition. It must be recognized, however, that freer trade would expose important groups of domestic producers to losses of material and human capital value and to the costs of adjustment to altered comparative advantage, losses which they now seek to avoid by using their political power to obtain protection from foreign competition. If those whose livelihoods are endangered by freer trade are to be deprived of these socially provided cushions against change, it is only just to provide some substitute form of compensation. This is the intention of the adjustment assistance provisions of the Trade Expansion Act: to assume governmental responsibility for part of the private cost of adjustment to change. It is both economically more efficient than providing governmental cushions against the need for change, and consis-

---

participation in it through bilateral aid giving is worth the political ill will participation generates.

tent with the philosophy of a free enterprise economy, which deliberately courts change effected through free competition. But since change results from many other causes than foreign competition, the principle of adjustment assistance in preference to politically legislated resistances to change should be applied in domestic policy generally, rather than be confined to international trade adjustment problems only.

It must be recognized that fundamentally the barriers imposed by developed countries to imports of agricultural products from the less developed are the consequence of the attempt to maintain farm incomes in face of the labor-displacing effects of the industrialization of agriculture, not by the economically rational policy of accelerating the movement of labor off the land, but instead by farm price supports. Similarly protection of labor-intensive, technologically unsophisticated domestic industry against low-wage foreign competition is prompted by the failure to devise and pursue adequate adjustment policies. Substantial progress toward liberalization of trade beneficial to the less developed countries is only likely to be politically possible in conjunction with replacement of domestic price-raising policies by mobility-increasing policies.

FOREIGN ECONOMIC AND TECHNICAL ASSISTANCE

There is a widespread and comfortable belief that the developed countries, particularly the United States, are providing foreign aid to the less developed countries on a generous and quite ample scale, and specifically that the present level of U.S. foreign aid is about right for the job. It is true that the level of gross foreign aid from the developed countries increased substantially in the years around 1960: but in recent years the volume of aid has increased relatively little. This fact has three important implications. First, during the initial stages of development, both the absolute magnitude of the net foreign aid required to sustain a given rate of growth and the ability to accelerate growth by absorbing more aid are likely to increase; thus over time a given flow of net aid becomes smaller relative to the amount that could be effectively used. Second, since most aid is in the form of loans that have eventually to be repaid, a given gross aid flow will be increasingly offset by the accumulation of interest and amortization payments on past aid, so that its net contribution of foreign exchange and of real current resources will diminish and may eventually even become negative—the debt service problem. If foreign aid is to provide a steady, let alone a rising, stream of foreign exchange and current real resources to the less developed countries, the amount of aid must rise steadily over time. Third, since the gross national products of the developed countries rise from year to year by several percent, a steady level of foreign aid is actually a declining level relative to the aid the developed countries initially considered themselves able to afford.

It has by now become a generally accepted rule of thumb among writers on aid that the developed countries should contribute a minimum of 1 percent of their national incomes to the less developed countries in the various forms of aid. The concept of aid in this context, however, is derived entirely from the foreign exchange contribution of capital flows to the annual balance of payments, not from any more fundamental concept of real resource transfers. It includes such economically disparate items as grants in cash and in kind, government loans of over one year, subscriptions to and purchases of debt from multilateral aid agencies, and net private long-term investment.[1] Such a rag bag of economically incomparable transactions makes a nonsense of the 1 percent standard. The same proportional contribution of "aid" from different countries may entail quite different proportional real resource contributions, and a country with a relatively high proportional contribution may in fact give a relatively low proportional contribution of real resources because its aid takes the form of loans rather than grants, or of loans at commercial interest rather than on

[1] UNCTAD recommended that each economically advanced country should endeavor to supply "financial resources" to the less developed countries of a minimum net amount approaching as nearly as possible 1 percent of its national income. "Financial resources" for this purpose are defined as:

"Official cash grants and grants in kind (including grants for technical assistance); sales of commodities against local currencies; government lending for periods of one year or more (net of repayments of principal); grants and capital subscriptions to multilateral aid agencies, and net purchases of bonds, loans and participations from those agencies.

"Private capital on the basis of net long-term movements, originating with residents of the capital-exporting countries. They are thus net of repatriation of principal, disinvestment, and retirement of long-term loans, portfolio assets and commercial debt. They are not net of reverse flows of capital originating with residents of the less developed countries, nor of investment income." (*Final Act of the United Nations Conference on Trade and Development* [United Nations, E/Conf.46/L.28, Annex A.IV.2, June 16, 1964], p. 86.)

concessional terms.[3] Moreover, it entails a much smaller real than nominal resource transfer for all aid-giving countries; yet the ethical justification of the 1 percent standard is clearly the reasonableness of a contribution of 1 percent of their incomes by the rich to the poor.

Increasing Levels of Assistance

Unfortunately statistics on the totals for individual aid-giving nations of the items classed as aid for the purpose of the 1 percent standard are not available. It seems reasonable to conclude from the available evidence that most of the aid-giving countries individually, and the developed countries as a group, fall substantially short of that standard, and that therefore they could increase considerably the external resources provided through aid to the less developed countries by bringing their separate contributions up to the 1 percent standard.

It is possible to estimate what could be done by applying the 1 percent standard to data on the aid commitments for 1962 of the members of the Development Assistance Committee of the Organization for Economic Cooperation and Development. The DAC definition of aid differs from the UNCTAD definition in excluding government loans of under five years maturity, repayments of past loans, and net private investment; hence the data, and the calculations based on them, must be regarded as illustrative of orders of magnitude only. The basic data on the aid commitments of nine DAC members are presented in Table 7, which shows that only two countries fulfilled the 1 percent standard and that collectively the nine countries fell short by 0.18 percent of their total gross national product. The final column of the table shows the additional aid (on this definition) that each country would have had to furnish to meet the 1 percent minimum; the total amounts to approximately $2.0 billion (to be compared with the current total aid given of under $8 billion, an increase of about 25 percent).

The calculation in Table 7 accepts the official definition of aid. From an economic point of view, however, the relevant measure of the contribution of foreign aid is the value or resource cost of the aid to the donor country, account being taken of the present value of future

[3] John A. Pincus in "The Cost of Foreign Aid," *Review of Economics and Statistics*, Vol. 45 (November 1963), p. 364, shows that when aid is revalued to obtain the net resource transfer as a proportion of national income, Portugal falls from first place to seventh while France rises from second place to first and the United States from third to second.

TABLE 7

Economic Aid Commitments and
Increases Required to Equal One Percent of Gross National
Product of Members of Development Assistance Committee, 1962

(In millions of dollars)

Country	Aid Commitment	Gross National Product	Aid as Percent of GNP	Aid Increase Required to Equal 1 Percent of GNP
Canada	$ 73.1	$ 37,000	0.19	$ 296.9
France	1,034.6	68,580	1.51	0
Germany	497.4	84,275	0.59	345.4
Italy	137.1	38,400	0.36	246.9
Japan	295.6	52,700	0.56	231.4
Netherlands	63.5	13,100	0.48	67.5
Portugal	60.2	2,800	2.15	0
United Kingdom	570.4	79,115	0.72	220.7
United States	4,975.0	553,600	0.90	561.0
Total	$7,706.9	$929,570	0.82	$1,969.8

Source: Data in first three columns from Pincus, in *Review of Economics and Statistics*, p. 364.

repayments of interest and principal and, in the case of grants in kind, of the difference between the valuation price and the alternative-opportunity cost of the goods concerned.[4] These two factors make the real cost of aid less than its nominal cost, and this fact suggests two possible alternative lines of action to increase the foreign aid contribution from the developed to the less developed countries.[5]

One possibility, which is suggested on the one hand by the demands of the less developed countries at UNCTAD for substantial softening of the terms of aid loans and easing of the debt service burden, and on the other hand by the political opposition in the United States to increases in the dollar level of foreign aid, would be to increase the real transfer involved in existing aid programs by softening the terms of

[4] Applying the present-value concept to the DAC figures, as Pincus and the calculations based on his work do, brings them closer to the UNCTAD concept by including all loans and netting out future repayments; private capital movements would presumably show a net gain for the country of origin on this concept.

[5] In this section of the argument the adjective "real" refers to the gift element in aid in money terms and ignores problems raised by differences between the prices of goods purchased under tied aid and world market prices.

loans in the many possible different ways that this may be done. The final extreme to which this policy could be carried would be to convert all loans into outright grants and to keep P.L. 480 commodity grants fixed in money terms but to value the commodities at world market prices, thus increasing the quantity of goods actually donated. This line of action of course assumes irrationality on the part of the aid donors, by assuming that the nominal but not the real level of aid is fixed; it is doubtful that any government suffers that severely from money illusion (though the U.S. Congress sometimes acts as if it does, or thinks the public does).

As the calculations in Table 8 show, a substantial amount of extra real aid could be squeezed out of the same nominal quantities by this means. The U.S. contribution could be increased by $1.3 billion, over a third of the current real contribution (third column), by giving all aid as grants, and by $1.9 billion if in addition commodity aid were kept constant in money terms but the goods supplied valued at world market prices. For the nine countries shown in the table, an extra $2.4 billion altogether (about 50 percent more than their total current real contribution) could be provided from existing nominal aid levels.

A second line of action would be to accept the standard of 1 percent of gross national product as applying to the real and not the nominal amount of foreign aid and to increase each country's aid contribution to fulfill that standard. This could be done in two alternative ways: by additional cash grants or by expanding existing aid programs while keeping their composition unchanged. Table 8 calculates the additional aid that would have to be provided by the individual countries and the total on each of these alternatives. In each case there are three alternative calculations for the United States and the total, depending on whether P.L. 480 commodity grants (A) cost the United States, and are valued at, Commodity Credit Corporation (CCC) prices; (B) cost and are valued at the world market price; or (C) cost the world market price and are valued at the CCC price for reckoning aid. The last of these probably is the most appropriate to use.

As Table 8 shows, to raise the real contribution of the United States to 1 percent of its gross national product in 1962 would have required additional cash grants of $1.9-$2.5 billion or proportional expansion of existing programs by $2.6-$4.1 billion, depending on how the cost of commodity grants was reckoned for aid burden and aid reporting calculations. Similarly, for the nine countries as a group the 1 percent

TABLE 8

Aid Commitments at Discounted Present Values and Increases Possible by Alternative Measures, for Members of Development Assistance Committee, 1962

(In millions of dollars)

Country	Value of Aid			Gross National Product	Aid as Percent of GNP[a]	Aid Increase Required to Equal 1 Percent of GNP	
	Nominal	Loans Discounted at Own Interest Rate	Difference			Cash Grants[b]	Nominal Value[c]
Canada	$ 73.1	$ 58.8	$ 14.3	$ 37,000	0.16	$ 311.2	$ 383.8
France	1,034.6	908.4	126.2	68,580	1.32	0	0
Germany	497.4	231.4	266.0	84,275	0.27	611.4	1,344.8
Italy	137.1	27.7	109.4	38,400	0.07	356.3	1,821.5
Japan	295.6	128.7	166.9	52,700	0.24	398.3	936.0
Netherlands	63.5	35.4	28.1	13,100	0.27	95.6	171.7
Portugal	60.2	6.2	54.0	2,800	0.22	21.8	213.4
United Kingdom	570.4	210.8	359.6	79,115	0.27	580.3	1,542.2
United States (A)[d]	4,975.0	3,661.0	1,314.0	553,600	0.66	1,875.0	2,562.9
United States (B)[e]	4,383.0	3,069.0	1,314.0	553,600	0.55	2,467.0	3,586.1
United States (C)[f]	4,975.0	3,069.0	1,906.0	553,600	0.55	2,467.0	4,070.5
Total with U.S. (A)	$7,706.9	$5,268.4	$2,438.5	$929,570	0.57	$4,249.9	$ 8,976.3
Total with U.S. (B)	$7,114.9	$4,676.4	$2,438.5	$929,570	0.50	$4,841.9	$ 9,999.5
Total with U.S. (C)	$7,706.9	$4,676.4	$3,030.5	$929,570	0.50	$4,841.9	$10,483.9

Source: Columns 1, 2, 4 and 5 from Pincus, in *Review of Economics and Statistics*, Tables 4 and 5, p. 364.

[a] Second column divided by fourth column.

[b] Computed by subtracting second column from 1 percent of fourth column.

[c] Increase required if additional aid were distributed among the same forms as in 1962 and in the same ratios; computed by dividing first column by fifth column and subtracting first column.

[d] Commodity aid valued at prices reported to the Development Assistance Committee.

[e] Commodity aid valued at world market prices.

[f] Reported prices for nominal value of aid, world market prices in discounted value.

122

standard would have required $4.2-$4.8 billion additional cash grants, or an expansion of existing aid programs totalling $9-$10.5 billion, depending on the assumptions. It appears from these figures that if the 1 percent standard were applied to determine the size of aid contributions by the developed countries and were maintained by increasing aid contributions each year as national income grew, the result would be to fill most and perhaps all of the "Prebisch gap" for 1970 of $10 billion, especially if allowance were made for the resulting reduction of debt service (or increase in gross capital flow required to offset it).

The calculations presented in Table 8 assume a contribution of resources worth 1 percent of gross national product, the donor being assumed indifferent as to whether the contribution is made by additional cash grants or proportional expansion of the existing program. It is appropriate at this point to recall Schmidt's analysis of the economics of charity[6]; by a simple extension of his analysis it can be shown that, for loan and grant alternatives involving an equal real cost to the donor (equal sacrifice of present value) the recipient country will derive a greater benefit from a loan than from a grant if the return on capital is higher in the recipient than in the donor country, and vice versa. If, as seems reasonable, the rate of return on investment is assumed to be higher in developed than in less developed countries, this would lead to the conclusion that providing foreign aid in the form of grants rather than loans would increase the effectiveness of foreign aid (assuming that donors rationally decide the amount of the real cost of the contribution they are prepared to make and seek to maximize its contribution to the income growth of the less developed countries). This theoretical point is reinforced by consideration of the debt service difficulties that some of the less developed countries have got into as a consequence of relying too heavily on borrowing.

Untying of Aid

Just as the real transfer of resources involved in a loan is less than the nominal amount implies, the purchasing power of aid is reduced below its nominal amount by the inefficiencies of the present system of aid provision. As pointed out in Chapter III, these reductions of purchasing power apply to both technical assistance and aid goods; the

[6] Wilson E. Schmidt, "The Economics of Charity: Loans versus Grants," *Journal of Political Economy*, Vol. 72 (August 1964), pp. 387-95; summarized in Appendix C.

most serious of them are the result of the interaction of several features of the present system, specifically the predominance of bilateral over multilateral aid and of project over program assistance and the country tying of aid. A change of emphasis in any of these respects would increase the efficiency of existing aid, as could an increase in the quantities of aid forthcoming and the numbers of countries supplying it.

The most serious problem arises from the combination of project assistance with country tying of aid. This problem could be relieved first by substituting multilateral (untied) aid for bilateral aid, or second, by changing bilateral aid policy, either by untying project aid or by providing relatively more program aid, from more countries, so that recipient countries would have more freedom to purchase aid goods and hire personnel from the lowest-cost source. None of these changes, however, would remove all inefficiencies. Project aid, even if bilaterally untied or provided multilaterally, may still exert pressure toward investment in projects favored by aid suppliers even though these may be of lower priority to the country receiving aid than others it cannot find aid finance for. Program aid tied to a purchase in the donor country may still require purchases of technologically inappropriate or overpriced equipment. The efficiency of aid would be increased most substantially by moving simultaneously toward more multilateral aid, untying of aid, and program rather than project assistance.

The seriousness of the inefficiencies associated with tying of aid depends on whether aid is by grant or by loan and whether it is project or program aid.[7] Tying is motivated by two considerations—balance-of-payments difficulties and covert protectionism—and its general effect is to raise the cost of aid goods and personnel. Where a given money amount of aid takes the form of outright grants, the effect of tying is simply to reduce the real value of the aid. This reduction (like the effects of giving loans instead of grants) should be taken into account in reckoning aid contributions or burdens. Where the aid is furnished by loans, however, the effect is to reduce the real value of the loan and thereby increase the real interest rate on it. It was partly the appreciation of this burdening effect of tying that led to the recommendation at UNCTAD of reverse tying of repayments, that is, obliging the donor

[7] Probably the most damaging inefficiency arises from the fact that tying not only prevents the recipient less developed countries from shopping for bargains among the developed countries, but also prevents them from buying from each other and so promoting each other's development through trade.

to accept repayment in the goods whose production facilities have been financed by the aid. There is a certain element of rough justice in this suggestion, given the prevalence of aid tying and the barriers to imports of industrial products into developed countries from less developed countries. But a more efficient solution would be for the element of excess cost imposed by tying to be given in the form of a grant and charged to some domestic expenditure account (as export promotion, domestic transfer, or domestic production subsidy) rather than against the foreign aid program.

Internationalization of Aid

The untying of aid, or the introduction of a scheme to compensate for the effects of keeping it tied, and the proposed shift from project to program assistance, are changes that could be readily introduced unilaterally by aid-giving nations. Further multilateralization of aid could be achieved by agreement among the aid-giving countries to expand the activities of the International Development Association, in which the weighted voting system gives them control over the allocation of aid funds. A far more important, and politically delicate, issue would be the internationalization of aid by the establishment of a new international agency (or the transformation of the International Development Association into an agency) not dominated by the aid-giving countries, which would distribute aid contributed on a large scale by the developed countries among the less developed countries.

The politics of the Cold War and the struggle for power in the Western world among the United States, Britain and France apart, there is much to be said for establishing such an agency. In particular, there is a great deal to be said for an institutional arrangement something like the conception of the Marshall Plan, involving all the developed countries and not just the United States on the capital-supplying end, in which the distribution of aid among the less developed countries would be largely their own responsibility, in cooperation with each other and with the developed countries as a group.[8] At present, with predominantly bilateral aid, the developed countries appear as competitors in giving aid in the individual less developed countries, and the latter appear as competitors for aid in the developed countries. As a result the donor countries (especially the United States, as the richest donor country) must both ration out the foreign aid and criti-

[8] The analogy of the Marshall Plan was suggested by R. A. Mundell.

cize the errors and deficiencies of the development plans of the less developed countries, and their criticisms are naturally interpreted as invented excuses for niggardliness. Put another way, the less developed countries now learn the lessons of each other's experience at second hand, through a suspect source; and, as UNCTAD demonstrated, it is only too easy for them to unite in blaming all their problems on the stingy graspingness of the developed countries, while insisting on reserving their domestic policies from outside criticism.

If the less developed countries were made collectively responsible for the distribution of foreign aid among themselves, they would be obliged to recognize, appreciate, and resolve the problems inherent in the allocation of a scarce supply of investible foreign aid funds. They would have to resolve problems now decided unilaterally (and for the most part individually) by the suppliers of aid—the problems of evaluating the efficiency of competing claimants in using funds and of striking the balance between equity and efficiency of distribution. In the process, they would have to become hardheaded and hardhearted about each other's economic policies and performances because in a real sense they would be investing their own money. The results in the initial stages might well be both acrimonious dispute and a deterioration of development performance; but the educational effects in the longer run could be of tremendous value in improving the efficiency of the use of foreign aid and of development planning in general.

PRIVATE FOREIGN INVESTMENT

Private foreign investment, especially direct investment, has many advantages over governmental capital transfers and technical assistance as a means of modernizing an underdeveloped country and implanting the automatic process of self-sustaining economic growth. From the point of view of the administration of a donor country that is committed to promoting growth but faced with an electorate that believes in free enterprise and a limited government budget, that is averse to government giving its hard-earned money away to foreigners, and that is fed up with foreign aid, the great political advantage of the government's promoting private investment is the appeal of doing something for business while demonstrating the superiority of the free enterprise system on the spot to the low-income peoples of the world. Furthermore, the costs of promoting private foreign investment appear in the budget not as a highly visible item for transfers to foreigners, but as a virtually invisible reduction in revenue from corporate taxation or increase in administrative expenditure, whose private benefits can be proclaimed without fear of censure for the public loss.

It is obviously possible to devise tax incentives that favor private investment in less developed countries. The United States currently provides significant incentives, both directly (e.g., through exemption of company operations in the less developed countries from the interest equalization tax and through extension to them of the investment credit) and indirectly (e.g., through the effects of depletion allowances on oil and other extractive activities in giving American enterprises a tax-based competitive advantage over the native enterprises of other countries).[9] Much more could evidently be done to stimulate private foreign investment in the less developed countries and, given opposition to increasing the foreign aid program as presently conceived and executed, action along these lines might be a reasonable partial substitute for, or a politically attractive complement to, increased intergovernmental foreign aid.

Policies for promoting additional private foreign investment, however, need to be designed with two considerations in mind, one economic and the other political. The economic point is that any foreign private investment involves a direct net loss of tax revenue to the United States to the extent that the government of the country invested in imposes taxes on the revenue from the investment that can be offset against U.S. taxes. This is of course not a reason for opposing the incentives for investment in less developed countries, since building up their governmental revenues is one of the objectives of assisting their development; it may well be that this method is preferable to direct transfers from the U.S. Treasury, which in any case may not be a feasible alternative. But it must be recognized that this method transfers to private enterprise the distribution among less developed countries of what are essentially government-provided aid funds. Moreover, as with any other scheme for subsidization of activities through tax incentives, some misallocation of resources between alternative investment opportunities will necessarily result.

The political consideration is that American private foreign investment, particularly direct investment, and most especially direct invest-

[9] The United Kingdom, apparently, is if anything even more generous than the United States in the tax advantages it gives its oil industry.

ment by the corporate giants of the United States economy, is unwelcome or at least ambiguously welcome in most of the less developed countries. Some of these countries already have good reason to believe that American development assistance is motivated in part by the desire to establish a place for the large international American companies in their markets, through legislative understandings banning the use of aid to finance public enterprise in the fields dominated by these companies and through the use of political pressure to inhibit acceptance of communist aid for the establishment of such enterprises. Tax incentives for private foreign investment could be interpreted as an effort to force U.S. corporate domination down the throats of the less developed countries, and so by sacrificing political goodwill offset the economic contributions private foreign investment could make.

It might therefore be worthwhile to explore the possibility of devising fiscal incentives for private foreign investment that would discriminate in favor of those forms of investment and types of economic activity that generate the least suspicion and ill will and against those that are potentially the most politically explosive. For example, less developed countries (judging by expressions of Canadian feelings in recent years) are more perturbed by foreign control of enterprises than by foreign ownership of the capital and hence prefer portfolio investment to direct investment. Accordingly, tax policy might discriminate in favor of investment in government and corporate bonds and other fixed-return instruments, where the less developed countries' financial systems are sufficiently developed for these to be available and tradable on an adequate securities market. Moreover, it could favor investment by mutual funds, investment trusts, life insurance companies, and other institutional investors not interested in control.

It is a well-confirmed fact that foreign-controlled operations in the extractive industries—especially the oil industry and refinery operations associated with it—are a focal point of political dissatisfaction, as are manufacturing industries in general and the automobile industry in particular (in less developed countries, there is almost invariably a political struggle to make the automotive firms conform to import-substitution policies considered politically and economically desirable, usually for imprecise nationalistic reasons). On the other hand, foreign operations in the service industries, particularly mass distribution, do not appear to generate political perturbation; yet foreign firms engaged in these activities can do a great deal to modernize the economy and raise living standards, by cutting distribution costs and also by promoting efficient production to reliable standards of quality by small-scale local enterprises. A third possible discrimination might favor activities that lend themselves to being turned over gradually or at some fixed future date to local owners over those that will always remain dependent on the parent company.

ENLARGING EXPORT OPPORTUNITIES WITHIN
THE GATT FRAMEWORK

The trade policies of the developed countries interpose serious impediments to international trade which bear especially heavily on the exports of the less developed countries. The less developed countries are heavily dependent on their exports of primary commodities whose entry—especially that of temperate agricultural products and their close substitutes—into developed countries is restricted not only by tariffs but by quota and other barriers designed to preserve the market for domestic producers. Furthermore, tariffs on industrial products (and the effective rates of protection of value added implicit in them) are especially high on the labor-intensive, technologically unsophisticated items that these countries are most capable, or least incapable, of producing at internationally competitive prices. In addition, exports of cotton textiles, which the "developing" countries have shown themselves capable of exporting in rapidly increasing quantities despite the relatively high tariffs of the developed countries, have been severely limited under the Long-Term Arrangement on Cotton Textiles established through GATT.

The existence of all these impediments implies that much could be done within the existing framework of GATT to open new export opportunities for the less developed countries. The most serious impediments are those that have been introduced since the establishment of GATT and in contravention of its principles and those of the International Trade Organization Charter that preceded it. Originally, the principles of GATT—protection by tariffs only (except during balance-of-payments difficulties), no new trade barriers, deliberate effort to negotiate tariff reductions—were intended to apply to trade in agricultural products as well as to trade in manufactures. The exigencies of their protectionist domestic agricultural policies, however, have led the developed countries—relying in part on the precedent of a waiver insisted on by the United States—to establish a different status in GATT for agricultural than for industrial products. Thus countries are permitted to guarantee domestic agricultural producers first claim on their markets and to enforce this claim by quotas and other trade barriers. Similarly the Cotton Textiles Arrangement—designed to prevent an expansion of exports by the less developed countries that existing high tariffs could not restrain—was developed to legitimize within GATT the "voluntary" restraint on Japanese exports that the United States had been insisting on, in contravention of the spirit of GATT.[10]

Removing GATT Barriers

A major improvement of the export opportunities of the less developed countries could be effected by the reduction and ultimate elimination of these new barriers to trade erected within the GATT framework, or (to put it another way) by restoring GATT to its original purposes. A significant improvement could be effected merely by enforcing from now on the prohibition of new barriers to trade, and by ensuring that the Cotton Textiles Arrangement operates so as to allow a steady expansion of exports by the less developed countries. Action along these lines, however, presupposes that the developed countries will be prepared to substitute policies of accelerated movement of labor off the land for policies of price maintenance for farmers, and that they will substitute adjustment assistance for protection of labor-intensive industries unable to compete with producers in lower-wage countries.

Beyond this, new export opportunities for less developed countries could be opened up by reduction of tariffs on industries in which the less developed countries have an existing or potential comparative advantage; generally speaking these are the industries on which the developed countries impose the highest tariffs, both nominal and effective. The commodities affected include processed foodstuffs and raw materials, to which the escalated tariff structures of the developed countries frequently give extremely high effective protection, and

[10] Lawrence Krause, in private conversation, has pointed out that the constriction of the expansion of cotton textile exports by the Cotton Textiles Arrangement has to a significant degree cancelled out the comparative advantage of the less developed countries in this industry, and has made unjustified the investments those countries have made in extending their productive facilities, investments involving a significant fraction of their scarce supplies of development capital.

which are sometimes given absolute protection through sanitary regulations and labeling requirements, and textiles and light consumers' goods such as toys and sporting equipment. In many of these industries the nature of the production process and the flexibility of the developed countries' industrial structure is such that greatly increased imports could be absorbed without appreciably disturbing the domestic economy. This is therefore likely to be the politically most feasible approach to the improvement of export opportunities for the less developed countries (the least feasible, of course, being relaxation of agricultural protectionism).

The GATT machinery for ensuring that the trade policies of member countries comply with GATT principles depends on negotiation and arbitration among the contracting parties. The machinery for reducing trade barriers involves negotiation among the members on the basis of reciprocity and thus makes it dependent on the willingness of more than one important trading country to reduce trade barriers. The bargaining principle, the principle of reciprocity, and the principle of nondiscrimination combined make GATT action dependent upon the trade policies and interests of the powerful trading nations. This is why in the past GATT has produced results injurious or not notably beneficial to the trading interests of the less developed countries—injurious in that it has allowed the increase in agricultural and other commodity protectionism demanded by domestic interests in the developed countries, not notably beneficial in that its principles of reciprocity and nondiscrimination have concentrated reduction of industrial tariffs on products in which the developed and not the less developed countries have a comparative advantage.

As has already been recognized within GATT, improvement of the export opportunities of the less developed countries is virtually impossible along the traditional lines of nondiscrimination and reciprocity. The less developed countries have little trade to bargain with and do not wish to jeopardize their development plans by bargaining with it. Furthermore, for developed countries the overspill to other developed nations of tariff reductions negotiated with less developed countries on a most-favored-nation basis is relatively too great to make bargaining with those countries attractive. Accordingly, the new GATT chapter on trade and development has recorded agreement that the developed countries do not expect reciprocity for reductions in trade barriers beneficial to the trade of the less developed countries, and that they should nevertheless make a concerted effort to effect such reductions in trade barriers.

Opening New Trade Opportunities

However, the opening of new trade opportunities for the less developed countries is still dependent on bargaining on the basis of reciprocity among the developed countries—and therefore on the willingness of more than one major country to reduce barriers that impede the exports of the less developed countries. This is the rock on which the current effort to assist the development through trade of the less developed countries is most likely to founder. While part of the intention of the Trade Expansion Act was to enable the United States to negotiate with the Common Market for general free entry of tropical agricultural and forest products and reduction of tariffs on industrial products of special interest to less developed countries, French insistence on maintaining the preferences granted by the Common Market to the associated overseas territories has blocked the former negotiation, and the general nature of the items on the Common Market's exceptions list indicates unwillingness to proceed very far with the latter.

As GATT is presently constructed, the combined effect of the principles of reciprocity from developed countries and nondiscrimination among countries is to put any individual developed country that wishes to reduce trade barriers for the benefit of less developed country exports on the horns of a dilemma. If it insists on both principles, the others can prevent it from achieving anything by refusing to negotiate. If it acts unilaterally, it must either reduce barriers on a nondiscriminatory basis, sacrificing reciprocity from the other developed countries whose exports are certain to increase (perhaps by far more than the exports of the less developed countries intended to be favored), or reduce them in a discriminatory fashion, introducing new preferences in contravention of GATT principles and exposing itself to retaliation by the other developed countries, whose exports are virtually certain to be injured by preferential tariff reduction for less developed countries.

The dilemma, however, is not a genuine economic dilemma: it derives not from economic principles but from the protectionist concept of the nature of the gains from freer trade that is embodied in the whole apparatus of GATT, and especially in the principle of reciprocity. That concept sees the gain from trade liberalization as the expansion of export markets and views the expansion of imports consequent on reduction of the country's own tariffs as a loss of domestic markets to the foreigner. The principle of reciprocity is the principle that the gain in exports must not be less than the loss of domestic markets; nonreciprocated tariff reductions by definition entail a net loss. If one really believes in the virtues of a free enterprise system, however (and understands what they are), this way of thinking is fundamentally nonsensical.

According to the theory of comparative advantage, the gains from trade liberalization come primarily from the country's reduction of its own trade barriers. The country is able to replace high-cost domestic by lower-cost foreign production and to shift the factors of production so released into the lines of production in which it is relatively efficient; it also increases its efficiency indirectly by exposing its producers to broader and more pervasive competition. The reduction of the trade barriers of other countries is, as a matter of general principle, irrelevant to the enjoyment of these gains. It becomes relevant only in certain special cases.

First, if the country has some monopoly-monopsony power in the world market, reduction of its trade barriers may turn its terms of trade against it by more than enough to offset the improvement in efficiency secured by tariff reduction. This is an "optimum tariff" situation, and from the point of view of maximizing its own welfare the country should exploit its monopoly-monopsony position, reducing its tariffs only if others reduce theirs sufficiently so that its welfare increases. (This case implies a concept of compensation in tariff reductions negotiated between countries with monopoly power, similar to but different from the conventional notion of reciprocity.)

Second, in the monetary economies of the real world, the real resource reallocations entailed in unilateral trade liberalization will generally have to be accomplished by reductions in money factor prices or in the exchange rate. If the country is in the Keynesian situation of downward rigidity of money wages and prices and refuses to alter its exchange rate, tariff reduction will tend instead to cause unemployment and a balance-of-payments deficit, since the resources displaced from import-competing industries will be unable to find employment in expanded exports, because export prices by assumption cannot fall to promote increased sales and production. This is obviously one of the major motivations for the reciprocity principle in the present international economy, with its defective international monetary system and the resultant concern with preserving balance-of-payments equilibrium. Nevertheless, the problem is one of short-run adjustment: a country with a diversified and flexible economy and a reasonable rate of growth of productivity should be able to absorb the effects of unilateral liberalization of trade, especially if the liberalization is phased over a period of years, without encountering serious balance-of-payments problems.

Third—a matter of more importance to other developed countries than to the United States, and of most importance to the less developed countries—the small scale and technological backwardness of domestic production may mean that little gain of real income can be realized by reduction of the country's trade barriers. Major gains may require the opening of foreign markets, and especially security of access to them, to permit realization of the economies of specialization and scale achievable from competing in a large market. This exception, however, does not imply that reciprocity is necessary to the realization of gains from trade liberalization. Rather, it indicates that two sorts of gains in efficiency from tariff reduction are possible, one accruing directly from the reduction of the country's own tariff and the other from the reduction of other countries' tariffs that may be negotiated in exchange under present tariff-bargaining procedures, and that the latter gain may be large by comparison with the former.

These exceptional cases apart, the general principle of comparative advantage indicates that unilateral tariff reduction involves a net economic gain to the country liberalizing trade, and that therefore from an economic point of view there is no dilemma. Unilateral reduction of a country's tariffs on a most-favored-nation basis would be fully consistent with the rules of GATT and give no cause for retaliation. While the country so doing would forego the gains from trade it might have obtained by negotiating reductions in other countries' tariffs, it would still enjoy the traditional gains in efficiency that result from the exploitation of comparative advantage.

Thus, if the other developed countries (and particularly the Common Market countries) refuse to cooperate with the United States in the negotiation of tariff reductions for the benefit of the less developed countries, and if the United States prefers to adhere to its traditional trade policy principle of nondiscrimination and to act within the existing GATT framework, but desires to open new export opportunities to the less developed countries, it could easily do so, both to its own long-run economic benefit and to theirs. It could unilaterally reduce its tariffs on products of special interest to the less developed countries and in so doing exploit the opportunity for product discrimination allowed by the most-favored-nation principle by concentrating its tariff reductions on those products in which the other developed countries have the least comparative advantage—choosing, for example, the products on which those countries impose high tariffs.[11] The United States could also, quite consistently with the principles of GATT, urge other developed countries that are disposed to assist the development through trade of the less developed countries to adopt similar policies of unilateral tariff reduction concentrated on goods of special interest to the less developed countries.

[11] The argument of the text is couched in terms of the broad principle of comparative advantage and ignores the complications that the theory of second best has shown to arise when partial and selective tariff reductions are considered. These complications, however, are relevant to the discriminatory policy suggested here. The standard analysis of the welfare effects of unilateral tariff reduction suggests that the gain to the tariff-reducing country is likely to be greatest from the reduction of the tariffs on the most heavily protected items, since the gain from trade expansion is greatest on these items and certain to outweigh any losses on trade diverted from other items on which the tariff is not reduced, so long as the tariff on the initially heavily protected items is not reduced below the tariff on the less heavily protected items; beyond that point it becomes necessary to balance probable losses from trade diversion against gains from trade creation. The analysis also suggests that the damage to the welfare of third parties that results from diversion of the exports of supplying countries from their markets to those of the tariff-reducing country is greatest when the latter reduces tariffs on the items on which the third parties impose their highest tariffs. Since developed countries typically impose tariffs at above-average rates on the industrial products in which less developed countries are specially interested, it would seem that a developed country that reduced tariffs on items of special interest to the less developed countries would both achieve substantial increases in its own economic welfare and impose substantial losses on other developed countries that failed to follow the same policy. Concretely, by following the policy suggested, the United States could both benefit itself and damage countries that refused to cooperate. The designing of an optimal strategy of unilateral tariff reduction to benefit the export trade of the less developed countries would, of course, require a much more sophisticated application of second-best theory than these tentative remarks suggest.

V

Arrangements for Trade in Primary Products

Exports of primary products are at the present time the overwhelmingly important source of earnings of foreign exchange and receipts of external resources by the less developed countries, accounting for some 85-90 percent of their total export earnings. Accordingly, changes in the developed countries' trade policies governing these products offer the largest opportunity for assisting their development. As demonstrated in Chapters III and IV, much could be done to increase the export earnings of the less developed countries by liberalization of international trade along orthodox lines, especially by reducing the protection accorded by the developed countries to their domestic agriculture and materials-producing industries, eliminating the protection accorded to processing industries by the escalation of tariff rates by stage of production, and abolishing the revenue duties imposed on tropical beverage products and bananas by the major European countries. Action along orthodox lines, however, presupposes that the developed countries will be prepared to dismantle the protectionist policies toward agriculture that they have been steadily building up for the past half-century or so, a change which few observers if any would be optimistic enough to consider likely. Less developed countries and their sympathizers have therefore concentrated their attention on schemes for new international arrangements to increase the earnings of the less developed countries from their primary product exports, and particularly on international commodity agreements. This chapter considers the possibility of assisting the less developed countries by such arrangements.[1]

[1] Much of the detailed information in this chapter and important aspects of

INTERNATIONAL COMMODITY AGREEMENTS

Most international trade experts, especially those in the United States, take a very dim view of international commodity agreements. They are extremely difficult to negotiate and administer, are unlikely to succeed in attaining their objectives, and are extremely likely to result in economic waste and the misallocation of productive resources. These judgments originate from a combination of a priori reasoning from the principles of economic efficiency and comparative advantage and observation of the unsatisfactory experience of past commodity agreements, whose negotiation and operation were guided predominantly by the commercial interests of the countries concerned. Against those judgments two arguments can be advanced. It can be argued, first (following the theory of second best), that if it is desirable to increase the export earnings of less developed countries as a substitute for an adequate level of development aid or because trade is morally superior to aid, and if the developed countries are unwilling to lower their trade barriers to imports from the less developed countries but are willing to consider international commodity arrangements, it is worth while to explore the possible benefits of such arrangements. The provision of the additional external resources by this means may be worth the costs of resource misallocation they entail. Second, it can be argued that if the developed countries accept the principle of using such arrangements deliberately to provide resources to the less developed countries, many of the practical difficulties that have beset these arrangements in the past could be resolved. This chapter thus explores the possible contribution to development through trade of international commodity arrangements, at the same time recognizing that in principle some combination of trade liberalization and cash transfers would always be more economically efficient. The possibilities are nevertheless rather limited, since the technical and economic characteristics of many commodities and the nature of the trade in them preclude the useful application of international commodity agreements.

---

its organization are derived from two extremely useful papers by Dr. Gerda Blau, in "International Commodity Arrangements and Policies," Food and Agriculture Organization of the United Nations, Commodity Policy Studies 16, Special Studies Program No. 1, Rome, 1964. While I am in sympathy with Dr. Blau's emphasis on international adjustment assistance, I do not share her institutionally associated enthusiasm for a "concerted attack" on commodity problems on all fronts.

International commodity agreements have been attempted ever since the 1920's, and since the collapse of commodity prices in the great crash of 1929-33 the need for such agreements has been widely asserted, especially in times of falling commodity prices such as preceded the convening of the United Nations Conference on Trade and Development. Detailed rules governing the nature and operating principles of commodity agreements were written into the Havana Charter of the proposed International Trade Organization; some of them survive in the rules of the General Agreement on Tariffs and Trade (GATT). Nevertheless, in the twenty years since the end of the World War II, international agreements have been concluded for only five commodities—wheat, sugar, coffee, tin and olive oil—and the agreements on olive oil and sugar currently do not influence international trade.[2] Moreover, the international wheat agreement (a multilateral contract originally specifying maximum and minimum prices at which participants were obliged to sell or purchase specified quantities) has survived only by dropping one of its initially most promising features— the obligation of consuming countries to purchase specified quantities at a minimum price—and its influence on the world wheat market has been steadily undermined by price maintenance practiced by the two leading suppliers—the United States and Canada—and supported by concessionary disposal of surplus stocks. Nor can the other two agreements be regarded as inspiring examples of this technique. The tin agreement, which is primarily a buffer stock arrangement buttressed by export controls, has functioned fairly satisfactorily recently owing to a world consumption-production relationship favorable to producers; in 1956-58, however, it suffered from a decline in demand that exhausted its financial resources and forced it to resort to sharp export restrictions, and in 1958 prices dropped temporarily due to an increase in Russian sales, an experience resolved by an agreement with the Russians to restrict their sales. The coffee agreement, initiated in 1963, involves the percentage adjustment of basic export quotas with a view to preventing a decline of prices below the 1962 level; it has encountered serious difficulties, first as a result of numerous requests for revisions of

[2] The olive oil agreement is concerned with the coordination of national policies, international trade in olive oil constituting only 5 percent of total production. The operating provisions of the sugar agreement (which provided for variable export quotas for the free market trade) were suspended in 1962 due to inability to agree on reallocation of quotas following the cessation of arrangements between the United States and Cuba.

basic quotas and then as a result of a sharp rise in coffee prices due to supply shortages in Brazil; experience with it does not yet permit evaluation of its effectiveness.

The difficulty of negotiating international commodity agreements arises, in the first place, from the fact that the agreements may be intended to serve a wide variety of purposes, including stabilizing the market, increasing export earnings, mitigating the impact of secular change, mitigating the damage to exporters from protection in importing countries, and organizing production, consumption and distribution comprehensively on a world scale. The chief practical difficulties have arisen from lack of clarity on the objectives sought and the ability of alternative forms of international arrangement to achieve them, together with divergence of interest among and between consuming and producing countries. Second, the rules of the Havana Charter envisage stabilization of the market and mitigation of the impact of secular change as the main objectives of international commodity agreements; they specify that agreements should include both producing and consuming countries, the two groups having equal voting strength. This institutional framework, and particularly the voting requirement, though ethically commendable, rules out the possibility of agreements to raise producer incomes unless this objective is deliberately accepted by consuming countries against their own economic interests (as in the case of U.S. support for the international coffee agreement). Third, each of the main forms of agreement has inherent weaknesses which may make them difficult or impossible to negotiate or operate. Multilateral contracts and buffer stocks require the ability to forecast price trends, and buffer stocks may exhaust their finances in coping with an unexpected downward price trend. Export restriction schemes assume national ability to control production or store goods and run the risk of being undermined by outside producer competition unless importing countries can be enlisted to police the restrictions. Fourth, the technical and economic characteristics of primary commodities frequently impose great obstacles to a workable international agreement. It is obvious that only cheaply storable commodities are suitable for buffer stock operations. It is not so obvious that ostensibly homogeneous commodities such as coffee, wheat, or tea come in a variety of grades whose price relationships may change rapidly with changes in taste or technology, posing serious problems for any price-stabilization scheme; that commodities very different in their physical characteristics may be close substitutes as inputs for producing a final product,[3] and that many more natural products than might appear at first glance face close competition with synthetic substitutes. Finally, important components of world trade in primary products are dominated by trade between producing and consuming developed countries, or producing and consuming less developed countries, or between developed producing and less developed consuming countries, in all of which cases an international agreement may be less attractive to one or both of the parties concerned than either bilateral negotiation or laissez-faire.

In the literature on the dependence of less developed countries on the export of primary products, two separate types of problems are distinguishable, each of which might be ameliorated by international commodity arrangements. The first is the instability of primary product prices and more generally of export earnings. This instability is alleged to bear especially heavily on less developed countries owing to their typical dependence on the export of a limited range of primary products; their growth is allegedly handicapped by the disruptive effects of uncertainty and variability of foreign exchange receipts on the formulation and execution of their development plans. Correspondingly, it is argued, stabilization of their export prices or export earnings by one form or another of international arrangement would facilitate their planned development by increasing the predictability and reliability of export earnings. The other problem is the level of export earnings and their purchasing power in terms of the industrial goods necessary for development investment; it is proposed that the level be raised by international commodity arrangements. While the former problem is less directly germane than the latter to the problem of external resources for development, it is obviously a part of the general problem of promoting economic development in the less developed countries by policy actions on the part of the developed countries.

METHODS OF STABILIZING EXPORT EARNINGS

Stabilization has been a motivating factor not only in the perennial demand for the extension of international commodity agreements—ex-

[3] For example, eight types of oil seeds compete with each other and with animal fat and fish oil in the production of edible oils; copper and aluminum are close substitutes for a number of industrial purposes.

pressed most recently and vociferously at UNCTAD—but also in the establishment of national and international governmental interventions in commodity trade (national interventions including in particular national marketing boards and the imposition of variable export levies). Unfortunately, one source of difficulty in designing such schemes of intervention, and in criticizing schemes that have been introduced, is the ambiguity of the notion of stabilization itself. Many different aspects of the conduct of international commodity trade could be the subject of stabilization operations, and stabilization of one may contribute little or nothing to the stabilization of, or may positively destabilize, another. For example, intervention may aim at stabilizing money prices to producers, money income of producers, purchasing power of the product over industrial goods or goods in general, or producer real income; stabilization of money prices will not stabilize but will instead destabilize money income if the main source of instability is unpredictable fluctuations in production, and stabilization of money prices or incomes will not stabilize purchasing power or real income if the general price level is changing.[4]

The Object of Stabilization

The precise object of stabilization has a significant bearing on the instrumentality required to effect it. In particular, if the object is to stabilize prices or incomes for a nation's domestic producers, measures can be applied on a national scale, provided that the national government has sufficient taxable capacity or borrowing power to finance possible transitory deficits. It follows that the demand for international stabilization must derive from the difficulties that fluctuations in export prices on earnings impose on governments of countries dependent on primary product exports attempting to plan their economic development and manage their domestic economies. The problems sought to be overcome by international measures are problems of governments, not necessarily of their citizens as individual producers and consumers.

In principle, national governments should be able to avoid the difficulties of fluctuations by basing their domestic and development policies on the normal or trend values of export prices or earnings,

[4] There is a vast literature, ranging from textbook treatments to journal articles, on the effects of stabilization measures on the stability of the various dimensions of international trade under varying elasticities of demand and supply and with instability originating alternatively on the demand or the supply side.

offsetting fluctuations around these values by alternating accumulations and decumulations of international reserves. Their inability to do so must be the result either of weakness in the formulation and execution of domestic policy or of unwillingness to invest in the accumulation of international reserves on the scale required to support domestic stabilization policies of the kind required. Accordingly, the demand for international stabilization arrangements is implicitly a proposal to relieve weak governments of a problem they are incapable of coping with or to provide a substitute for international reserves of a magnitude they are not prepared to accumulate. Since commodity price stabilization typically involves substantial costs of operation, whereas creation of monetary reserves is in principle virtually costless,[5] solution of the problem of export price or earnings instability through provision of reserves or borrowing facilities would appear to be economically superior to the direct establishment of stabilization schemes. This indeed seems to be the trend in current thinking on the problem of instability.

The argument for international schemes for stabilizing primary product prices rests on the assumption that the governments of less developed countries are afflicted with especially severe problems of economic planning and management owing to fluctuations in their export earnings associated with the dominance of primary products in their exports. The facts responsible for this assumption are well known: the variability of supply of and demand for individual primary products, the low elasticities of both supply and demand, the specialization of less developed countries on one or a few primary product exports, and the concentration of their exports on one or a few developed-country markets.

These facts, however, while constituting potential causes of and reasons to expect exceptional instability of export earnings, do not suffice to establish the existence in reality of such exceptional instability, which is an empirical question not resolvable by theoretical speculation. Though the assumption that less developed countries are subject

---

[5] While the creation of money is costless, the expenditure of it by the recipient involves a transfer of resources to him from the rest of the community. To avoid this it is necessary to provide incentives for the recipient to maintain his money balance intact on the average over time. The problems arising from the fact that money is costless to create from the social point of view but cannot be allowed to be so treated by private individuals or governments are central to the welfare economics of money.

to exceptional instability of export earnings has become an orthodoxy of development economics, the scattered empirical evidence so far presented in support of it has not been strikingly convincing. The problem has recently been subjected to a major econometric investigation by Alasdair MacBean,[6] who finds that the empirical evidence does not support the orthodox assumption.[7]

MacBean finds that less developed countries are not significantly more subject to instability of export earnings than developed countries, and specifically that three plausible reasons for expecting greater instability have little value in explaining the instability that actually exists—commodity concentration of exports, proportion of primary goods in total exports, and geographical concentration of exports (which actually has a negative relationship with instability). While certain less developed countries have suffered from especially severe instability of export earnings, MacBean points out that the reasons have usually been particular to the country concerned and associated with domestic developments, often with political disturbances. He further finds that variations in export quantities have been an important source of export instability, which implies that price stabilization might aggravate rather than ameliorate instability; that there is little relationship between export fluctuations and variations in domestic economic variables, a fact he attributes to the operations of built-in stabilizers and especially to high marginal propensities to import; and that there is no evidence that instability of export earnings has retarded economic growth in the less developed countries.

These findings, which are contrary to what MacBean himself had expected, lead him quite justifiably to the position that international schemes for stabilizing primary product prices or the export earnings of less developed countries are very unlikely to contribute much to the economic welfare of less developed countries, and in particular are unlikely to contribute enough to justify the costs of establishing and operating them, and that a few national schemes would suffice to take care of the really serious problems. This position seems fully warranted

[6] Alasdair MacBean, *Export Instability and Economic Development* (London: Allen and Unwin, and Harvard University Press, to be published).
[7] Earlier studies, broadly consistent with MacBean's findings, also fail to provide support for the orthodox assumption. See Joseph D. Coppock, *International Economic Instability: The Experience after World War II* (McGraw-Hill, 1962), and Michael Michaely, *Concentration in International Trade* (Amsterdam: North Holland Publishing Co., 1962).

by the empirical analysis MacBean presents in his study. That analysis also explains why so few international price stabilization schemes have in fact been established. Gerda Blau has remarked[8] that the paucity of such agreements indicates that neither exporting nor importing countries have been willing to pay a substantial premium for the implicit insurance against the risk of large price changes; MacBean's analysis suggests that, so far as the less developed exporting countries are concerned, this unwillingness reflects a rational appreciation of the extremely limited value of such insurance in the stabilization of export earnings.

Methods of Stabilizing Commodity Prices

Despite the fact that stabilization of the money prices of commodities will not necessarily stabilize, and may destabilize, money and real export earnings, international arrangements to stabilize commodity prices could serve useful purposes for the less developed countries. While stabilization of money or real export earnings would obviously be more helpful, it would be extremely difficult if not impossible to accomplish through international commodity agreements on traditional lines; and while various schemes could be adopted for achieving the same results by compensatory financing of fluctuations in export earnings, these schemes might be equally or more difficult to negotiate and would not eliminate other problems associated with fluctuations in commodity prices. International commodity agreements could stabilize prices over the short run; this partial contribution to stability would be more valuable (in the more fundamental sense of stability or predictability of money or real export earnings) the smaller the random or "natural" element in variations of output of the product.[9] Stabilization

---

[8] *Op. cit.*, p. 7.

[9] It is necessary to distinguish between stability in the sense of a stable or steadily changing magnitude over time and stability in the sense of a predictable magnitude on which planning can reliably be based. Some methods of price stabilization simply fix the price without controlling the quantity sold by individual supply sources; the planners can then plan output to obtain the foreign exchange earnings they need or predict their foreign exchange availabilities from forecasts of the likely output of private producers. Other methods of price stabilization rely on control of individual national outputs or exports; in this case the planners can only predict their foreign exchange availabilities, but cannot plan them or rely on their magnitude being steady over time. In both cases variations of actual from expected outputs due to the hazards of climatic conditions remain as a source of unavoidable instability.

It is true but not practically relevant that perfect future markets with competi-

of prices could in particular eliminate or ameliorate a problem that afflicts producers of commodities such as tree crops with a long gestation period and subject to substantial variations of demand. A temporary increase in demand of these crops tends to raise prices sharply due to the inelasticity of current supply, thus motivating the development of synthetic substitutes less subject to unpredictable price fluctuation and inducing investment in increased production capacity which comes into operation after demand has subsided and reduces prices and earnings.[10] This consideration provides a reason for maintaining that price stabilization, if it could be efficiently performed, might contribute more to stabilization of and an increase in the export earnings of less developed countries than MacBean's statistical evidence might suggest.

The international commodity agreements negotiated in the period since the war exemplify the three alternative methods of price stabilization: buffer stocks, export restriction schemes, and multilateral contracts. A fourth method of stabilization—price compensation agreements —was recommended to UNCTAD by Professor James Meade[11] and deserves discussion as a possibly superior alternative to the multilateral contract.

BUFFER STOCKS. Buffer stock schemes entail setting a maximum and a minimum price for the commodity, to be maintained by purchases for or sales from the stock. They may start with either a stock of the commodity—in which case they can effectively only hold the price

---

tive speculation and arbitrage on an adequate scale would stabilize commodity prices without government intervention, and that planners armed with sufficient information and sophisticated forecasting techniques could profit from exploiting fluctuations in market prices; the essence of the problem is the cost of collecting and analyzing information and the desirability of certainty and simplicity of information about future prices.

[10] If the supply curve is fixed, demand varies, and total production per period on the average is the same whether price is stabilized or not, price stabilization through a buffer stock reduces total earnings if production responds to price without a lag, because in the absence of stabilization larger quantities are sold at the high price than at the low price. (See Herbert Grubel, "Foreign Exchange Earnings and Price Stabilization Schemes," *American Economic Review*, Vol. 54 [June 1964] pp. 378-85.) But the reverse is true, at least for simple models of supply response, if production responds to market prices with a lag, because then the lower prices are earned on the larger quantities. These points are illustrated in Appendix E.

[11] J. E. Meade, "International Commodity Agreements," *Lloyds Bank Review*, No. 73 (July 1964), pp. 28-42.

down to the maximum—or with a stock of money—in which case they can effectively only hold the price up to the minimum—or with stocks of both the commodity and cash, in which case they can stabilize in both directions. The advantages of a buffer stock scheme are that it need not include all the major producing or consuming countries nor involve restriction of production or exports by the producing countries. Its disadvantages are the capital and storage costs of operating the stock, which may be substantial, especially in commodities which come in a variety of grades differing in technical characteristics important to the user. In addition, effective operation requires that the resources of the buffer stock be large enough to absorb prospective excesses of demand or supply at the stabilization prices, the amount of resources required depending on the range between the two prices and the extent to which the equilibrium price in the absence of stabilization would persistently fall above or below that range. If the buffer stock's resources are inadequate—as they may be if tendencies toward high or low prices are persistent, and necessarily must be if the long-run equilibrium price falls outside the selected range of stabilization prices—the buffer stock will exhaust either its capital or its stocks and lose its power to stabilize the price. If the selected price range is too low, the stock will end its phase of stabilization with a profit and can be reconstituted to stabilize prices within a higher price range. If on the other hand the selected price range is too high, the stock will end its stabilization phase with a stock of the commodity bought at prices above the current market price and hence will have suffered a capital loss. The risk of such a loss, which might well be substantial, is a major deterrent to the participation of consuming countries in buffer stock schemes.

EXPORT RESTRICTION. Export restriction schemes seek to stabilize the price indirectly, by controlling the quantities marketed by means of national quotas for production or export by the supplying countries. To be effective, such schemes require the participation of the major producing countries. Since they necessarily give an incentive for participants to evade their quotas and for outside producers to expand their production, their effectiveness further depends on the inclusion of the major consuming countries and on their agreement to enforce the quotas in their importing policies. In favor of export restriction schemes it is argued that they avoid the capital investment, problems of stock management, and risk of capital loss involved in a buffer stock scheme.

In reality, they pass these problems back to the individual producing countries, which must keep productive capacity or stocks ready for use when export quotas increase and cope with decreases in export quotas either by accumulating stocks or by taking resources out of production of the commodity.

The arguments against export restriction schemes are that they tend to promote resource misallocation, protect inefficient producers at the expense of efficient producers, and restrict the average level of production. These arguments are derived from practical experience with such schemes; in principle, these effects could be avoided by sufficient flexibility in the reallocation of quotas. Probably a more important problem is the difficulty countries experience in abiding by their quotas, especially when they lack facilities to store unusually large crops. Restriction schemes have the advantage over buffer stocks of being applicable to perishable commodities such as bananas. The most important problem in operating them—essentially the same problem as for buffer stocks, though it appears as a question of predicting quantity rather than price—is the difficulty of predicting the aggregate quantity that will be demanded at the target price or range of prices. Both the buffer stock and the export restriction schemes seek to stabilize the price received by exporters. Therefore if successful they will achieve whatever advantages are possible by stabilizing the expansion of consumption and production and improving the efficiency of investment in new capacity.

MULTILATERAL CONTRACTS. By contrast, the multilateral contract aims to avoid the transfers of real income between consumers and producers implicit in price swings without interfering with marginal adjustments by producers and consumers to such swings. It specifies a maximum price at which producing countries are obligated to sell stipulated quantities to consuming countries and a minimum price at which consuming countries are obligated to purchase stipulated quantities from producing countries. The advantage to producers obviously depends on price fluctuations being primarily the result of demand changes, while the advantage to consumers presumably depends on price fluctuations being primarily the result of supply changes.[12] The advantages

---

[12] If fluctuations were due to supply changes, producer real income might be destabilized; if fluctuations were due to demand changes, consumer real income might be destabilized, though the presence of demand changes makes analysis of welfare effects on consumers difficult.

claimed for the multilateral contract are that it requires neither the building and operation of stocks nor restriction of trade or production[13] and that it permits efficient marginal adjustment to temporary variations in the scarcity or abundance of the commodity. Whether the latter advantage outweighs the disadvantage of the effects of variation in the world market price of marginal supplies in destabilizing investment in the expansion of capacity is an important question that cannot be answered with the information currently available.

The effectiveness of the multilateral contract in avoiding random real income transfers depends on the range between the maximum and minimum prices and on the proportion of the trade covered by the contract (as well as on the nature of the factors causing price variations). The chief problem for this scheme as for the others is to forecast the normal or long-run equilibrium price; if this falls outside the price range of the scheme, the result will be a regular transfer of real income from one party to the other—as indeed happened under the initial international wheat agreement, which transferred income from producing to consuming countries.

The Meade price compensation scheme is essentially a superior version of the multilateral contract. It envisages establishment of a normal price and a normal trade quantity by agreement between producing and consuming countries, bilaterally or multilaterally, and complete or partial compensation by one party to the other for deviations of the value of the normal trade volume from its normal value. The advantages of this scheme over the multilateral contract are that compensation is paid directly between governments, leaving them the utmost freedom in raising or disposing of the compensation; it can be scaled flexibly in any way desired, so that, for example, the proportion of compensation could be increased as the deviation of prices from the normal level increased. Further, the "normal" price and quantity could be chosen to yield a net transfer on average to the producing country or countries—though it is difficult to imagine political circumstances which would make a visible transfer of this kind politically more acceptable than foreign aid. The chief question about the scheme is the same as that raised by multilateral contracts: the relative advantages and disadvantages of preserving marginal price variations.

[13] It is an interesting theoretical question whether the obligations to sell at prices below world market prices or to buy at prices above world market prices would encourage or discourage private accumulation and decumulation of stocks.

Again, the chief practical problem is to forecast the long-run equilibrium price, errors resulting in a steady transfer of income from one party to the other.[14]

The crucial difficulty in all price-stabilization schemes is to forecast the long-run equilibrium price. This is an inherently risky venture, but if price stabilization is considered important enough for the less developed countries it would seem possible to improve on past performance by investment of resources to improve techniques for forecasting commodity prices. International commodity agreements would then have a better chance of success and be more attractive to the developed and less developed countries concerned. On the other hand, a real improvement in forecasting accuracy might be sufficient by itself to evoke stabilization of markets for primary products through speculation and arbitrage by private traders, without the need for international agreements.

Compensatory Financing of Fluctuations in Export Earnings

The difficulties of organizing international commodity arrangements, the risk that they may fail to achieve their stabilization objectives and the fact that price stabilization may contribute little to the stabilization of export earnings have recently generated interest in schemes for tackling the problem of fluctuations in export earnings directly, through compensatory financing. Depending on how they are financed and operated, such schemes may be designed either to stabilize the earnings of a country over time without altering their total (except incidentally, through the payment of interest on the finance) or to involve a regular transfer of real resources from the developed to the less developed countries. In the first case they are strictly financing schemes (except to the extent that soft-loan terms imply a transfer to the coun-

---

[14] The effectiveness of the Meade scheme in stabilizing export earnings depends on whether the chief source of price instability is demand or supply variation. Meade shows that his scheme would destabilize earnings if supply variations are the source of price changes; but his enthusiasm for the theoretical beauty of his scheme leads him to conclude, without justification, that the problem could be handled by an appropriate schedule for partial compensation. Both Meade's and other writers' adoption of a too aggregative approach lead them to overlook the fact that price stabilization or compensation would be of no help to a country whose production varied substantially, if the effects of these variations on price were negligible either because the country produced a negligible portion of the total supply or because variations in individual countries' outputs averaged out.

try receiving finance), while in the second case they partake of the character of social insurance.

The first type of scheme is exemplified by a proposal put forward by the Organization of American States (OAS) in 1961 and by the system of compensatory finance introduced in 1963 by the International Monetary Fund (IMF). The OAS scheme envisaged the establishment of a special revolving fund, by contributions of $1,200 million from the developed countries and $600 million from the less developed countries; the fund was to be used for compensatory financing of a proportion (two-thirds up to a maximum of 20 percent of previous exports) of any shortfall of export proceeds below their average in the previous three years, for less developed countries only, the loans to be repaid in a maximum of five years irrespective of the subsequent development of the borrowers' export proceeds. Under the IMF scheme, less developed countries may temporarily borrow 25 percent of their IMF quotas, subject to Fund approval, if their export earnings fall below a recent moving average; the theoretical combined maximum of borrowings under this scheme is $800 million. The limited magnitude and duration of compensatory finance under this scheme was criticized at UNCTAD; the Conference recommended action to make additional medium-term credit available for compensatory financing of shortfalls of export earnings.

The second type of scheme is represented by a proposal advanced in 1961 (prior to the OAS scheme) by a group of United Nations experts.[15] This proposal recommended the creation of a Development Insurance Fund, into which developed countries would contribute a percentage of their national income and less developed countries a proportion of their export receipts; in return, member countries could claim automatic compensation for a decline in export proceeds from the average of the preceding three years, such compensation covering a proportion (50 percent being recommended) of the shortfall above a minimum shortfall of 5 percent for which no compensation would be payable. Two alternative types of compensation were considered, a mixture being recommended: a nonrepayable cash settlement and a contingent loan that must be repaid if the export proceeds of the subsequent five years exceed the three-year base period average by enough to allow it, but otherwise not. This scheme would entail an automatic

[15] *International Compensation for Fluctuations in Commodity Trade* (United Nations, 1961).

transfer from the developed countries (which would put in the bulk of the money) to the less developed countries (which would take out the bulk of it), thus giving the scheme its social insurance character and also making it implicitly a method of increasing the flow of aid from developed to less developed countries.[16]

Leaving aside the question of social insurance and implicit resource transfers to the less developed countries,[17] compensatory financing of fluctuations in export proceeds has the apparent advantage over price stabilization schemes of directly attacking the source of the less developed countries' difficulties (or asserted difficulties). Such schemes however, have costs, both of administration and of foregone earnings on alternative investments of the capital, that must be weighed against the increase in stability of export earnings the schemes can achieve. Moreover, it does not necessarily follow that schemes designed to stabilize export earnings will in fact achieve much or even any additional stability, especially if compensation is partial and the repayment of the compensatory finance must follow a fixed schedule, so that the results may well not justify the cost.

The importance of this last point is illustrated by the results of empirical tests of various automatic schemes for compensatory financing of short-term fluctuations of export earnings performed by three members of the International Monetary Fund staff.[18] They tested 137 different schemes, devised by varying the provisions of the OAS scheme relating to the weighting system employed to establish the norm, the aggregate debt limit imposed on the borrowing country, and the repay-

[16] The U.N. experts estimated that in 1953-59, on the basis of 50 percent compensation above a 5 percent minimum reduction and assuming compensation entirely by cash settlement, the scheme would have transferred annually $241 million from high-income to low-income countries (Blau, *op. cit.*, p. 18). If full compensation were paid after the 5 percent reduction, this figure would be doubled, to $482 million.

[17] An arrangement of this kind might be politically acceptable as a way of transferring additional external resources to the less developed countries. The objections to it are that the resulting distribution of aid would be rather arbitrary and that aid policy already takes account of the balance-of-payments situations of the recipient countries, so that little is to be gained by giving additional aid in this particular form.

[18] Marcus Fleming, Rudolf Rhomberg, and Lorette Boissonneault, "Export Norms and Their Role in Compensatory Financing," *International Monetary Fund Staff Papers*, Vol. 10 (March 1963), pp. 97-149. Part I of their paper is concerned with the intricate question of devising and estimating a satisfactory norm, Part II with the tests referred to here.

ment of the debt. The tests involved determining the extent to which each scheme would have brought export "availabilities" (proceeds plus borrowings less repayments) for each country to a target level (designed to lie between the ideal norm and the actual level, to take account of the interrelation of export income and import demand). The main finding was that none of the schemes would have brought export availabilities closer to the target by more than a limited extent, and that some would have increased rather than reduced the deviation.[19]

These results suggest that compensation schemes of this kind could make only a limited contribution to stabilization of export earnings. Whether that contribution would be worth its cost depends on the value assigned to the stabilization that could be achieved, a matter on which economics can offer no adequate guidance.

METHODS OF INCREASING EARNINGS FROM EXPORTS OF PRIMARY PRODUCTS

While stabilization of primary product prices or export earnings might be of significant help to less developed countries, and the desirability of such stabilization is a part of the case for international commodity agreements, the chief concern of the less developed countries is evidently with increased opportunities for export earnings from primary products. Apart from trade liberalization along orthodox lines, such opportunities could be provided in a variety of ways, of which the extended use of international commodity agreements is only one; in fact, commodity agreements are unlikely to be applicable to more than a handful of commodities. Other approaches could usually be applied by unilateral action by individual developed countries and do not necessarily require international collaboration or agreement, though the motivation and implementation of them might be strengthened by international action. Nevertheless, for comprehensiveness and to avoid an undue emphasis on the commodities suitable for treatment by

[19] The authors' statistic has a value of zero for perfect compensation and unity for no compensation; some of the schemes yielded a statistic in excess of unity. The OAS scheme yielded a statistic of 0.92, and the best scheme a statistic of 0.77, implying removal of less than a quarter of the instability; counting only the years in which the schemes would have affected export availabilities, the corresponding statistics are 0.86 and 0.62, implying that the best scheme would have eliminated less than 40 percent of instability. These statistics are averages for all countries; individual countries would have done much better in some cases and worse in others.

commodity agreements that has tended to distort contemporary consideration of possible actions in the commodity field, it is necessary to survey all the main approaches that have been suggested in recent years, placing special emphasis on the potentialities of international commodity agreements.

General Considerations

What can be done to increase the export earnings of the less developed countries from their primary commodity production, and how it can be done, depends in large part on the economic philosophy of the governments and public opinion of the developed countries, and particularly on the precise character of the protectionist support for agricultural and other primary products. Protectionism involves reserving first claim on the domestic market to domestic producers, predominantly with the objective of raising their incomes or maintaining their incomes in a desired relation with other incomes. Protectionist groups might be persuaded by a variety of means to modify their policies for the benefit of the less developed countries.

For example, protectionists might be persuaded to allocate a larger or increasing share of the domestic market for primary products to less developed countries, provided that the allocation was strictly controlled by quotas and other safeguards. Or, since protectionist policies imply a certain lack of concern about imposing implicit taxes—in the form of higher prices—on domestic consumers for the benefit of domestic producers, it might be possible to induce the public to accept policies enabling producers in less developed countries to benefit from these same high prices on the exports they are allowed to sell to developed countries, in place of present policies which absorb the difference between domestic and foreign prices into domestic tax revenue by tariffs or levies. This is the recommendation of the Prebisch report and also the point of the French plan for organizing commodity markets. Protectionists might even welcome increases in less developed countries' export prices to the levels of domestic prices in the developed countries as a means of disguising the extent of the burden imposed on consumers by protectionist policies. For the same reason—the protectionist fondness for preserving the outward appearance of national competitiveness and of determination of prices by free competition—protectionist policy-makers might be willing to tolerate international commodity agreements designed to raise prices by restricting output, since such agreements would still result in an apparently competitively determined world market price.

In considering the contribution to development that policy changes of these kinds might make, it is important to recall the analysis of the relative benefits of aid and trade to the less developed countries, and particularly that the benefit from trade is measured not by the foreign exchange earned but by the increase in the value of the output of domestic resources that trade permits. On the lines of comparative cost doctrine, as modified to take account of exchange-rate rigidity, this increase results from the opportunity to obtain foreign products more cheaply than by the alternative of import substitution. In the context of trade in primary commodities, however, which is subject to considerable restriction by the protective policies of the developed countries, the important new possibility arises of obtaining more foreign resources through increases in the price of each unit of primary output, permitted by policy changes that would allow less-developed-country producers to enjoy the same prices as developed-country producers. Given the relatively low elasticities of demand for many primary products, and the long-run elasticity of supply of them from the less developed world, the less developed countries might well gain more, in the way of additional external resources for development, from such policy changes than from a liberalization of trade in primary products.[20]

Similarly, the relative inelasticity of demand for certain primary products suitable for output-restricting, price-raising commodity agreements would permit the less developed producers as a group to increase their real incomes by exploiting their collective monopoly power and so might benefit them considerably more than trade liberalization would. In this connection it should be noted, first, that the rational objective of international commodity agreements should be to exploit the collective monopoly power of the less developed producers so as to maximize their real incomes. There is no economic sense (though there may be considerable political shrewdness) in the Prebisch argument that commodity agreements should seek to preserve some purchasing power

---

[20] As explained in greater detail in Chapter II, higher prices for existing exports would involve a direct transfer of real resources from developed to less developed countries; liberalization would involve no transfer, but a gain for both sides from a fuller exploitation of comparative advantage. The gain to the less developed countries in the first case would be the increase in price on the existing volume of trade; in the second it would be the saving of excess cost of import substitutes made possible by the expansion of export earnings permitted by trade liberalization.

parity relationship between primary commodities and industrial products. Second, and more important, maximizing real income is not the same thing as maximizing foreign exchange earnings, unless the resources employed in primary production have no alternative opportunity cost or alternative use. Otherwise, as standard monopoly theory demonstrates, the optimal policy involves restricting output below the level that would maximize total revenue.

The confusion of optimal policy with maximization of foreign exchange earnings is a consequence of approaching the problem of development from the balance-of-payments rather than the real-resources point of view. It has produced at least two fallacious conclusions in recent writings on international commodity agreements: that international commodity agreements could be useful only for commodities for which the demand is inelastic (at least in the neighborhood of historically experienced price levels);[21] and that where demand is of greater than unitary elasticity, less developed countries should seek to lower their prices through increased productivity, devaluation, or both.[22]

Neither of these conclusions is theoretically correct. For each elasticity of demand greater than unity, there is a corresponding optimal degree of export restriction, diminishing as the elasticity increases. For elasticities of demand less than unity, restriction should be applied until it encounters an elastic range on the demand curve and then should be further increased until it reaches the optimal degree of restriction. Further, it does not seem valid to argue that export restriction through commodity agreements is not to be recommended if the long-run demand elasticity is substantially above the short-run elasticity. Given that the less developed countries are anxious to industrialize as rapidly as possible, and in so doing expect to increase the flexibility of their economic structures, it might well be an optimum strategy for them to attempt to maximize their profits from primary production over the short run, at the expense of future earnings, in order to secure their development objectives.[23] (Whether this would be so

[21] This assumption has been made by John A. Pincus, *Economic Aid and International Cost Sharing* (The Johns Hopkins Press, 1965), and accepted by MacBean, *op. cit.*

[22] This is the position taken by Grant L. Reuber, *Canada's Interest in the Trade Problems of Less-Developed Countries* (Montreal: The Canadian Trade Committee of the Private Planning Association of Canada, May 1964).

[23] Exploitation of the collective monopoly power of the less developed countries necessarily wastes resources through distorting allocation, from a world point of view. These wastes might be tolerated, as falling on the rich countries, especially

would depend on the rate at which the policy-makers discounted the future profits sacrificed by such a strategy.)

The foregoing argument is subject to one potentially important qualification because it implicitly assumes that exports of the commodities in question are not already restricted. As is well known, a country can restrict its exports so as to exploit its monopoly power in the world market either directly by a tax or other type of restriction on exports, or indirectly by import duties and equivalent interventions that draw resources out of exports into import-substituting activities. Thus, the exports of a group of producing countries might already be restricted by their import tariff structures sufficiently or more than sufficiently to exploit their collective monopoly power in their export markets. Given the levels of protection practiced in the typical less developed country, this might well be the case for producers of primary products for which the demand elasticity is appreciably in excess of unity; and in such cases further export restriction would not be beneficial. But it could not be the case for products for which the demand elasticity is less than unity in the neighborhood of historically experienced prices, for restriction of exports of such products would raise total revenue while releasing resources presumably possessing some alternative use value.

Since it is impossible to ascertain whether less developed countries are over- or under-exploiting their monopoly power in commodities with elastic demands, while they must be under-exploiting it for commodities with inelastic demands in the current price range, it seems reasonable pending further research to accept maximization of foreign exchange earnings as a safe minimal standard for optimal commodity agreement policy, and inelasticity of demand at current prices as a criterion for selection of commodities for agreements, in spite of the theoretical objection to these standards.[24]

---

if (as has sometimes been proposed) the commodity agreements followed a two-price policy, charging monopoly prices to the developed countries and marginal cost prices to the less developed countries. From the standpoint of world economic efficiency, and the welfare of the developed countries, it would be preferable for the developed countries to use income transfers to bribe the less developed countries not to exploit their monopoly power; this would be the equivalent of providing deficiency payments, which is the superior method of maintaining producers' incomes. In part, foreign aid may play this role at the present time.

[24] If less developed countries are over-exploiting their collective monopoly power in commodities in elastic demand, Reuber's policy recommendations are correct within the range between the actual and the optimum degree of export restriction.

Alternative Commodity Arrangements

As is evident from the wide variety of restrictions on trade in primary products surveyed in Chapter III, and the interrelation of these variations with the nature of the commodities and especially whether they compete directly, do not compete, or compete indirectly with commodities produced in the developed countries, it is extremely likely that different approaches to international commodity arrangements would be called for, or would be most likely to be successful, for different commodities. The different approaches would offer different potential benefits to the less developed countries, some involving expanding markets for exports at current prices and therefore requiring additional resources in production and others involving raising prices for existing export volumes. The benefits would be distributed among countries according to their shares in the production or export of the commodities affected and would not appear to be subject to the control of the developed countries, facts which might be considered drawbacks. The same objections can be raised to trade liberalization, however; moreover, most of the alternatives would involve some sort of quota system, controlled by the developed countries, which could be used to distribute the benefits according to some canon of fairness and to put pressure on the beneficiaries to use their gains in ways conducive to their economic development.

The main alternative approaches that have been considered or recommended are:

(1) **Quota restriction agreements** aimed at raising prices and exploiting collective monopoly power. These are most readily applicable to only a few tropical products that function as consumption goods rather than industrial materials.

(2) **Levies on imports** by developed countries from less developed countries, to be refunded in whole or in part. This is the French plan for organization of markets. The levies would be of two types: (a) Where developed countries' domestic prices of products partly imported from less developed countries are above world market prices, the levy would be imposed at a variable rate to raise the prices of imports to the domestic level (the intention would be to encourage exporting countries to raise their export prices sufficiently to make the levy unnecessary). (b) On primary products not produced in the developed countries (tropical products) the levy would be a tax on consumers and

could be used in place of a commodity agreement to exploit the monopoly power of the less developed countries' products. Given the inelasticity of demand for such products, a refundable levy of this kind would increase the export earnings of the less developed countries concerned by far more than would the elimination of taxes and tariffs.[25]

(3) Quantitative guarantees of access for producers in less developed countries to markets in which protected domestic production is important. This is intended both to increase imports in a controlled way and give the exporter some certainty about the amounts he will be allowed to export. This approach would probably be most appealing to the United States, in terms of consistency with past American policy.

(4) Compensation from developed to less developed countries in part payment for the effects on the latter's exports of adverse trends, whether arising from the natural working of market forces or from obstacles to competition imposed by policy. In the extreme, this approach would involve acceptance of the Prebisch demand for "compensatory finance"; a milder version of it is represented by proposals that have been advanced for international schemes of "adjustment assistance" for less developed countries experiencing difficulties with their export earnings from primary products.

All of these alternatives involve accepting the fact of protectionist policies in the developed countries and attempting either to restrain their harmful effects on the less developed exporters, to draw the exporters into the protective system, or to compensate them in part for the damage done them by protectionist policies. While the general concept of these approaches is scarcely appealing to believers in the virtues of freer international competition, specialization and division of labor, it has the attractions of practicality in the contemporary protectionist world and might also serve as a stepping stone to a more wholehearted pursuit of liberalization of world trade in primary products.[26]

Gerda Blau has presented some "illustrations" of the potential contributions of these policy approaches to the export earnings of the

[25] The notable exception is sugar, where elimination of tariffs and other protection would lead to substantial replacement of domestic beet sugar production by tropical cane sugar.

[26] As noted in previous chapters, the trend in primary commodity policy in the postwar period has been toward more and not less protection. Against this background even a modification and rationalization of the trend could appear genuinely progressive.

less developed countries, together with those of policies strengthening or weakening market forces. Table 9 reproduces these illustrations. The first two columns show the maximum trade to which the measures described might be applied. For the relevant types 5 to 8, column four represents Dr. Blau's view of what might reasonably be expected to be achievable in practice, type 8 requiring a particularly arbitrary judgment of what developed country taxpayers might stand, and column three shows the quantitative implications. These estimates are not additive; and it should be recalled that price increases entail more gain than quantity increases.[27] The figures do not suggest that such approaches could work wonders for the export earnings and trading gains of the less developed countries. But these are rough guesses only, and incorporate a judgment of political practicality, whereas what are required are detailed estimates of the maximum economic potentialities of these approaches.

Such detailed estimates have been made, for the possibilities of increasing export earnings through international commodity agreements, by John Pincus.[28] He uses a variety of criteria to select commodities meriting priority for control schemes, including: (1) importance in the export trade of less developed countries, preferably of a large number of them; (2) unimportance in the export trade of developed countries; (3) relatively unfavorable free-market earnings prospects due to sluggish export demand or rapid supply growth; (4) the three economic characteristics of (a) inelastic demand over the price range being considered for support, (b) prices that can be supported individually, rather than requiring joint control over a variety of commodities, and (c) amenability to effective national marketing and control systems.

These criteria lead to the selection of coffee, tea, cocoa, bananas and sugar as priority candidates for support. Pincus estimates[29] that mo-

---

[27] The column showing the group on which the cost falls must be interpreted as referring to the short-run effect; some of the policies would benefit the country adopting them, while others would entail transfers of real resources.

[28] *Op. cit.*, Chap. 6, "Burden Sharing and Commodity Policy."

[29] Pincus' procedure (obscurely described, *op. cit.*, pp. 166-67, and implicit in his table, p. 185) is to choose a "monopoly" price by a judgmental process that apparently involves the assumption that elasticities are really higher than statistical estimates indicate, and then to use the statistically estimated elasticities to estimate the quantities that would be sold at the monopoly prices selected. It would have been better practice, and easier for the reader to follow, to estimate maximum revenues for alternative elasticity estimates, rather than choose prices with one set of elasticities in mind and calculate revenues by reference to another (lower) set

TABLE 9

Estimated Effects of Commodity Policies on Exports of Less Developed Countries

Possible Types of Policy Measures	Shares of Underdeveloped Group's Total Exports of Primary Products Which Might Be Affected (Total Exports, 1959–61 Excluding Petrol = 100)		Assumed Increase in Earnings (Illustrative)		Incidence of Cost (If Any) in Importing Country Falling on:
	$ Billion	Percent	$ Billion	Percent	
A. Strengthening market forces					
1. Lessening agricultural protection and related effects in both importing and high-income exporting countries	4.0	30	*	(mainly volume)	Agricultural producers
2. Abolishing revenue duties	5.0	37	0.2	(inelastic demand; 10% for part of volume)	Taxpayers
3. Lessening differential duties for raw and processed goods and other measures encouraging exports of products in processed form	10.6	80	0.5–1.0	(mainly for advantage of "value added" for share of unchanged total volume)	Some industrial sectors
B. Weakening market forces					
4. Understanding re regulating expansion of synthetics	6.5	50	*		Community
C. Making the best of status quo re market forces					
5. Quota restriction agreements (aiming at raising prices)	3.3	25	0.3	10% (price)	Consumers
6. Refundable import levies	7.3	55	0.7	10% (price)	Consumers
7. Quantitative guarantees of access (might be quota agreement as under 5, but not for primary purpose of raising prices)	4.8	36	0.5	10% (volume)	Domestic producers
8. Compensation, in part, for effects of adverse trends, whether arising from working of market forces or from obstacles to working of market	13.2	100	0.3	2%[b]	Taxpayers

Source: Blau, "International Commodity Arrangements and Policies," p. *47*; detailed figures are given in *ibid.*, Table 5/II, p. 30. ᵃ Range of possible alternative policies is too wide for any meaningful quantitative assumptions, even purely illustrative, to be inserted here. ᵇ See reference to type 8, p. 159.

Commodities for which above measures might be applied: 1. Temperate-zone foods and some temperate-zone raw materials; tropical agricultural products competing with temperate-zone; tobacco. 2. Tropical beverages, sugar, tobacco. 3. Most commodity categories (see *ibid.*, Table 5/II, p. 30). 4. Raw materials, oils. 5. Mainly tropical beverages. 6. Most commodities other than raw materials (if importers cooperate) of which: (a) Commodities with internal reference price in importing countries (some temperate-zone products, sugar, oil, rice); (b) No internal reference prices in importing country (tropical products). 7. Temperate-zone foods, tropical competing with temperate. 8. All commodities.

nopoly pricing of these commodities would have raised export earnings in 1961 from \$4,358 million to \$5,042 million, or by \$684 million, an increase of 15.7 percent; an alternative estimate of the maximum revenue obtainable, based on Pincus' elasticity estimates, indicates maximum foreign exchange earnings of \$5,254 million, an increase of about \$900 million or 20.6 percent; on the other hand, if Pincus' monopoly prices are taken to represent revenue-maximizing prices, the implied elasticities indicate a maximum revenue of \$4,800 million, an increase in foreign exchange earnings of only about \$44 million or approximately 10 percent. Most of this increase in revenue would go to the countries of Latin America, and the burden imposed on the United States as compared with the European countries would be disproportionately light.

As mentioned previously, there are good theoretical reasons for rejecting the restriction of commodity agreements to commodities for which the demand is inelastic, as well as for rejecting the objective of maximizing export earnings.[30] Such action would probably broaden

---

of elasticities; the results of doing so are presented in the text. The ratios of the elasticities implied by the prices selected to the elasticities stated are as follows: sugar 1.30, coffee 1.12, tea 1.95, cocoa 1.52, bananas 1.03. The stated elasticities make the demand for tea least elastic, followed by cocoa and coffee with the same elasticity; the elasticities implied by the selected prices place coffee demand as the least elastic, followed by tea and then cocoa demand.

Using Pincus' definitions,

$$e = \frac{(Q' - Q)/Q}{(P' - P)/P}, \quad Q' = [(P' - P)/P] \, [e \, Q + Q],$$

where P and Q are free market prices and quantities; revenue $R = P'Q'$ is maximized when $P'/P = (e - 1)/2e$; at that price $Q'/Q = (1 - e)/2$ and $P'Q'/PQ = -(1 - e)^2/4e$ (e must have a negative sign). This last relationship was used to calculate maximum revenues from the commodity agreements in Pincus' five commodities.

[30] Using the same notation as in note 29, and assuming that P is the alternative opportunity cost of production, profit [expressed by $(P' - P) \, Q'$] is maximized when $P'/P = (2e - 1)/2e$, $Q'/Q = 1/2$, and total profit equals $-PQ/4e$; applying this formula to Pincus' elasticity figures yields \$2,598.4 million as the maximum monopoly profit that could be extracted by international commodity agreements in Pincus' five commodities. This is obviously a substantial figure.

The loss of consumers' surplus (the "collection cost") entailed in transferring this amount of resources to the less developed countries [$1/2 \, (P' - P) \, (Q - Q') = -PQ/8e$] would be 50 percent of the amount transferred, i.e., \$1,299.2 million.

If the alternative opportunity cost of resources used in the industry is a fraction x of P, social profit [expressed by $(P' - xP)Q'$] is maximized when $P'/P =$

L

the range of commodities eligible for agreements and correspondingly broaden the dispersion of the benefits from higher prices among the less developed countries.

Once one begins to think seriously about commodity agreements as a means of increasing external resources, one is forcibly struck by their relative inefficiency as a means of taxing the richer consuming countries to raise resources for development of the poorer countries, and inevitably drawn to the consideration of more efficient methods of international taxation. This process has led Boris Swerling, an established expert on commodity problems, to recommend an international tax on petroleum products and to suggest that tolls on international waterways should be converted into international taxes to raise revenue for development assistance.[31] These suggestions attach insufficient weight to the facts that the developed countries are apparently not yet ready to accept an international tax system, and that the proposal to raise prices by commodity agreements is inherently an effort to establish such a system by subterfuge. But the growing concern with the equity of international burden-sharing in defense and foreign aid is a portent of a trend in that direction; it may ultimately lead to recognition of the need for, and acceptance of, a rational international tax system for the finance of development assistance and other international endeavors.

$[e(1 + x) - 1]/2e$, $Q'/Q = [1 - e (1 - x)]/2$, and total social profit equals $-PQ$ $[1 - e (1 - x)]^2/4e$. The size of x could be identified with the reciprocal of the ratio of domestic to world market prices of protected import substitutes.

[31] Boris Swerling, *Current Issues in Commodity Policy* ("Essays in International Finance," No. 38; Princeton University Press, 1962), especially pp. 14-17, and "Financial Alternatives to International Commodity Stabilization," *Canadian Journal of Economics and Political Science*, Vol. 30 (November 1964), pp. 526-37.

VI

Trade Preferences
for Manufactured Goods

The preparatory work for the United Nations Conference on Trade and Development, and the conference itself, produced two proposals for changes in policy with respect to trade in manufactured products. The more important, novel, and controversial proposal, on which the conference was unable to reach agreement, was for the establishment of preferences in the markets of developed countries for exports of manufactures and semimanufactures by the less developed countries. The other proposal was for preferential arrangements for trade among the less developed countries in manufactured products. This proposal attracted relatively little discussion, presumably because it involves no change in the trade policies of the developed countries, but merely an extension of their tolerance of the protectionist policies of the less developed countries to the sanctioning of overt discrimination against their exports.

Both proposals violate the nondiscrimination principle of the General Agreement on Tariffs and Trade and the GATT ban on new preferential arrangements other than customs unions and free trade areas embracing the bulk of the trade of the participating countries. This, however, does not mean that the proposed trading arrangements would necessarily be economically disadvantageous. The postwar development of the theory of customs unions and of commercial policy changes, culminating in the theory of second best, has shown that in a tariff-ridden world economy there is no a priori reason for believing that nondiscrimination among import sources is economically superior to discriminatory trading arrangements. It has demonstrated also that the question of whether a discriminatory tariff reduction improves or worsens the efficiency and economic welfare of the countries involved and the world as a whole depends on the empirical circumstances of the particular case.

Both the theory of second best and modern welfare economics (as well as ordinary common sense) indicate that policy changes that secure desirable results in terms of income distribution or other objectives at the cost of reduced economic efficiency may constitute improvements on a balance of gain and loss, and may legitimately be recommended if no more efficient method of achieving the same objectives is feasible or acceptable. Finally, inconsistency with GATT principles is not an insuperable institutional objection to the proposals for changes, since GATT principles may be modified by the contracting parties if such modification serves the basic objectives of the Agreement; under Article XXV of the Agreement a member may be relieved of its obligations under GATT by a two-thirds majority vote of the members, a majority which the less developed countries command.

This chapter considers the two proposals for altering existing arrangements governing trade in manufactured goods. Attention is devoted primarily to the possibilities of preferential treatment of exports of manufactured and semimanufactured goods by less developed to developed countries as a means of promoting the growth of the less developed countries. Some brief observations only are offered on the subject of preferential arrangements for trade in manufactured goods among less developed countries.

TRADE PREFERENCES
IN DEVELOPED-COUNTRY MARKETS

At the United Nations Conference on Trade and Development, the U.S. delegation adopted a position of adamant opposition to the demand of the less developed countries for preferences for their exports of manufactured and semimanufactured goods. This position has subsequently been reiterated by official spokesmen and defended, supported, or rationalized, at least in broad terms, by various academic experts.[1]

[1] For a dispassionate exploration of the possibility of assisting the less developed countries by trade preferences in manufactured goods, concluding with extreme skepticism, see Gardner Patterson, "Would Tariff Preferences Help Economic Development?" *Lloyds Bank Review*, No. 76 (April 1965), pp. 18-30. The argument in this chapter draws on Patterson's exposition, though disagreeing with his central theme.

Apart from the traditional commitment of the United States to the principle of nondiscrimination, which is largely responsible for its dogmatic stance on the question, the reasons underlying American opposition to or skepticism about the desirability and probable contribution of preferences to the development of the less developed countries are of two broad sorts: administrative-political and economic. The administrative-political arguments possess a certain prima facie cogency; the economic arguments, on the other hand, appear to have been insufficiently thought out and to have been strongly influenced by the political convenience of the conclusion they arrive at.

Administrative and Political Arguments
Against Preferences

The chief administrative and political arguments against the adoption of preferences for manufactured exports by less developed countries are four in number.[2] In the first place it is argued that the establishment of preferences would inevitably generate—and in fact discussion of them has already generated—serious political frictions among and between the developed and the less developed nations. Among the developed countries, some favor preferences for selected products only and others preferences for all manufactures, some favor nondiscriminatory preferences for all less developed countries and others preferences for selected less developed countries or preferences differentiated according to each country's stage of development. Moreover, some developed countries are peculiarly vulnerable to the discrimination against their manufactured exports that preferences for less developed countries would invoke. The important cases are Japan, which exports goods of a type closely competitive with the labor-intensive goods in which the less developed countries have a comparative advantage, and countries such as Canada and Australia which, though developed, tend to be weak competitors in the world market for manufactures.

Among the less developed countries, for their part, there are conflicts of interest between the members of the British Commonwealth and the associated overseas territories of the Common Market, which currently enjoy preferences respectively in the markets of the United Kingdom and the Common Market countries that they would stand to lose, and other less developed countries that would tend to gain from preferences, partly at their expense. There are also conflicts between the

[2] Patterson, *op. cit.*, pp. 28-30. Patterson presents these as "costs" of preferential arrangements, rather than as arguments against them.

more advanced and the more backward less developed countries, since the former stand to gain more and the latter less, the freer the competition between less developed countries allowed by the preferential arrangements adopted. A serious attempt to initiate preferences for manufactured exports by less developed countries would undoubtedly exacerbate these frictions. On the other hand, it can be argued that if preferential arrangements promise to yield a significant contribution to the economic development of the less developed countries, these frictions should be resolvable by the normal procedures of international negotiation; if necessary, measures could be devised to compensate developed or less developed countries adversely affected by the arrangements.

In the second place it is argued, quite convincingly, that preferential arrangements of the type proposed would involve a great deal of governmental surveillance and control of trade, and correspondingly large administrative costs. The arrangements, it is asserted, would entail exceptions for certain commodities, require validation of the origins of commodities enjoying the preferences, and probably necessitate a complex system of quotas to prevent undue disturbance of domestic markets and to equalize the distribution of the benefits of preferred market entry among the beneficiary less developed countries. These administrative problems and costs, however, have to be weighed against the potential contribution of the arrangements to the growth of the less developed countries.

In the third place, it is argued, the establishment of preferences would create powerful vested interests opposed to further nondiscriminatory tariff reduction through GATT, since such reduction would reduce the value of the preferences enjoyed by the less developed countries. This argument, however, does not present the whole picture. The vested interests would be those of the less developed countries which could only exert political pressure externally on the developed countries. They would be bound to be less powerful than the domestic interests now vested in national tariffs. Moreover, once these national vested interests were subordinated, domestic political pressures for all-round reduction of trade barriers might be strengthened. Further, the argument assumes that in the absence of preferences there would be a strong inclination on the part of the developed countries to pursue trade liberalization through GATT. This is a questionable assumption, for it is very possible that an unsatisfactory outcome of the Kennedy Round and the unwillingness of the United States and other developed countries to reduce tariffs unilaterally on a most-favored-nation basis may leave preferential trading arrangements as the only feasible and acceptable method of assisting the less developed countries through changes in their trade policies.

In the fourth place it is argued that the establishment of preferences for less developed countries' exports of manufactures requires United States participation. Other developed countries presumably will not establish such preferences unilaterally for fear of having their markets glutted by exports from less developed countries, while the less developed countries now enjoying Commonwealth and Common Market preferences will not surrender them unless they receive compensation through preferential access to the American market. From this conclusion it is further argued that while Congress might be willing to empower the Administration to offer preferential access for manufactured exports from less developed countries either unilaterally or by negotiation of a multilateral scheme with other developed countries, a Presidential request for such authority might open a Pandora's box of congressional interventions in the trading privileges of particular less developed countries. It might also offer Congress the opportunity to graft new protective devices for domestic industry onto the arrangements and to use trade policy as an instrument for punishing or rewarding particular developed countries. The fear of what might happen if Congress gained control of a discriminatory United States tariff policy appears to be a powerful underlying factor in the aversion of American officials and academic experts to any form of preferential trading arrangements for less developed countries.[3] How far this fear is justified is a crucial question of political judgment, beyond the scope of this study. Clearly, however, the strength of this argument depends on how great a contribution to development preferential arrangements might make, as well as on how firmly public opinion and the Congress endorse this means of promoting development.

Economic Arguments Against Preferences

All of the political-administrative arguments are inconclusive and depend for their strength on the implicit assumption that the contribution that trade preferences could make to the development of the less

---

[3] Several officials who made this point in discussions cited the administration of the sugar quotas as a leading example of what they feared.

developed countries is relatively small. The economic arguments used to support this assumption are essentially the same as those used to support the assertion that the barriers imposed by the developed countries to the development through trade of the less developed countries are relatively minor. These arguments, discussed in Chapter III, rest on the small volume of existing exports of manufactures by less developed countries, the small number of the exporters and the narrow range of products exported, the low average tariff levels of the developed countries, and the prospect that these tariff levels will be substantially reduced in the Kennedy Round. On the other hand, as maintained in Chapter III, the small existing volume of trade may reflect the influence of trade barriers and certainly does not prove inability to benefit from the reduction of trade barriers, especially in the longer run. Reference to tariff averages conceals the tendency for tariffs to be exceptionally high on the labor-intensive, technologically simple products in which the less developed countries are likely to have a comparative advantage. A number of commodities in this category are on the exceptions lists presented by the developed countries to GATT and so will not be included in the Kennedy Round of tariff reductions. Finally, and most important, what matters for trade is not the tariff rates on commodities but the effective rates of protection of value added implicit in the whole tariff schedule. These effective rates tend to be high on exports or potential exports of less developed countries both because the escalation of tariff rates by stage of production makes effective rates on finished goods higher than nominal rates and because the nominal rates on goods of interest to the less developed countries tend to be exceptionally high. Judged in terms of effective rather than nominal rates, preferences are likely to be considerably more effective in improving the competitive position of less developed countries in the markets of developed countries than might appear from consideration of nominal tariff rates alone.

The argument that preferences in industrial products would be unlikely to contribute much to the development of the less developed countries has been presented in the most careful detail by Gardner Patterson.[4] He points out that in order for a preference to be helpful to less developed countries' exports, the exporter's price must be less

[4] *Op. cit.,* pp. 25-28.

than the domestic price in the preference-giving country[5] and must exceed competitors' prices by less than the amount of the preference margin given. The room for the latter condition to be fulfilled, he argues, is rather restricted: the tariff levels of the developed countries average about 15 percent and will, he reckons, be reduced to 10 percent by the Kennedy Round; moreover, developed countries would be extremely reluctant to grant zero tariffs to the less developed countries and would be more likely to settle for the 50 percent minimum preference suggested by some of the less developed countries at UNCTAD. He therefore concludes that what is under discussion is a 5 percent average margin of preference and that even this would be subject to exceptions, notably for cotton textiles. He then poses the question: "How many cases are there where a 5-7 percent price advantage would be a decisive factor in making it possible for less developed countries to take markets in developed nations away from both domestic producers in those countries (including all members of any regional group) *and* from producers of comparable manufactured goods in other industrial countries?" His answer is "some, but not many." "Excluding those goods for which most-favored-nation reductions would probably be as effective as preferential ones (leather and wood manufactures, some textiles, rugs, some drugs, etc., come to mind) the most likely candidates would seem to be in such products as pottery, toys, sporting goods, footwear and rubber manufactures."[6]

This argument is unsatisfactory even in its own terms as an evaluation of the potentialities of trade preferences for less developed countries. In the first place, it is not legitimate to argue that a policy has limited economic potentialities by assuming that it will be applied only to a limited extent, as Patterson does in assuming preferences of 50 percent only; to do so is to confuse a judgment about governmental behavior with an assessment of economic facts. In the second place, it is not valid to exclude goods on the grounds that a nondiscriminatory reduction of the tariffs applicable to them would be equally effective; to do so is to assume without warrant that such a reduction will in fact occur, as well as to ignore possible differences in the benefits of the two

[5] In this connection, Patterson makes the relevant but frequently overlooked point that the less developed countries will have to compete with the lowest-cost producing countries in the European Economic Community (EEC) and the European Free Trade Association (EFTA).

[6] Quotations from Patterson, *op. cit.*, p. 27.

alternative policies to the less developed countries.[7] The main objections to the argument, however, concern its reliance on average tariff rates[8] and, more fundamentally, its use of nominal rather than effective rates of protection.

Assessing Advantages of Preferences

The competitive advantages that preferences in industrial products might give to less developed producers must be assessed in terms of the resulting reduction of the effective protection enjoyed by producers in the developed countries against less developed producers and of the margin of effective preference given less developed over developed exporters. Because of the way in which effective rates of protection are determined by the tariff structure, a preferential tariff reduction on a particular commodity must reduce the effective rate of protection of producers in the preference-granting country against producers in the preference-receiving country by at least the same percentage as the reduction in the tariff rate and possibly by much more, or may even result in negative protection.[9] Similarly, the margin of preference over

[7] Grant L. Reuber (*Canada's Interest in the Trade Problems of Less-Developed Countries* [Montreal: The Canadian Trade Committee of the Private Planning Association of Canada, May 1964], pp. 23-27) has compared three tariff strategies for increasing the earnings of less developed countries from exports of manufactures not subject to quantitative restrictions. These are: reduction of most-favored-nation rates to zero and elimination of existing preferences, reduction of preferred rates to zero and reduction of most-favored-nation rates sufficiently to maintain existing preferences (both strategies being consistent with GATT), and elimination of tariffs applicable to less developed countries combined with maintenance of tariffs applicable to developed countries (the extreme possibility of trade preferences). He concludes that the third (preferential) strategy would be most beneficial to the less developed countries; using a 12 percent estimate of average tariff rates and an assumed demand elasticity of two, he estimates that this strategy would increase less-developed-country exports of the goods in question (which account for about 5 percent of their total exports) by 25 percent (p. 26), or about $600 million per year (p. xii). This estimate is subject to the same major objections as are Patterson's less quantitative arguments, and for that reason is probably a substantial underestimate of the possibilities; nevertheless, it does indicate that the possibilities of preferences in industrial products for less developed countries are by no means negligible.

[8] For comparison with Patterson's assumption of an average nominal tariff rate of 15 percent, see the nominal tariff rates shown in Table 10, especially in the category of consumer goods.

[9] The effective rate of protection of a production process j is $T_j = (t_j - \Sigma_i a_{ji} t_i)/v_j$, where the t_i represents the tariff rates of the tariff schedule, v_j is the value added in the process per unit value of output, and a_{ji} is the cost, per unit value of output of j, of the input of commodity i into the process j, all values being

foreign competitors granted to the preference-receiving country is (approximately) measured not by the number of percentage points by which the tariff applied to that country is reduced below the general rate, but by that number divided by the ratio of value added to value of output.[10]

It may be useful to illustrate these points by some hypothetical examples. First, suppose that for a given commodity, materials account for half the world market price and that the commodity is subject to a tariff of 10 percent but the materials are admitted free of duty to a particular country. The effective rate of protection of the processing of the materials into the product is then 20 percent (10 percent of the foreign price, applied to the half of that price that represents processing costs); a 50 percent preference would reduce the nominal

---

reckoned at world market prices. The elasticity of T_j with respect to t_i is $t_j/(t_j - \Sigma_i a_{ji} t_i)$. Assuming that T_j is initially positive, this elasticity has a minimum value of unity (when $\Sigma_i a_{ji} t_i = 0$), and must be greater than unity if any t_i is positive. A preference will provide negative protection to the production process against producers in the preference-receiving country (i.e., will result in the tariff structure imposing a tax on the domestic operation of the process as compared with its operation using inputs obtained at world market prices) if the preferential tariff rate t_j is less than $\Sigma_i a_{ji} t_i$.

One implication of this analysis is that the Kennedy Round might conceivably have a much greater effect in liberalizing international trade than estimates of the likely percentage reduction in tariff rates resulting from it would suggest.

It should be noted that granting a preference to a product used as an input in other production processes will increase the effective protection of those processes, if some part of the preference is reflected in a lowering of the domestic price of the input on which the preference is given. Thus the granting of preferences on some exports of less developed countries might be so arranged as to increase the overall domestic protection against competition from foreign countries, including the less developed.

[10] Let t_j be the initial tariff applicable to all suppliers, p_j the proportion by which the preference reduces it for the preference-receiving country, and v_j the ratio of value added to value of output in the production of competitors ($1 - v_j$ being the ratio of value of inputs to value of output, these inputs being assumed to be available to the preference-receiving country at the same world market price as competitors pay). Define C_j as the ratio by which the preference allows the cost of value added in the preference-receiving country to exceed that in the competitor countries; C_j is determined by the condition that the prices of exports from the two sources in the protected market concerned be equal, which is $1 + t_j = [1 + (1 - p_j) t_j] [1 + C_j v_j]$. This yields $C_j = p_j t_j / (1 + t_j - p_j t_j) v_j$; for small tariff rates and substantial proportional preferences $C_j \approx p_j t_j / v_j$.

For some purposes it may be appropriate to assume that capital is internationally mobile and to conduct the analysis in terms of the effective rate of protection of value added by labor.

rate of protection against preferred producers by 5 percentage points, from 10 percent to 5 percent, but the effective rate by 10 points, from 20 percent to 10 percent; and it would give them a nominal preference margin against foreign competitors of 5 percentage points, but an effective margin of 10 points in the processing of the materials. Similarly, a 100 percent preference would reduce the effective rate against preferred producers by 20 percentage points, and give them an effective preference margin of 20 percentage points against foreign competitors. Second, making the same cost assumptions, suppose that both the materials and the finished product are subject to a tariff of 10 percent, so that the effective rate of protection of the processing is 10 percent. In this case a preference of 50 percent, reducing the nominal rate of protection against preferred producers by 5 percentage points, would completely wipe out the effective protection of domestic producers against competition from preferred producers (assuming that the latter could buy materials at world prices), since the 5 percent tariff levied on imports of the finished good would just offset the 10 percent disadvantage on half their costs imposed on domestic producers by the duty on materials. A preference of 100 percent would impose a cost disadvantage of 10 percent on the domestic producers, because of the higher materials cost imposed on them by the duty on materials, for which they would receive no compensation via the tariff on the final product. In this second case, the margins of preference enjoyed by preferred producers over their foreign competitors would be the same as in the first case.

These theoretical considerations are important because effective rates of protection of manufactured goods in developed countries are both higher in general than nominal tariff rates and relatively high on the processing of primary products and the manufacture of consumer goods, in which the less developed countries are likely to have an actual or potential comparative advantage.[11] Their practical importance is demonstrated by the data presented in Tables 10, 11, and 12. Table 10 shows nominal and effective tariff rates for a number of industries (the effective rates are those used in Table 4, Chapter III; the industries are grouped as in Table 3, Chapter III). Table 11 separates the effective tariff rates of Table 10 into two components, the subsidy to domestic value added implicit in the tariff rates applicable to the output of the

---

[11] See Chapter III, Tables 3, 4, and 5.

industry, and the average rate of taxation of value added in the industry implicit in the tariffs levied on the products of other industries which this industry uses as inputs.[12] The granting of a preference to less developed countries on the product of that industry alone, other tariffs remaining unchanged, would reduce the subsidy—so far as competition with the preference-receiving countries were concerned—without reducing the implicit tax on production. In the extreme case of a 100 percent preference on the product, domestic producers would have a disadvantage by comparison with their competitors in the preference-receiving country—would receive negative protection—to an extent measured by the implicit rate of taxation of value added (assuming that these competitors could purchase inputs at world market prices). Table 12 shows the nominal and the effective rates of preference over their developed-country competitors in the major developed-country markets that less-developed-country producers would enjoy in consequence of a preference at the rate of 100 percent on the individual products for which calculations are presented; it is assumed in each case that no other tariffs are changed and that competitors in both developed and less developed countries use the same input-output ratios for purchased inputs and can purchase these inputs at world market prices.[13]

The clear implication of the theoretical considerations and empirical evidence is that, despite impressions to the contrary derived from contemplation of nominal tariff levels, preferences in developed-country markets for exports of manufactures and semimanufactures might well exercise a powerful influence in expanding the export earnings and promoting the industrialization of the less developed countries. The potentialities of such preferences consequently deserve serious exploration. Such an exploration would be desirable, first, because the less developed nations appear to be convinced that further liberal-

[12] In terms of the formula of note 9, $T_j = t_j/v_j - \Sigma_i a_{ji} t_i/v_j = S_j - T_j$, where S_j and T_j are the proportional rates of subsidization and taxation of domestic value added in industry j imposed by the country's tariff structure.

[13] Or that they impose the same average rates of protection on these inputs. On these assumptions, and using the same value-added ratios for the preference-giving, preference-receiving, and nonpreferred countries (as is done in the computations), the effective preference rates of Table 12 are identical with the implicit rates of subsidization of Table 11. The reasons why these assumptions may well not be realized in practice are discussed later.

The proviso that only one tariff rate at a time is changed in constructing Table 12 should be emphasized; on this point see note 9.

TABLE 10

Nominal and Effective Tariff Rates on Manufactures of Export Interest to Less Developed Countries[a]

(Percent)

Industry[b]	United States Nom-inal	United States Effec-tive	United Kingdom Nom-inal	United Kingdom Effec-tive	Common Market Nom-inal	Common Market Effec-tive	Sweden Nom-inal	Sweden Effec-tive	Japan Nom-inal	Japan Effec-tive
Intermediate Products I[c]										
Thread and yarn (21)	11.7	31.8	10.5	27.9	2.9	3.6	2.2	4.3	2.7	1.4
Wood products including furniture (29)	12.8	26.4	14.8	25.5	15.1	28.6	6.8	14.5	19.5	33.9
Leather (35)	9.6	25.7	14.9	34.3	7.3	18.3	7.0	21.7	19.9	59.0
Synthetic materials (39)	18.6	33.5	12.7	17.1	12.0	17.6	7.2	12.9	19.1	32.1
Other chemical materials (40)	12.3	26.6	19.4	39.2	11.3	20.5	4.5	9.7	12.2	22.6
Average of nine manufactures that make up Intermediate Products I	8.8	17.6	11.1	23.1	7.6	12.0	3.0	5.3	11.4	23.8
Intermediate Products II[d]										
Textile fabrics (22)	24.1	50.6	20.7	42.2	17.6	44.4	12.7	33.4	19.7	48.8
Rubber goods (37)	9.3	16.1	20.2	43.9	15.1	33.6	10.8	26.1	12.9	23.6
Plastic articles (38)	21.0	27.0	17.9	30.1	20.6	30.0	15.0	25.5	24.9	35.5
Miscellaneous chemical products (43)	12.6	15.6	15.4	16.7	11.6	13.1	2.5	0.0	16.8	22.9
Ingots and other primary steel forms (49)	10.6	106.7	11.1	98.9	6.4	28.9	3.8	40.0	13.0	58.9
Metal manufactures (56)	14.4	28.5	19.0	35.9	14.0	25.6	8.4	16.2	18.1	27.7
Average of ten manufactures that make up Intermediate Products II	15.2	28.6	17.2	34.3	13.3	28.3	8.5	20.8	16.6	34.5

Consumer Goods										
Hosiery (23)	25.6	48.7	25.4	49.7	18.6	41.3	17.6	42.4	26.0	60.8
Clothing (24)	25.1	35.9	25.5	40.5	18.5	25.1	14.0	21.1	25.2	42.4
Other textile articles (25)	19.0	22.7	24.5	42.4	22.0	38.8	13.0	21.2	14.8	13.0
Shoes (26)	16.6	25.3	24.0	36.2	19.9	33.0	14.0	22.8	29.5	45.1
Leather goods other than shoes (36)	15.5	24.5	18.7	26.4	14.7	24.3	12.2	20.7	23.6	33.6
Bicycles and motorcycles (64)	14.4	26.1	22.4	39.2	20.9	39.7	17.1	35.8	25.0	45.0
Precision instruments (66)	21.4	32.2	25.7	44.2	13.5	24.2	6.6	9.1	23.2	38.5
Sport goods, toys, jewelry, etc. (67)	25.0	41.8	22.3	35.6	17.9	26.6	10.6	16.6	21.6	31.2
Average of ten manufactures that make up Consumer Goods	17.5	25.9	23.8	40.4	17.8	30.9	12.4	23.9	27.5	50.5
Investment Goods										
Nonelectrical machinery (58)	11.0	16.1	16.1	21.2	10.3	12.2	8.8	11.6	16.8	21.4
Electrical machinery (59)	12.2	18.1	19.7	30.0	14.5	21.5	10.7	17.7	18.1	25.3
Average of five manufactures that make up Investment Goods	10.3	13.9	17.0	23.0	11.7	15.0	8.5	12.1	17.1	22.0
Average of 34 manufactured goods included in categories above	11.6	20.0	15.5	27.8	11.9	18.6	6.8	12.5	16.2	29.5

Source: Bela A. Balassa, "Tariff Protection in Industrial Countries: An Evaluation," *Journal of Political Economy*, Vol. 73 (December 1965), Tables 1 and 5; the effective tariff rate for Swedish precision instruments has been corrected after correspondence with Professor Balassa.

a Tariff averages are weighted by the combined imports of the countries.
b Numbers in parentheses are the classification numbers used in the input-output tables from which effective tariff rates were derived.
c Manufactures whose main inputs are natural raw materials.
d Intermediate goods at higher levels of fabrication.

TABLE 11

Implicit Rates of Subsidization
and Taxation of Domestic Value Added
in Manufactures of Export Interest to Less Developed Countries

(Percent)

Industry	United States		United Kingdom		Common Market		Sweden		Japan	
	Subsidy	Tax	Subsidy	Tax	Subsidy	Tax	Subsidy	Tax	Subsidy	Tax
Intermediate Products I[a]										
Thread and yarn (21)	41.8	10.0	37.5	9.6	10.4	6.8	7.9	3.6	9.6	8.2
Wood products including furniture (29)	29.1	2.7	33.6	8.1	34.3	5.7	15.5	1.0	44.3	10.4
Leather (35)	32.0	6.3	49.7	15.4	24.3	6.0	23.3	1.6	66.3	7.3
Synthetic materials (39)	48.9	15.4	33.4	16.3	31.6	14.0	19.0	6.0	50.3	18.2
Other chemical materials (40)	32.4	5.8	51.1	11.9	29.7	9.2	11.8	2.1	32.1	9.5
Intermediate Products II[b]										
Textile fabrics (22)	75.3	24.7	64.7	22.5	55.0	10.6	39.7	6.3	61.6	12.8
Rubber goods (37)	25.8	9.7	56.1	12.2	41.9	8.3	30.0	3.9	35.8	12.2
Plastic articles (38)	52.5	25.5	44.8	14.7	51.5	21.5	37.5	12.0	62.3	29.6
Miscellaneous chemical products (43)	28.0	12.4	34.2	17.5	25.8	12.7	5.6	5.5	37.3	14.4
Ingots and other primary steel forms (49)	117.8	11.1	123.3	24.4	71.1	42.2	42.2	2.2	144.6	85.5
Metal manufactures (56)	36.9	8.4	48.7	12.8	35.9	10.3	21.5	5.3	46.4	18.7

Consumer goods										
Hosiery (23)	67.4	18.7	66.8	17.1	49.0	7.6	46.3	3.9	68.4	7.6
Clothing (24)	67.8	31.9	68.9	28.4	50.0	24.9	37.8	16.7	68.1	25.7
Other textile articles (25)	57.6	34.9	74.2	31.8	66.7	27.9	39.4	18.2	44.9	31.8
Shoes (26)	35.3	10.0	51.1	14.9	42.3	9.3	29.8	7.0	62.8	17.6
Leather goods other than shoes (36)	36.9	12.4	44.5	18.1	35.0	10.7	29.1	8.3	56.2	22.6
Bicycles and motorcycles (64)	37.9	11.8	59.0	19.7	55.0	15.3	45.0	9.2	65.8	20.8
Precision instruments (66)	38.9	6.7	46.7	2.5	24.6	0.3	12.0	2.9	42.2	3.7
Sport goods, toys, jewelry, etc. (67)	50.0	8.2	44.6	9.0	35.8	9.2	21.2	4.6	43.2	12.0
Investment goods										
Nonelectrical machinery (58)	22.5	6.3	32.9	11.7	21.0	8.8	18.0	6.4	34.3	12.9
Electrical machinery (59)	23.0	4.9	37.2	7.2	27.4	5.9	20.2	2.5	34.2	8.9

Source: Computed from Table 10; value-added coefficients supplied by Bela A. Balassa.
a Manufactures whose main inputs are natural raw materials.
b Intermediate goods at higher levels of fabrication.

TABLE 12

Nominal and Effective Preference Rates
on Manufactures of Export Interest to Less Developed Countries
Conferred by 100 Percent Preferences Granted by Developed Countries

(Percent)

Industry	United States		United Kingdom		Common Market		Sweden		Japan	
	Nom-inal	Effec-tive	Nom-inal	Effec-tive	Nom-inal	Effec-tive	Nom-inal	Effec-tive	Nom-inal	Effec-tive
Intermediate Products I[a]										
Thread and yarn (21)	11.7	41.8	10.5	37.5	2.9	10.4	2.2	7.9	2.7	9.6
Wood products including furniture (29)	12.8	29.1	14.8	33.6	15.1	34.3	6.8	15.5	19.5	44.3
Leather (35)	9.6	32.0	14.9	49.7	7.3	24.3	7.0	23.3	19.9	66.3
Synthetic materials (39)	18.6	48.9	12.7	33.4	12.0	31.6	7.2	19.0	19.1	50.3
Other chemical materials (40)	12.3	32.4	19.4	51.1	11.3	29.7	4.5	11.8	12.2	32.1
Intermediate Products II[b]										
Textile fabrics (22)	24.1	75.3	20.7	64.7	17.6	55.0	12.7	39.7	19.7	61.6
Rubber goods (37)	9.3	25.8	20.2	56.1	15.1	41.9	10.8	30.0	12.9	35.8
Plastic articles (38)	21.0	52.5	17.9	44.8	20.6	51.5	15.0	37.5	24.9	62.3
Miscellaneous chemical products (43)	12.6	28.0	15.4	34.2	11.6	25.8	2.5	5.6	16.8	37.3
Ingots and other primary steel forms (49)	10.6	117.8	11.1	123.3	6.4	71.1	3.8	42.2	13.0	144.4
Metal manufactures (56)	14.4	36.9	19.0	48.7	14.0	35.9	8.4	21.5	18.1	46.4

Consumer goods										
Hosiery (23)	25.6	67.4	25.4	66.8	18.6	49.0	17.6	46.3	26.0	68.4
Clothing (24)	25.1	67.8	25.5	68.9	18.5	50.0	14.0	37.8	25.2	68.1
Other textile articles (25)	19.0	57.6	24.5	74.2	22.0	66.7	13.0	39.4	14.8	44.9
Shoes (26)	16.6	35.3	24.0	51.1	19.9	42.3	14.0	29.8	29.5	62.8
Leather goods other than shoes (36)	15.5	36.9	18.7	44.5	14.7	35.0	12.2	29.1	23.6	56.2
Bicycles and motorcycles (64)	14.4	37.9	22.4	59.0	20.9	55.0	17.1	45.0	25.0	65.8
Precision instruments (66)	21.4	38.9	25.7	46.7	13.5	24.6	6.6	12.0	23.2	42.2
Sport goods, toys, jewelry, etc. (67)	25.0	50.0	22.3	44.6	17.9	35.8	10.6	21.2	21.6	43.2
Investment goods										
Nonelectrical machinery (58)	11.0	22.5	16.1	32.9	10.3	21.0	8.8	18.0	16.8	34.3
Electrical machinery (59)	12.2	23.0	19.7	37.2	14.5	27.4	10.7	20.2	18.1	34.2

Source: Computed from Table 10; value-added coefficients supplied by Bela A. Balassa.
[a] Manufacture whose main inputs are natural raw materials.
[b] Intermediate goods at higher levels of fabrication.

ization of international trade along traditional lines within the GATT framework will be of little benefit to them, and that preferential entry to developed-country markets will enable them to expand their exports of manufactures in competition with those of the developed countries. Whether this belief is correct or not, the political and economic interests of the United States in the less developed countries, and the U.S. concern with providing its contributions of development assistance in the most effective form, suggest that the belief should be acknowledged and given serious consideration in developing policy recommendations.

Second, the major European countries, in their statements and voting behavior at UNCTAD, revealed considerable sympathy with the notion of trade preferences in manufactured products for less developed countries, even though there was sharp disagreement over whether preferences should be selective or general. The United States was relatively isolated in its blanket opposition to preferences. As leader of the Western world, and a leader committed to the solution of political and economic differences by negotiation and discussion, it cannot hope to sustain an isolated position. Either it must produce a case against preferences, and an alternative solution to the problems preferences are intended to deal with, sufficiently compelling to persuade the other developed countries, or (what is probably the more realistic alternative) develop its own policy on preferences to reconcile the differences.

Finally, future progress toward trade liberalization within the existing institutional framework of GATT depends, because of the principles of nondiscrimination and reciprocity, on the willingness of major trading countries to bargain with each other for reciprocal tariff reduction. How far the Kennedy Round negotiations between the United States and the Common Market will be successful in reducing tariffs is a major uncertainty at present. More important is the question whether their result will be to prepare the way for yet another round of negotiations or to terminate progress toward liberalization along the GATT route in favor of completion of the establishment of the EEC and the EFTA and the regionalization of world trade that these externally protected and internally free-trading blocs would entail. In the latter event, if the United States wished to continue to press for freer trade, both in the general interest of its objectives with respect to the free world economy and the particular interest of promoting the development of the less developed countries through trade, it would be obliged to abandon either the principle of reciprocity or the principle of nondiscrimination. Because of the prevalence of the protectionist conception of the gains from free trade from which the reciprocity principle is derived, it might well be necessary to abandon the principle of nondiscrimination, and to negotiate preferential tariff reductions with countries or regional groupings of countries that were prepared to reciprocate. Preferential treatment of the exports of less developed countries, probably on a basis of discrimination among such countries, would complement this sort of policy, on the already accepted principle that developed countries should not expect reciprocity from less developed countries.

The Arguments for Preferences

The central argument for tariff preferences for the manufactured exports of less developed countries advanced at UNCTAD was for temporary preferences; the argument was derived from infant-industry considerations and alleged to be a logical extension of the infant-industry argument. In one respect it is, not a logical extension, but an empirically motivated analytical revision of the infant-industry argument, for it incorporates the observation that the process of acquiring efficiency in production through experience requires access to a large competitive market and is unlikely to be carried out successfully in the small national market made available by infant-industry protection on traditional lines. In two significant respects, however, the argument is something different from and more debatable than the infant-industry argument.

INFANT-INDUSTRY PREFERENCES. The infant-industry argument envisages a social investment by the consumers of the country imposing the infant-industry tariff, financed and disbursed through higher prices paid by consumers and received by producers as a result of the tariff; in return the country acquires an industry able to compete at world market prices while the producers earn higher incomes than they would have earned without the social investment. In contrast, the argument for tariff preferences is an argument for a social investment by the consumers of the developed countries, the return on which will accrue to the producers of the less developed countries except to the extent that the maturation of the infant industry actually has the effect of reducing world market prices.

Therefore the argument for preferences is an argument for a particular form of transfer of external resources from the developed countries for investment in the industrialization of the less developed countries. The question naturally arises as to the relative merits of this method of collecting and transferring the resources and choosing the investments, as compared with the more straightforward method of transferring resources as foreign aid and choosing the investment projects as part of the normal routine of development planning. The answer obviously must be that preferences could provide resources that would not be made available through the more orthodox aid alternative.

The more important difference between the tariff-preference and infant-industry arguments concerns the choice of industries and the amount of protection afforded them. Rational implementation of the orthodox infant-industry argument would involve first selecting the industries that could—after an initial period of protection—compete in the world market while yielding a socially satisfactory return on the investment and then granting these industries the temporary protection required to establish them. Under the tariff-preference scheme, however, at least in its more general forms, selection would be based on the extent to which the developed countries protected the industries, those most heavily protected being given the greatest incentive to establish themselves in the less developed countries.

Politically this is a dubious scheme because it would provide maximum incentives for the establishment in the less developed countries of the very developed-country industries that have in the past shown most political power to obtain protection from foreign competition. This would seem likely to militate against preferences unless they were accompanied by quota and other safeguards designed to minimize their inherent threat to existing protectionist interests. The tariff-preference scheme is economically dubious because it provides maximum incentives for the establishment of the industries whose costs will have to fall most below those in the preference-giving countries if they are to survive the termination of the preference. While the most heavily protected industries in the developed countries are likely to include those in which the less developed countries have a potential comparative advantage, it is very unlikely that they generally represent the best infant-industry prospects for the less developed countries. Generally speaking the developed countries have designed their tariffs to protect

their industries from each others' competition, and that competition is
at least as likely to be based on abundance of capital or technological
superiority as on the low-wage labor and abundance of raw materials
that constitute the potential comparative advantage of the typical less
developed country.[14]

These doubtful features of tariff preferences relate to a scheme in
which a standard preferential margin for less developed countries is
applied to the existing national tariff schedule of one or more developed countries. The problems indicated could be avoided by two
alternative preferential arrangements. One would involve giving each
less-developed-country industry the same absolute preference margin.
Ignoring certain difficulties associated with the difference between
nominal and effective preference margins, this alternative would be
equivalent to an export subsidy on industrial exports by less developed
countries or (again with certain obvious qualifications associated with
differences in the effects on imports) to a devaluation coupled with an
aid transfer. This alternative would ignore differences in the infant-industry potentialities of different lines of production, letting experience
determine which industries should survive. The other alternative
would be to examine the various industries for infant-industry potentialities and provide the required protection by specific adjustment of
the margin and duration of the preference for each product. The
difficulty with this alternative, aside from its cumbersomeness, is that
existing developed-country tariffs might not be high enough for preferences to provide the required protection,[15] additional subsidies being
required. In any case, implementation of the infant-industry argument
in the context of a tariff-ridden world market could be more conven-
iently and simply effected by the use of production subsidies to industries genuinely qualifying as infants.

However, even where infant-industry conditions exist—an empirical
issue concerning which the ratio of unsupported assertion to empirical

[14] These points would lose some of their force if it could be assumed that investment decisions in the preference-receiving countries were guided entirely by consideration of those countries' comparative advantages after the preferences termi-
nated; but this would involve a deliberate decision to renounce opportunities for
profits in the interim period (commonly put at a minimum of ten years), which
seems very unlikely.

[15] Patterson, op. cit., p. 26, emphasizes the point that the levels of developed-
country tariffs are now too low to enable as much protection of infant industries
to be given through tariff preferences as has in the past been conferred by infant-
industry tariffs.

evidence is probably unexcelled in any other field of economics—these conditions do not logically lead to the recommendation of a tariff. Instead, they lead to the recommendation of a subsidy, either on the production of the industry or on whatever aspect of its initial operations (creation of infrastructure, training of labor)[16] generates the difference between social and private return on which the argument depends. The use of the tariff, which entails a distortion of consumption choices contributing nothing to the attainment of the objectives of the policy, has to be justified by the infeasibility of the economically superior subsidy method, so that resort to infant-industry tariffs appears as a second-best policy. Correspondingly, the recommendation of tariff preferences from developed countries, with their inefficiencies, appears as a third-best policy recommendation.

OTHER PREFERENCES. Other arguments have also been advanced for tariff preferences. One asserts that the temporary extension of preferences would enable producers in less developed countries to lower their costs to the competitive level through reaping economies of scale. This argument differs from the infant-industry argument in positing no divergence of social from private returns in investment, but instead assuming a lack of the capital, entrepreneurship and marketing ability required to establish industry on the appropriate scale and the consequent need to provide special incentives to attract the required managerial resources. The assumption that these resources do not exist locally implies that they will be attracted from the outside, presumably from established enterprises located in the preference-giving country or in competitor countries not favored by the preference.

Since the argument assumes that the industry eventually would be competitive, and that outside enterprises are free to establish it, it must further assume either that such enterprises must be bribed to do so by the extra profits provided by the preference, or that establishment of local operations is unprofitable without the temporary subsidy pro-

---

[16] It is frequently argued that the training by a firm of workers who then move on to other employers imposes a private loss on the firm to which there corresponds no social loss (e.g., Patterson, *op. cit.*, p. 24). This is only true if the firm, and not the worker, bears the cost of the training; institutional arrangements such as apprenticeship or other means of paying low wages to trainees generally permit the firm to make the worker bear the expense of his training where this risk of loss exists.

vided by the preference but profitable with it.[17] In either case, the temporary preference is, as before, a transfer from the developed-country consumers, used for a particular kind of investment. While it might conceivably make a powerful contribution to the development of exporting industries in the less developed countries, there is a distinct possibility that foreign enterprises might be rationally motivated to remain only as long as the subsidy lasted.

Another argument frequently used stresses the divergence between private industrial costs and real social costs created by social security legislation, wage policies, and other cultural or institutional factors that make the cost of labor to industry exceed the value of its marginal product in the agricultural or subsistence sector. In the same category belong arguments resting on divergences of private and social opportunity costs created by protectionist policies and overvaluation. These conditions would argue for permanent rather than temporary subsidies to offset the alleged divergences of social from private opportunity costs as a first-best policy, and consequently for permanent protection as a second-best policy (and therefore for permanent preferences as a means of imposing the costs of the required subsidies on the consumers of the developed countries).[18]

Tariff Preferences in the Light of Effective Protection Theory

The modern theory of customs unions and preferential tariff reduction is an extremely complex exercise in general equilibrium analysis, much too elaborate to deploy in analyzing all the alternative preferential tariff systems that have been proposed in connection with UNCTAD. It is also primarily concerned with static considerations of efficiency of resource allocation and hence does not deal with the dynamic growth-generating effects that are hoped for from preferences for less developed countries. Moreover, it rests heavily on the assumptions of perfect competition and especially of homogeneity of the product

[17] The latter assumption applies also to the establishment of operations by local entrepreneurs.

[18] Patterson, *op. cit.*, p. 25, points out that these divergences could be offset by subsidies arranged by the government of the country, but that this would raise the practical problem of inviting the imposition of countervailing duties by the importing countries. This seems incorrect, for the proper subsidies would be on the production of goods, not on exports of them, and so should not appear as dumping in export markets.

supplied by different national producers, and has not yet been revised to incorporate the theory of effective protection. Briefly stated, its central principles are as follows: A preference will result in an increase in the efficiency of utilization of the world's resources if its effect is to shift production of a given good from a higher-cost to a lower-cost national source, or consumption from higher-cost to lower-cost goods satisfying the same want. Conversely, a preference will result in reducing the efficiency of utilization of the world's resources if it shifts production or consumption from lower-cost to higher-cost sources of supply. Any specific preference or preferential arrangement will have effects of both kinds, and its net effect can only be evaluated by a quantitative comparison of the gains with the losses in efficiency.

In the literature on customs union theory, the efficiency-increasing shifts are identified with "trade creation"—a shift from protected higher-cost domestic goods to lower-cost imports from the preference-receiving country. Efficiency-reducing shifts are identified with "trade diversion"—a shift from lower-cost imports from non-preference-receiving countries to higher-cost imports from preference-receiving countries. This identification, however, derives from the practice of traditional theory of identifying the protective effects of tariffs on the location of production with the nominal tariffs on commodities produced. The recognition that what really matters is the effective rates of protection of value added implicit in national tariff structures requires a re-exploration of the effects of preferences in these terms. Such a re-exploration indicates that trade creation may entail losses from increased inefficiency, whereas trade diversion may entail gains from reduced inefficiency. The former possibility arises when the effect of the preference is implicitly to subsidize imports whose real cost is greater than the cost of the domestic goods they replace. The latter possibility arises when the money prices of imports from the preference-receiving country, relative to the prices of imports from nonpreferred countries, overstate the relative real costs of such imports. Both possibilities are associated primarily with the money-cost-raising effects of tariffs on inputs into the production process. Pending further theoretical and empirical investigation, however, these possibilities should probably be regarded as potentially significant qualifications to a general rule, and the general principle that trade creation increases and trade diversion decreases the efficiency of utilization of world resources be retained as a broad rule of thumb for the evaluation of preferential schemes.

The essentials of the economic theory of preferences, as modified by the concepts of the theory of effective protection, can be presented in some simple exemplary cases.[19] To simplify the analysis, it is assumed that preferences are given at the rate of 100 percent of the existing tariff; this assumption arbitrarily excludes consideration of the important point that not only the magnitude of the gain or loss resulting from preferences, but the question of whether the result will be a gain or loss, will depend on the preference rate given. The problem is further simplified by assuming for the most part that supplies of competing goods from nonpreferred countries are available at constant costs and that these costs represent the alternative social opportunity costs of producing the goods so that changes in these countries' export volumes give rise to no gains or losses for them.

RESULTS OF PREFERENCES FOR STANDARDIZED GOODS. The simplest case to start with is that of a homogenous commodity (say, standard metal screws), the world supply of which is perfectly elastic, and of which the less developed country supplies only a small part of the total import requirements of the developed country that accords it a preference. Initially, the preference-receiving country would be enabled to raise the price it charges from the world market price to the domestic price of the preference-giving country. It would thereby receive a windfall gain equal to the tariff revenue formerly collected on its exports to the preference-giving country; the latter country would lose the same amount of revenue. The initial effect would therefore be equivalent to a transfer of the tariff revenue previously collected from the developed to the less developed country. The higher price received for its exports, however, would encourage the less developed country to increase its production for export, which would replace exports from the rest of the world to the preferential market.[20]

[19] Readers impatient with formal economic reasoning may consider the preceding brief sketch of general principles adequate for their purposes and proceed directly to the next section.

[20] A complication here, and a source of policing problems in actual preferential arrangements, is that the preference-receiving country would have an incentive to export that part of its output it previously consumed itself, replacing it by imports from the rest of the world, and also to import the commodity from the rest of the world for re-export to the preference-giving country. To the extent that they occurred, these changes in trade patterns would increase the transfer to the preference-receiving country; any transport costs involved in them would constitute a waste of world resources and a reduction in the amount of the transfer. This source of waste is emphasized by Jaroslav Vanek, "Discriminatory Liberalization of

This increase in production would depend on the competitive advantage conferred by the preference-giving country's initial tariff rate on the preference-receiving country and on the elasticity of supply in the preference-receiving country, which in the long run would include the effects of new investment stimulated by the preference. Normally the expansion of production would occur at rising costs, which would absorb part (approximately half on the average) of the transfer implicit in the premium price on the additional exports from the preference-receiving country paid by the preference-giving country. The excess of the cost of this increment in supply above the cost at the world market price would represent the economic waste resulting from the discrimination in favor of the preference-receiving source of supply over other world suppliers, if money costs of factors of production in the less developed country corresponded to real social costs. The total loss to the preference-giving developed country would in this case be the excess of the price paid for all imports from the preferred source over the world market price; the net transfer to the preference-receiving country would be this amount less the excess cost of the additional production stimulated by the preference. The less developed country would also gain by any excess of the money costs of the factors of production used to produce the additional output above the real social cost or alternative opportunity cost of these factors (their productivity in the subsistence or import-substitution sectors of the economy), and by any excess of the prices of imported inputs over their world prices due to tariffs imposed on them. These gains—which increase the transfer received by the less developed country—should be deducted from the excess cost of the incremental supplies to arrive at the net waste of world resources. It is conceivable that the result would be a net cost saving and an increase in world efficiency.

The rest of the world, owing to the assumed perfect elastictiy of world supply of the good, would neither gain nor lose from the initiation of the preference, since the resources formerly employed in pro-

Imports of Manufactures from the LDCs by Advanced Countries: A Comment" (unpublished manuscript). Such effects on trade patterns and their consequences could be prevented by origin rules and by countervailing tariffs imposed on imports of the preferred commodity into the preferred producing country. A more likely source of waste, much more difficult to police, would be relocation of production facilities of the rest of the world in the preferred-producer country; of course, this would be a welcome consequence of the preference for the preference-receiving country.

ducing the good would simply be transferred to other lines of production in which they would earn the same incomes. This point is of importance in relation to the assessment of the damage inflicted by preferential trading arrangements on outside (nonpreferred) parties and of
the compensation it may be considered desirable or appropriate to give
them for such damage. It is sometimes assumed that the damage to outside parties is measured by the volume of trade they lose. In the long
run and in strictly economic terms,[21] this is incorrect; the true long-run
damage to outside parties is measured by any reduction in prices or incomes they will have been obliged to incur as a result of having had to
shift exports to other markets, or to shift the resources formerly used to
produce these exports into other lines of production.[22] In the present
case, this loss by assumption is zero; some temporary losses would, of
course, be incurred in effecting the requisite shifts of resources.

In the foregoing case, the effect of the preference is to divert production from other world suppliers to those in the preference-receiving
country, giving them a windfall gain and—on the assumption that
money costs reflect real costs—leading to a waste of resources; this
effect, a pure case of trade diversion, is due to the assumption that the
supply capacity of the preference-receiving country is small in relation
to the import demand of the preference-giving country. If on the contrary it is assumed that the supply capacity of the preference-receiving
country is large relative to the import demand of the preference-giving
country, so that whatever happens the preference-receiving country
must sell at the world market price, the effect of the preference will be
to pre-empt the import market of the preference-giving country for
supplies from the preference-receiving country and lower the price of
the product in that market to the world market price. In this case the

[21] As contrasted with the protectionist philosophy that places value on exports of
industrial goods per se.

[22] The Australian preferential scheme proposed in 1965 contemplated compensating nonrecipients of preferential treatment by paying them the duties that would
have been collected on any loss of their exports to Australia resulting from the
preferences. In terms of the economic theory of preferences this superficially equitable arrangement is clearly nonsensical. At one extreme the exporter might be
able to sell the unwanted goods at the same price in some other market, yet collect
compensation for losses not in fact incurred; at the other extreme the exporter
might be obliged to reduce prices in all markets by the amount required to offset
the effects of the preference on his Australian sales, thereby maintaining Australian
sales and failing to qualify for any compensation despite his loss of revenue from
all markets.

preference-receiving country derives no benefit whatsoever from the preference. Any benefit accrues to the preference-giving country, through two routes: a gain in welfare from expansion of total consumption of the good, and a cost saving through substitution of lower-cost supplies from the preference-receiving country for higher-cost domestic supplies, both of which are trade-creating effects.

There is not necessarily a net cost saving, however, because any substitution of preferred-country output for domestic output that results from negative protection of the latter (consequent on removal of the implicit subsidy rate without removal of the implicit tax rate imposed by the country's tariff structure) involves a substitution of higher-cost for lower-cost supplies and so entails a loss. This loss from what may be termed subsidized trade creation must be deducted from the gain from unsubsidized trade creation (that associated with the reduction of the effective rate of protection to zero); there will be a net gain or loss (approximately) according to whether the effective protection rate exceeds or falls short of the implicit tax rate. The magnitude of this gain or loss depends on the difference between the effective protection rate and the implicit tax rate and on the elasticity of supply in the preference-giving country; in the long run, that elasticity of supply will be determined by the response of investment in productive facilities to the loss of protection.

As in the previous alternative, the outside countries neither gain nor lose, owing to the assumed perfect elasticity of supply and correspondence of money to real costs. (If outside supply were imperfectly elastic, the rest of the world would lose owing to the rise in the price of the product consequent on the elimination of part of the preference-giving country's domestic supply, since the rest of the world is by assumption a net importer of the commodity from the preference-receiving country.)

RESULTS OF PREFERENCES FOR DIFFERENTIATD GOODS. The foregoing example illustrates the alternative trade-creating and trade-diverting effects that preferences may have and also the novel possibility, introduced by the theory of effective protection, that trade creation will result in economic losses to the extent that it is implicitly subsidized. The example involves primarily the response of producers in the countries concerned to price changes consequent on the preference. The same possible alternative effects can occur with respect to consumption. Consider a case in which the preference-giving developed country, an outside developed country, and the preference-receiving less developed country produce variants of an industrial product (say, women's handbags)—products that are close but not perfect substitutes for one another, compete in the market of the preference-giving country, and are produced competitively under constant costs such that their prices in that market are initially equal. In this case, the preference results in the price of the less developed country's handbags being reduced in the preference-giving country's market. This price reduction will have two sets of effects (for simplicity, the argument ignores the possibility of an increase in total consumption of handbags).

First, it will induce substitution of the less developed country's handbags for those of the preference-giving country in the latter's consumption—a trade-creating effect. So far as consumption is concerned, this will involve a gain for the preference-giving country. The magnitude of this gain will depend on the amount of trade created. This will depend on the height of the initial tariff, which will determine the proportional reduction of the price of the less developed country's product, and on the elasticity of substitution between the two countries' products in consumption in the preference-giving country, which will determine the amount of trade created in response to this price reduction. The average gain per unit increase in imports of handbags will be half the initial tariff rate multiplied by the price of a handbag. With respect to production, however, the country will lose—as a result of the reduction of domestic production of handbags—the implicit taxes formerly collected on the handbags no longer produced. This is another example of loss from subsidized trade creation; the loss per handbag no longer produced is measured (approximately) by multiplying the price of the domestic handbag by the implicit rate of taxation of value added and the ratio of value added to price. The loss on the production side will outweigh the gain on the consumption side (approximately) if the proportion of implicit taxes in the price of the domestic product is over half the proportion of tariff proceeds in the landed (tariff-inclusive) price of the imported product.

Second, the preference will induce substitution of the less developed country's product for the outside developed country's product—a trade-diverting effect. The magnitude of this effect will depend, in parallel fashion to that of the trade-creating effect, on the initial height of the tariff and the elasticity of substitution in consumption between the products of the two countries in the consumption of the preference-giving country. Trade diversion will involve a loss to the preference-giving country because (owing to the tariff and the preference) the product of the nonpreferred country will be worth more to consumers in the preference-giving country than it costs the country, whereas the product of the preference-receiving country will not. The average loss per handbag import diverted will be half the tariff rate multiplied by the price (net of tariff) of an imported handbag.

In this case the preference-giving country may either gain or lose, depending on the balance of the effects analyzed;[23] but it makes and the less developed country receives no transfer. The latter gains only to the extent that the opportunity cost of the resources used to produce its export product is less than their money value. As in the previous case, the outside developed country by assumption neither gains nor loses; it would lose to the extent that it had to reduce its prices to sell its export good elsewhere, or shift the resources used in producing it to other lines of production yielding lower incomes.

Both of the examples just discussed assume some pre-existing exports of the less developed country, unchanged conditions of demand and supply, and perfect competition in production, all of which assumptions are unrealistic and abstract from some of the conditions at which the argument for preferences (especially temporary preferences) is directed.

USE OF PREFERENCES TO INITIATE TRADE. It is possible that preferences could be used to initiate trade; for instance, assume that the cost of producing the less-developed-country product is greater than the world market price in the standard screws case, or too much to attract purchases in the handbags case, and that the rate of protection is sufficiently high for the preference to lead to the initiation of exports from the less developed to the preference-giving developed country. The chief analytical differences would be that in the trade-creating version of the standard screws case the transfer would be smaller relative to the associated economic waste, while in the trade-diverting ver-

[23] Its welfare will be unchanged if the trade created through substitution of the preference-receiving country's product for the domestic product is equal to the trade diverted to the preference-receiving country through substitution of its product for the product of the outside developed country and if implicit taxes on domestic production are zero. It should be noted that this simple rule holds only for a 100 percent preference.

sion the gain to the preference-giving country would be smaller and the results would entail inefficiency in production from the world point of view as contrasted with nondiscriminatory free trade (unless the excess money costs of production in the less developed country do not reflect excess real costs). In the handbags case, the amounts of both trade creation and trade diversion, and the associated net gain or loss, would simply be smaller.

To take account of the dynamic aspects of the argument for temporary trade preferences advanced at UNCTAD, the analysis can be developed in terms of either the screws or the handbags case as modified in the preceding paragraph, by assuming that once the opportunity to export is opened by the preference, the cost curve falls and the industry in the less developed country becomes able to compete without preference with suppliers in the developed countries. An alternative modification of the handbags case, corresponding to what some proponents of preferences have in mind concerning consumers' goods, would introduce the assumption that once the less developed country established a foothold in the market, demand would grow as its national style became established, so that eventually the product would be able to sell without the aid of the preference.

PREFERENCES UNDER IMPERFECT COMPETITIVE CONDITIONS. This last modification introduces the question of the effects of preferences under imperfectly competitive conditions as contrasted with the perfectly competitive conditions so far assumed. Such conditions modify the preceding analysis in two important ways. First, the analysis of the production effects of preferences illustrated that a preference might induce either a pure transfer of former tariff revenue from the preference-giving to the preference-receiving country, or an expansion of production in the latter with no resource transfer, or a combination of the two, depending on the elasticity of supply. Correspondingly, the less developed country would benefit either by transfers of additional external resources entailing no resource cost to itself, or by additional exports whose value would depend on there being an excess of the money values of the factors used in producing them over alternative opportunity cost, or by some mixture of the two. The outcome would be determined by supply conditions, and outside its control. Under imperfectly competitive and especially under monopolistic or joint-profit maximizing organization of the less developed suppliers, the benefit would

N

tend to be greater than under perfect competition, as a result of the profit-maximizing efforts of the suppliers to choose the best combination of higher prices and larger sales quantities. (This tendency, however, would be weaker, the more the producers' private costs exceeded the social opportunity costs of the factors of production they employed.)

The second way in which imperfection of competition modifies the analysis is that, in the type of case exemplified by handbags, imperfect competition among national producers would introduce the possibility of producers in the preference-receiving country choosing the optimal strategy for investing the additional revenues permitted by the preference in the expansion of future sales and profits. They might either initially charge low prices to introduce their brand to the market, or charge prices to the consumers in the same range as the developed-country producers' prices, and use the excess revenue to fatten distributive margins or to mount advertising campaigns.

EFFECTIVENESS OF PREFERENCES. As the examination of these various cases indicates, the giving of preferences results in trade-creation and trade-diversion effects which may occur either in production or in consumption. In the presence of imperfectly elastic supplies it also involves transfers from the preference giver to the preference receiver and from outside countries to one or the other. On the consumption side, the magnitudes of the trade-creating and trade-diverting effects depend on the effects of the preference on the relative prices of commodities from the different sources, and therefore on the levels of the existing nominal tariff rates on which the preferences are based. On the production side, however, the magnitudes of these effects depend respectively on how the preference alters the effective rate of protection of producers in the preference-giving against producers in the preference-receiving country, and the margin of preference it establishes for producers in the preference-receiving country over their competitors in nonpreferred countries. These effects depend in a complex way on the input-output structure of industrial production in the various competing countries; and they may be very great, even though nominal tariff rates on commodities appear to be low and the preferences conferred are substantially less than 100 percent.

For this reason it is argued that trade preferences for less developed countries might have very substantial effects in shifting industrial production toward the less developed countries—whether for good or ill depending on the complex of consequences analyzed above. This conclusion is reinforced by recognition that "elasticity of supply" is in the long run a response of new investment decisions to changing competitive opportunities, and that such responses are facilitated by the present international mobility of capital, technology, and managerial skill. In such a world, apparently quite small preferences might be immensely effective in inducing domestic producers in preference-giving developed countries or in their developed competitor countries to shift their operations to preference-receiving less developed countries, because the relevant consideration would be the effective rate of protection of, or margin of preference on, value added by labor. Unfortunately, both knowledge of the determinants of international investment decisions and the data required to calculate the effects of preferences of various kinds on the incentives to alter industrial location are almost completely lacking. This is one of the major reasons why preferential schemes are inevitably discussed in association with devices for quota and other controls on trade volumes.

In conclusion, it should be emphasized that once the complexities of effective protection are taken into account, it is no longer true that trade-creating and trade-diverting effects of preferences can be identified with efficiency-increasing and efficiency-reducing effects. Trade-creating effects may involve the subsidization of imports by comparison with domestic production and hence increase rather than reduce inefficiency. Similarly, trade-diverting effects may increase efficiency by shifting production toward sources of supply whose real costs of production are lower even though their money costs are higher.

Alternative Systems of Preferences

The various possible economic effects of tariff preferences have been illustrated in two simple examples of internationally traded goods designed to take account of relevant aspects of the argument for preferences for less developed countries. What was proposed at UNCTAD, however, was an international system of preferences on manufactures and semimanufactured products to be extended from developed countries to less developed countries, justified by the infant-industry argument and intended to be equitable from the point of view of both developed and less developed countries. The design of such a system is an impossible task, given the inevitable conflicts among the objectives sought, their ambiguity, and the difficulties of using preferences to achieve them. It is no wonder that the conference was unable to arrive at any sort of consensus on the problem.[24]

The proponents of preferences (the less developed and the majority of the developed countries) took the stand—in opposition to the supporters of the traditional GATT approach—that the GATT principle of nondiscrimination would be satisfied by general preferences applying to all less developed countries, without discrimination, in all manufactures and semimanufactures. Thus preferences would have been allowed on products already exported by some less developed countries —including goods such as cotton textiles which had already been disrupting the markets of developed countries—which products could scarcely be described as suitable candidates for infant-industry protection. Consequently the necessity of allowing exceptions had to be recognized; but this raised the problem of how exceptions should be determined. The essential difficulties here were that developed countries differ in their vulnerability to competition from less developed countries and that less developed countries differ in their ability to export. It soon appeared that these difficulties could not be readily resolved by establishing positive lists of industries eligible for preferences or negative lists of industries or products not eligible for preferences.

The next problem was whether the quantities to be imported by the various developed countries under preferential arrangements should be subject to restriction—a question of assuring equity in the distribution of the burden assumed by developed countries—and if so how those maxima were to be determined; again there appeared to be no fully satisfactory solution. A third problem involved recognition of differences in the ability of the less developed countries to take advantage of preferences—implicitly a conflict between nondiscrimination among these countries and equitable distribution of the benefits of preferences among them—and the difficulties of overcoming this by differentiation of preferential rates or allocation of quotas on a country-by-country basis.[25] The solution of the fourth problem, involving

[24] See *Preferences: Review of Discussions*, Report by the Secretary-General of the Conference (United Nations Conference on Trade and Development, TD/B/AC.1/1, 23 March 1965). The description of the contents of this document in the text is intended as a logical chronicle rather than a descriptive chronicle of the UNCTAD discussions.

[25] The discussion apparently did not consider the obvious solution, especially to problems arising from the mismatching of equitable quotas and ability to deliver, of making the quota rights marketable among the less developed countries.

the duration of preferences, depends on whether the maturation of the less developed economy as a whole or of individual infant industries in the economy is the criterion of "development."

A fifth problem was how to define an equal degree of preference by developed countries, given the variations in their tariff rates. Equal percentage preferences would entail the granting of larger trade advantages by the higher tariff countries; equal absolute percentage margins would entail larger sacrifices of protection by the low tariff countries.[26] A related series of difficulties arose from the less developed countries' desire to have preference rates differentiated to favor products in which they might expect to have a comparative advantage. A sixth problem was how to arrange the transition to a general system of preferences in such a way as to avoid economic loss to the British Commonwealth members and the associated overseas territories of the Common Market that already enjoy preferences. A final problem was which developed countries should or would give preferences, and specifically how the communist countries could be meaningfully included in a world preferential system; the general difficulty was that the fewer the preference-giving countries the stronger the likely impact on their economies and hence the smaller the extent of the preferences they would be willing to establish.

These various problems illustrate, but by no means exhaust, the contents of the Pandora's box of new causes of international dissension opened by the proposal to use trade preferences as a tool for promoting economic growth in the less developed countries. The reason for the difficulties is simple, obvious, and insuperable: tariffs are inherently discriminatory between domestic and foreign producers, preferences involve discrimination between categories of foreign producers, and a nondiscriminatory system of discrimination is a contradiction in terms. The only possible means of reconciling all the conflicting interests would be the negotiation by each developed country with each less developed country of the terms of preference (preferential margin, duration of preference, and quantity of imports to which the preference applies) for each commodity. This was the proposal (the "Brasseur plan") supported by the French delegates to UNCTAD; its administrative

[26] The problem of ensuring equity and efficiency in a system of preferences to be given by countries with differing tariff structures is far more difficult than the conference's discussions seem to have appreciated. Vanek, *op. cit.*, shows that either these countries must equalize their tariffs or they must establish quotas for each preference-receiving country in each product.

and diplomatic cumbersomeness and its inherent risks of political and economic dependence of particular less developed on particular developed countries appalled the vast majority of the representatives present.[27]

The difficulties encountered in the discussion of trade preferences in manufactured goods at UNCTAD, however, are in large part a consequence of the attempt to reconcile conflicting objectives while preserving the semblance of adherence to the GATT principles of international trading relationships, and in particular to provide what is essentially additional foreign aid under the guise of expansion of trade opportunities. Thus the initial emphasis on preferences from all developed countries entails the protectionist notion of the GATT philosophy that tariff reduction involves a national sacrifice which ought to be reciprocated, in this context by equal sacrifice by all developed countries for the sake of the less developed countries. Similarly, the emphasis on preferences for all less developed countries represents an effort to create a fictitious compliance with the principle of nondiscrimination, a principle which is supported by no economic rationale and whose sole function is to prevent the undermining of tariff agreements by subsequent bargains between the parties to the agreement and other trading partners. And finally, the emphasis on the infant-industry argument for tariff preferences, which both arouses the deepest suspicions of international trade theorists and if taken seriously tremendously complicates the design of any preference scheme, derives from the exception allowed by the GATT rules for infant-industry protection and the use that has been made of it in defense of the protectionist policies of the less developed countries.

PREFERENCES REGARDED AS AID. If preferences are regarded as a form of aid to less developed countries rather than as a commercial policy, and considered rationally in that light, many of the current difficulties disappear or at least appear far less intractable. In particular, each developed country has in providing aid maintained its autonomy in deciding the amount and form of aid it is prepared to give and had the

---

[27] On the basis of some twenty developed nations and seventy less developed nations, one thousand products would require nearly one and a half million bilateral negotiations. Many of these negotiations, of course, would not be worth while to the individual less developed countries; on the other hand, the number of tariff items on which negotiations might be worth while for one or more pairs of countries is obviously many times one thousand.

freedom to increase that amount and alter its form, even though concepts of equity in the distribution of the aid burden have been developing in recent years and countries have been restrained from increasing their aid commitments for fear of the effects on their balances of payments. Similarly, in the allocation of its aid each developed country has maintained its freedom to concentrate its aid on countries in which it has political interests and to use it to compete for political influence with other developed countries and to reward or punish the recipients for their behavior and performance. In short, aid is bound neither by the principle of reciprocity nor by the principle of nondiscrimination. It should be possible to use the conception of preferences for less developed countries as a form of aid to free the treatment of them within GATT from the shackles of those principles and to allow GATT members so motivated to extend preferences as they wish to the less developed countries they choose to assist, while retaining the GATT machinery for the discussion and rectification of the injuries that such policies may impose on other members.

The rational use of trade preferences as a means of giving foreign aid to less developed countries may be conceived of in terms of two alternative types of rationality, those of the protectionist and of the free trader. The protectionist viewpoint is worth exploring specifically because it has impeded and threatens to completely block progress toward trade liberalization along traditional lines and so may make the trade-preference approach the only means available of helping the less developed countries through trade policy. The free trade viewpoint is a necessary guide to the design of preferential arrangements that will be most efficient, or least inefficient, from the joint perspective of assisting the less developed countries and working toward a more liberal international trading system.

A PROTECTIONIST'S VIEW OF PREFERENCES. The protectionist point of view[22] involves a preference for production to be carried on by residents of the country rather than foreigners. This preference, based on the belief that in some relevant sense foreigners are less deserving or desirable

[22] For a fuller discussion, see Harry G. Johnson, "An Economic Theory of Protectionism, Tariff Bargaining, and the Formation of Customs Unions," *Journal of Political Economy*, Vol. 73 (June 1965), pp. 256-83; for the application of the same framework of analysis to the economic policies of less developed countries, see Johnson, "A Theoretical Model of Economic Nationalism in New and Developing States," *Political Science Quarterly*, Vol. 80 (June 1965), pp. 185-96.

than residents and should be discriminated against, is reflected in a willingness to pay a premium price to have goods produced by residents rather than foreigners, the premium being furnished through tariff protection. In this way of thinking tariff reduction involves a national loss, by leading to the replacement of domestic by foreign production of the previously protected commodity; that loss must be compensated for by an expansion of domestic production for export made possible by tariff reduction by the other countries—the principle of reciprocity.

To a protectionist, a preference involves discriminating less against the residents of the preference-receiving country than against other foreigners and treating them more like residents of his own country. Preferences are therefore justifiable, in general terms, if there is some reason for regarding the countries suggested for preference as more like residents than other foreigners—geographical propinquity, common cultural background, common political interests—or for regarding them as more worthy than other foreigners—amenability to political influence, deservingness of favors on humanitarian grounds. In short, a protectionist regards preferences as a legitimate gesture of friendship. At the same time, a rational protectionist would be more willing to give preferences to a foreign country or group of countries the more likely were they to spend their earnings on the exports of the protectionist country.[29] Thus, from a protectionist point of view, there are strong reasons for confining trade preferences to those less developed countries with which the preference-giving country has particularly close political, cultural and economic ties. Pursuit of this policy by the developed countries would probably lead to a regionalization of world trade into north-south developed–less-developed blocs, Europe taking primary responsibility for Africa, and the United States for Latin America, leaving Asia rather poorly provided for by Commonwealth preferences and whatever the Russian bloc was prepared to do along preferential lines.

In the choice of goods for preferential treatment, rational protectionism would give priority to preferences that diverted trade from other foreign countries over those that created trade at the expense of domestic producers. It would seek to prevent trade creation and to control the amount and allocation of the benefits (from a protectionist viewpoint) of trade diversion to the preferred countries through quo-

[29] This consideration also justifies the tying of foreign aid.

tas. Thus rational protectionism would concentrate the granting of preferences on goods with which, in spite of the tariff, nonpreferred foreign producers were able to compete in its domestic market, and in which the preferred producers competed more closely with nonpreferred foreign producers than with domestic producers.[30] Further, in the interests of maximizing the transfer element involved in the preferences, rational protectionism would give priority to preferences on commodities in which the preference-receiving country was most competitive or nearly competitive with nonpreferred producers.[31] Finally, rational protectionism would avoid giving preferences to industries with infant-industry characteristics; those industries' maturation would threaten an eventual loss of production by domestic residents, unless their products were closely substitutable for nonpreferred foreign products but not for domestically produced products. In general a protectionist use of trade preferences to promote the development of the less developed countries would (rationally) bias such development toward self-sufficiency or toward competitiveness with other developed countries than itself.

A FREE TRADER'S VIEW OF PREFERENCES. From the point of view of a free trader—defined in this connection as one who desires changes in trade policy to lead as far as possible in the direction of a more efficient allocation of world resources in production and consumption —the desirable characteristics of a system of trade preferences are naturally quite different. To begin with, a free trader would not share the protectionist's political reasons for wishing to discriminate among less developed countries nor would he value the likelihood of their purchasing his country's exports. He might, however, wish to discriminate as a means of giving aid through trade on charitable grounds or of achieving greater world efficiency: for example, according to the relative poverty of the candidates for preferences and strength of their claim for resource transfers, according to their effectiveness in using their domestic and foreign resources to promote their own development, or according to the extent to which their protective and exchange-rate policies

[30] This would accentuate the tendency toward regionalization of world trade.

[31] It may also be in the interest of the preference-giving country to give preferences on certain less competitive goods if the partner receiving the preference attaches a great deal of prestige to appearing to be a competitive producer and exporter of those goods. Such a preference would also recommend itself as a means of maximizing the economic dependence of the preference-receiving on the preference-giving country.

corresponded to the requirements of rationality and efficiency.[32] Such discrimination, however, he would probably prefer to have implemented through choice of products rather than through choice of countries, on the grounds that an equal preference for all less developed countries in the same product would ensure that imports from them would be most efficiently allocated among competing sources and best reveal the comparative advantages of each country in the different industries.[33]

With respect to the choice of goods on which preferences should be given, the economic-efficiency criterion suggests that preferences should be concentrated on products offering the greatest prospect of trade creation, through the expansion of consumption and the replacement of domestic production, and the least prospect of diversion of trade from nonpreferred sources (subject to the qualifications explained previously). In general terms, this would imply giving priority to products that the less developed countries have already shown a capacity to export competitively (in contrast to the infant-industry arguments for confining preferences to products they cannot export competitively at present) and especially to products in which they account for a relatively large share of world trade (on the presumption that this would minimize the potential losses from trade diversion).[34] Among such products, priority should be given to those enjoying the heaviest nominal and effective rates of protection. The preferences given on products so selected should be permanent and not temporary,[35] since their effect would be

[32] He would, however, take the position that so far as possible discrimination between countries on these criteria should be effected through the allocation of foreign aid, rather than through trade policy.

[33] Actually, second-best theory indicates that a nondiscrimination rule of this kind cannot be justified on theoretical grounds, once it is recognized that goods in the same tariff classification may be differentiated, so that reduction of the tariff on imports from one source might lead to trade creation and from another source to trade diversion. But it could be argued that there is a broad presumption in its favor, and more important that any possible inefficiencies resulting from its application would be far outweighed by the advantages of the rule in checking protectionism.

[34] A particularly strong case can be made for preferential or free entry for natural products in processed form, including such items as wrought metals, fats and oils, and canned fruits and vegetables, where the processing is most economically performed at or near the point of production of the raw product, since this would result in virtually pure trade creation.

[35] As a compromise with the protectionist position, they might be given subject to withdrawal on the graduation of a beneficiary country into the category of a developed country.

to increase world efficiency and benefit the preference-giving country, and they should be applicable to whatever quantity of exports the less developed countries are capable of providing, rather than subject to global or individual country quotas, so as to maximize the benefits to all parties. This general enjoinder on quotas, however, is conditional on the preferences being granted on a permanent basis, or for a long period. If they are granted for a relatively short period only, quotas might be required to prevent overinvestment in productive facilities in the less developed countries designed to exploit the preference while it lasts. Finally, it should be noted that contemporary customs union theory indicates a presumption that partial preferences are more likely to produce an improvement in the efficiency of resource allocation than would completely free entry of preferred goods;[36] this point, however, might be outweighed by the beneficial effects of the simplification of customs administration procedures for duty-free entry of preferred goods.

The economic-efficiency approach to preferences carries a strong presumption that they should apply to all less developed countries without discrimination. That presumption, however, rests on the usual trade-theory assumption that cost conditions are given, or will be altered appropriately in face of changing conditions by the private investment decisions of entrepreneurs, in an environment of competition. It requires modification if preferences are employed either to establish an infant industry whose costs are expected to fall or to encourage the reorganization of an existing protected inefficient industry to

---

[36] This point can be arrived at as follows. Assume a nonhomogeneous commodity produced at constant costs in the preference-giving, the preference-receiving, and the nonpreferred country, producers in the latter two countries initially being subject to the same tariff rate. The welfare and efficiency effects of preferential tariff reduction can be analyzed in terms of its effects on the tariff revenue collected. An initial small preferential tariff reduction would entail very little loss of tariff revenue on any trade it diverted from the nonpreferred to the preference-receiving country, the difference in tariff rates being slight, whereas it would entail a large gain of tariff revenue on any trade it created. As the tariff on imports from the preference-receiving country is successively reduced, however, the loss of tariff revenue per unit of trade diverted rises toward the initial tariff collected per unit and the gain of tariff revenue per unit of trade created falls toward zero; if each successive increase in preference both diverts and creates trade there will be some preferential tariff rate between the initial tariff rate and zero below which the loss from trade diversion will exceed the gain from trade creation. If, for example, the preference created and diverted equal amounts of trade, the optimal preferential tariff rate would be 50 percent of the initial tariff rate.

take advantage of the scale economies that a large market would permit. Both the infant-industry and scale-economy rationales for preferences assume deficiencies in the system of private competitive entrepreneurship that will succumb to the bribery of higher profit opportunities. To give entrepreneurs the assurance that these profits will in fact be earned if they go to the effort of finding the necessary capital and organizing or reorganizing industry in the appropriate way, it might well be necessary to ensure them of a monopoly of the profit opportunity created by the preference. This could be accomplished by restricting preferential entry in the products concerned to producers in one or at most a few less developed countries, rather than generalizing it to all less developed countries. This technique of assigning preferences in particular industries to particular countries could be especially effective, and indeed, would probably be necessary, if the total amount of imports eligible for preference were narrowly restricted by the protectionist interests of the preference-giving country. The assignment of minuscule quotas to a large number of less developed countries could obviously do nothing to encourage industrial organization for large-scale and low-cost production. The technique could, however, also be used to avoid creating the opposite type of problem, that generous preferences for a particular industry might encourage indiscriminate investment in productive facilities by a number of less developed countries on a larger scale than the world market could digest. In either case the principle of nondiscrimination among less developed countries would have to be implemented by attempting to arrive at an equitable division of the preferred industries among the less developed countries.[87]

Concluding Observations on Preferences

The proposal for developed countries to extend preferences on imports of manufactures and semimanufactures to the less developed countries as a means of promoting the economic growth of the latter raises a host of difficult problems. Nevertheless, it has been argued that, contrary to superficial appearances, preferences might be an extremely powerful tool for stimulating industrial development in the less developed countries, the reasons being largely inherent in the recently developed theory of effective protection. Given the emphasis placed by the less developed countries on their need for such preferences and the possibility that the

_____
[87] I am indebted to John Pincus for this point.

formation and policies of the European Common Market will block further progress after the Kennedy Round toward trade liberalization along traditional GATT lines, the possibilities of using trade preferences to promote development deserve serious consideration.

Unfortunately, it is not possible to estimate how much could be done by this means for the less developed countries, by the United States acting unilaterally or in concert with other developed countries, let alone to produce comparative estimates of the probable effects of alternative systems of trade preferences on the volume and gains from trade of the less developed countries.[38] The conceptual framework required to tackle these empirical questions in the scientifically proper fashion has only recently been developed and its empirical application requires extensive collation and manipulation of data on tariff rates and on the industrial input-output structure that are notoriously difficult to mesh together. In addition, much of the argument for preferences as presented at UNCTAD hinges on whether and to what extent preferential market access would permit less developed countries to reap economies of scale in production or to lower costs through the accumulation of experience; this is a question on which, despite the hoary history of the infant-industry argument, international trade specialists have developed neither the theoretical conceptualization nor the empirical evidence that is required to pass an empirical judgment.

If preferences for less developed countries are to be seriously consid-

[38] Exploration of these problems would require empirical investigation not only of the effective preference margins the developed countries would give, but of the costs of production in the less developed countries, which would determine their ability to take advantage of preferences. One indication of the potentialities of preferences would be the total customs revenue now collected by developed countries on their imports from less developed countries, which revenue might be transferred back to the less developed countries via preferences. The total customs revenue collected on imports of manufactured goods from less developed countries into the United States, United Kingdom, European Economic Community and Sweden in 1962 has been estimated at $306 million, made up as follows: United States $140 million, United Kingdom $89 million, European Economic Community $71 million, Sweden $6 million. The estimate, by V.N. Balasubramanyam, applies Bela Balassa's average tariff rates on industrial products to trade data obtained from the *Foreign Trade Analytical Abstracts* of the Organization for Economic Cooperation and Development. To allow for Commonwealth preference for members and EEC preferential treatment of associated overseas territories, sterling area imports are excluded from the figures for the United Kingdom and imports from Africa from the figures for the EEC; if these imports were not excluded, the estimated total duty collected would be $390 million. Unfortunately, the data required to make the same calculation for Japan are not available.

ered, a great deal of theoretical and empirical research needs to be done on the infant-industry and scale-economy arguments. More generally, it is necessary to determine what factors account for the inability of less developed countries, and specifically of the "developing" countries that already produce manufactures for the home market, to export in competition with the developed countries in spite of their comparative advantages in availability of materials and low-wage labor, and how significant these factors are empirically. Chapter II suggested that a major part of the explanation is to be found in the import-substitution and currency-overvaluation policies typically pursued by the governments of less developed countries, and that the cost disadvantages resulting from these policies may frequently be far greater than the competitive advantage that could be conferred by preferences from the developed countries.[39] If this suggestion is confirmed by further empirical research, it would imply that neither preferences nor nondiscriminatory tariff reduction would help the less developed countries unless they were prepared to make major changes in their tariff and exchange-rate policies. Thus, the developed countries could legitimately insist on such policy changes in the less developed countries as a condition for trade concessions.

PREFERENTIAL ARRANGEMENTS AMONG LESS DEVELOPED COUNTRIES

The proposal at UNCTAD for preferential arrangements for trade in manufactured goods among less developed countries was based on the same sort of argument as the case for preferences in developed-country markets: the need for a market larger than the protection of the national market could provide, in order to foster the development of infant industries and to permit the exploitation of economies of scale, and the inability of producers in the less developed countries to export in competition with producers in the developed countries. Such preferences would be negotiated among the countries of a region, or of a like-minded group, for the manufactured products they agreed upon, and would stop considerably short of a free trade area. Hence they would be in violation of the principles of GATT. However, there was

---

[39] There is some general evidence suggesting that the tax policies of less developed countries may impose especially heavy tax burdens on industries producing potentially exportable manufactures.

little discussion of the proposal at UNCTAD and the reaction of the developed countries to it appears to have been generally sympathetic, presumably because their trade in manufactures with the less developed countries is both relatively unimportant and limited, at least on a superficial view, by those countries' receipts of foreign exchange rather than by their tariffs.

The GATT principle of nondiscrimination and ban on new preferences except for customs unions and free trade areas are not consistent with either the political principle of treating all foreign countries equally or the economic principle of maximizing real income through promoting the most efficient attainable allocation of productive resources in the world economy. There is therefore no compelling reason for opposing the proposal for preferences among a group of less developed countries on grounds of its inconsistency with GATT principles. The facts that these preferences would involve only less developed countries and that prevailing political sentiment favors giving such countries the maximum possible latitude within the GATT system, however, do not provide valid grounds for giving a blanket endorsement to such preferences. There is, in fact, good reason for not endorsing them without investigating their economic aspects in the same way as preferences from developed to less developed countries.

This analytical task can be considerably simplified by assuming, as seems reasonable, that preference-induced changes in the demand of the less developed countries for the manufactured goods to which preferences would apply would be small in relation to total world production and consumption; thus the developed-country producers could shift the goods to other markets, or the resources used in producing them to other activities, without appreciable change in their prices or the incomes of their producers. In other words, it is reasonable to assume that any potential or actual trade diversion resulting from group preferences would inflict no significant damage on the developed-country suppliers, and correspondingly would yield the less developed countries no benefits in the form of improved terms of trade with the developed countries. The analysis then need consider only the effects on the participating countries; the concern of the developed countries in such arrangements can be considered to be confined to their potential effects on development.

From one point of view, of course, it could be argued that if one is prepared to assume that preferential arrangements among less developed countries would impose no economic cost on the developed countries, the latter have no legitimate concern with the terms of the arrangements. The principle of freedom of contract should rule and should by itself guarantee that any resulting preferential arrangements will be beneficial to all participants. This argument, however, assumes that the governments of less developed countries fully understand their own interests and how these will be affected by preferential arrangements; moreover, it ignores the fact that as providers of foreign assistance for economic development, the developed countries have a legitimate concern for the efficiency with which development is planned and promoted in the less developed countries.

Preferences to Expand the Industrial Base

In analyzing the effects of preferential arrangements among less developed countries, it is necessary at the outset to distinguish two alternative standards of economic welfare that might be applied. In the policies of many less developed countries, economic development appears to be identified with expansion of the industrial structure, regardless of whether the cost of production of industrial products is above the price of such products in the world market. If these policies are regarded as representing rational social choice, it must be assumed that the social value of having additional industrial facilities as a symbol of development achievement is worth the loss of material consumption imposed by the higher costs of domestic production as compared with importing.[40] On this basis, anything that lowers the cost of establishing additional facilities for industrial production in the less developed countries increases their welfare and contributes to their development. Preferences in manufactured goods among a group of less developed countries would permit such a reduction in the cost of establishing additional industrial production by the group by enabling the group to produce each industrial good in the member country possessing a comparative advantage in supplying it (instead of each country producing its own requirements) and to enjoy whatever economies of scale and infant-industry maturation the larger size of the pooled markets would allow.

Allowing less developed countries to negotiate whatever such arrangements they considered desirable would therefore contribute to their economic welfare and promote their economic development, in

---

[40] On this approach, see the works cited in note 28.

the special sense that identifies development with industrialization. The only problem that would arise on this approach would derive from the fact that, since the granting of a preference to another less developed country entails a sacrifice of actual or potential domestic industrial production by the preference-granting country, which must be compensated by receipt of a reciprocal preference on industrial production in which it has a comparative advantage within the group, the possibilities of improvement depend on the extent to which the preferences can expand the markets for lines of industrial production in which the various countries have comparative advantages within the preferential group. The distribution of comparative advantages in industrial production among the countries of the group might be such that some countries had few or no industrial products they could produce at lower prices than the others, or that cost differences among the countries were so negligible that preferences could not be negotiated to mutual advantage.[41]

Preferences to Establish an Efficient Economic System

The foregoing analysis assumes both that the governments of the less developed countries understand the interests of their peoples and how best to serve them, and that the objectives they define for themselves should be accepted unquestioningly by the developed countries. The alternative analytical approach—which appears more realistic and relevant for the developed countries to adopt in determining their attitude to preferential arrangements among less developed countries—is to assume that, regardless of how governments in less developed countries may visualize their objectives, the true interests of their peoples lie in

---

[41] The problems and possibilities of preferential arrangements among less developed countries, envisaged from this analytical point of view, are dealt with in detail by C. A. Cooper and B. F. Massell, "Toward a General Theory of Customs Unions for Developing Countries," *Journal of Political Economy*, Vol. 73 (October 1965), pp. 461-76.

In any grouping of countries, it might be possible for the more powerful to exert pressure on the weaker to participate in preferential arrangements that imposed a welfare loss on the weaker countries by obliging them to provide a market for the high-cost products of the more powerful countries even though their industrial products were unable to compete with industrial production in the rest of the region, or to compete on a scale sufficient to be compensatory. For this reason, even if the developed countries accepted the definitions of economic welfare and development employed in the foregoing analysis, they would have some obligation to exercise surveillance over less developed countries' preferential trading arrangements to protect the weaker from the rapacity of the stronger.

o

achieving the most efficient possible economic system, and to evaluate proposed preferential arrangements in that light. This involves applying the economic analysis of preferences for exports of manufactured goods, with the two differences that effects on outside countries can be ignored and that the effects of the preferences on the joint economic welfare of the preference-giving and preference-receiving countries must be considered.

In terms of the static-efficiency considerations of that analysis, preferential trading arrangements among less developed countries will improve their economic efficiency, and hence contribute to the economic development of the group, to the extent that they create trade by leading to substitution of lower-cost for higher-cost production within the group. Conversely, preferential arrangements will worsen efficiency and retard economic development to the extent that they divert trade from outside sources to higher-cost sources within the group. In terms of the dynamic arguments for preferential arrangements based on scale-economy or infant-industry considerations, preferences will contribute to welfare and development only if, in fact, costs are reduced as the arguments claim they will be, and the cost reduction yields an adequate social return on the investment implicit in the use of preferences.

These propositions imply that the developed countries should favor and seek to promote preferential arrangements among less developed countries for trade in the products of industries already established within the group, particularly products in which the group is close to self-sufficient, since they offer the maximum opportunity of gain from trade creation and the minimum risk of loss from trade diversion. By contrast, the developed countries should regard with extreme skepticism preferential schemes to establish new industries based on scale-economy and infant-industry arguments; the establishment of such industries necessarily involves trade diversion which can be economically justified only by a strong probability that costs will in fact fall sufficiently to make the industry economic.[42] Such a policy stance would, however, be sure to arouse dissension between the developed and the less developed countries, since the governments of the latter

---

[42] Given the distortions of costs in less developed countries introduced by import substitution and currency overvaluation, it is quite possible that the establishment of some such industries would be justified even if costs could not be reduced to the world level. The complications of optimal investment decision in an environment of distorted factor and commodity prices would have to be tackled in any evaluation of such proposals.

generally seek tenaciously to maintain any industrial activity they have been successful in establishing, regardless of its excess cost, and view preferential arrangements as a way of establishing still more industry without sacrificing what they already have.

The protectionist policies of the less developed countries are frequently an important factor in fostering inefficiency in their economies and inhibiting their economic development. The developed countries could probably help to ameliorate this problem by attempting, in connection with any decision to modify the GATT rules to allow preferential arrangements for less developed countries, to establish some sort of internationally agreed maximum rate of protection[48] that could possibly be justified by the familiar arguments for protection in less developed countries, and to insist that it not be exceeded in any new preferential arrangements. In the longer run, the same objective of curbing the excesses of protectionism in less developed countries might be served by the negotiation and implementation of such new preferential arrangements, since this would oblige the participating less developed countries to take a critical interest in each others' protective policies.

[48] Ideally, the effective and not the nominal rate.

VII

International Monetary
Reform

Some of the important impediments in contemporary aid and trade policies to the development of the less developed countries stem from the concern of the developed countries with actual or potential balance-of-payments problems and therefore from the functioning of the present international monetary system. Because the connection between the functioning of the international monetary system and the process of development of the less developed countries is remote, it is rarely appreciated by those directly concerned with development problems. On the other hand, the notion that the creation of money entails someone getting something for nothing is only too readily grasped; consequently the growing recognition of the need for reform of the present international monetary system has evoked a host of proposals designed to capture the "something for nothing" as additional development assistance for the less developed countries. Thus it is desirable to consider those aspects of the problem of international monetary reform that are relevant to the problems of the less developed countries. To this end, this chapter[1] discusses the general interest of the less developed countries in a properly functioning international monetary system, describes the nature of the present problem of international monetary reform, and analyzes various proposals designed to link international monetary reform with the provision of increased development assistance to the less developed countries. It concludes with a critical evaluation of the most far-reaching proposal, that of Hart, Kaldor, and Tinbergen for an international commodity-reserve currency;

[1] This chapter is a revised version of Harry G. Johnson, "International Monetary Reform and the Less Developed Countries," *The Malayan Economic Review*, Vol. 11 (April 1966), pp. 1-20

the amount of space devoted to their scheme is accounted for by the professional eminence of its proponents and the publicity the plan has attracted, and not by any likelihood of its being adopted.

A PROPERLY FUNCTIONING INTERNATIONAL MONETARY SYSTEM

A properly functioning international monetary system may be described as one that provides a combination of international liquidity and adjustment mechanisms adequate to permit rectification of balance-of-payments disequilibria without imposing severely deflationary policies on the deficit countries or obliging them to resort to balance-of-payments restrictions on current and capital account transactions. Over the long run it provides a rate of increase of international liquidity adequate to support a steady growth of world production, trade and payments at levels as close to "full employment" of world resources as possible. Such an international monetary system would contribute substantially to the promotion of the economic development of the less developed countries, and particularly to their growth through trade, in two major ways: first, by modifying or removing the need for various policies designed to protect the balance of payments of the developed countries that currently impede the development of the less developed countries, and secondly by establishing an international monetary framework within which the natural processes of diffusion of economic development throughout the world economy could operate with maximum force.

Many of the trade and aid policies of the developed countries that impede the efficient development of the less developed countries are directly or indirectly the result of their concern with actual or potential balance-of-payments deficits, a concern aggravated by the deficiencies of the present international monetary system. The outstanding example is the tying of aid to expenditure in the donor country and the various inefficiencies it produces: in the case of the United States, the progressively restrictive tying of aid in the past several years has been the direct consequence of the Administration's concern to remedy the country's chronic deficit; in other donor countries, the protectionist motive for aid tying is probably predominant though the balance-of-payments motive was strong in the European countries during the period of dollar shortage and probably continues to be influential, especially in the United Kingdom and France. Balance-of-payments considerations also undoubtedly reinforce the unwillingness of all the developed countries to expand the scale of their aid to the less developed countries, so that the defects of the present international monetary system may be held partially responsible for the problem of the "external resources gap" with which UNCTAD was concerned.

Under the present rules governing international economic relations, embodied in the General Agreement on Tariffs and Trade and the Charter of the International Monetary Fund, protection is to be implemented solely by tariffs; quantitative import restrictions are sanctioned, however, in cases of balance-of-payments deficits.[2] While GATT principles call for such restrictions to be applied in as nondiscriminatory a fashion as possible and to be removed as soon as the need for them has passed—and GATT has striven with considerable success for the implementation of these principles and particularly for the elimination of European quantitative restrictions established during the period of dollar shortage—there is a strong tendency for such restrictions to be influenced by protectionist considerations and to be perpetuated for the same reason. Such quantitative restrictions are likely to be especially disadvantageous to the less developed countries for several reasons. First, insofar as protectionist considerations influence their design, the restrictions are likely to be directed against imports in which less developed countries have an actual or potential comparative advantage.[3] Second, such restrictions usually base import quotas on past trade and thus discriminate against new and rapidly expanding sources of supply. Third, the disruption of trade and the uncertainty associated with the imposition of quantitative restrictions are likely to bear especially heavily on less developed countries owing to their lower degree of di-

[2] In fact, as evidenced by the vociferous protests against the use of temporary tariff surcharges by Canada in 1962 and Britain in 1964, the paradoxical principle has been established that only tariffs are to be used for permanent restriction of imports and only quantitative restrictions for temporary restriction of imports. There is no obvious reason for believing this to be the most efficient deployment of the two instruments for achieving those policy objectives; for example, temporary tariff surcharges have the advantage over quotas of being more quickly applicable and of automatically tending to exercise deflationary pressure on the domestic economy through the additional tax revenue collected.

[3] As mentioned in Chapter III, it is very difficult to obtain concrete information on the discriminatory effects of quantitative restrictions, especially as between developed and less developed countries.

versification both in variety of products and range of alternative markets for particular products.

Balance-of-payments difficulties have increasingly generated a third type of governmental intervention in international transactions, control over private international capital movements. The United States has deliberately excepted capital movements to less developed countries; the European countries probably follow similar discriminatory practices in their capital market policies, at least with respect to investment in their former colonies. Therefore the net effects of intervention in private international capital flows may actually be to further rather than to impede the development of the less developed countries through private foreign investment. As a general proposition, however, it seems likely that the less developed countries as a group stand to lose rather than gain from the trend toward reliance on capital market interventions, for any fragmentation of the world economy by the erection of new barriers to international competition is likely to be detrimental to them.

These considerations suggest that the less developed countries would benefit substantially from the establishment of an international monetary system that provided a more adequate combination of liquidity and adjustment mechanisms. The most important contributions of such a system would be to remove the inhibitions to expansion of aid generated by fear of consequent balance-of-payments difficulties and to facilitate the untying of aid, thus increasing its efficiency. In addition, less developed countries would benefit significantly from the removal of restrictions dictated by balance-of-payments difficulties, whose effect is frequently to protect production in the developed countries and to aggravate uncertainty in international trade.

The less developed countries have, however, a far more important interest in the establishment of an international monetary system that would promote the growth of world production and trade at high levels of employment and activity by providing an adequate secular expansion of international liquidity. As explained in Chapter II, a competitive international economic system contains various automatic mechanisms that tend to diffuse development from the primary centers of growth to the less developed periphery. These mechanisms—which encourage transfer of the production of commodities requiring scarce natural resources and of products characterized by high labor-intensity and low technological sophistication from the center to the periphery—operate with most efficiency, and least resistance from the center countries, in an environment of high employment and steady growth of productivity in the developed countries.

The transmission process is stimulated by the pressure of demand in the developed countries and the availability of actual or potential lower-cost supplies in the less developed countries, based on natural resources or the abundance of low-wage labor. Political resistance to the transmission process—expressed in protectionist policies for domestic activities threatened by competition from the less developed countries—is stimulated by aversion to loss of income and the costs and uncertainties of converting resources to higher-income activities. Maintenance of high levels of employment and activity in the developed countries provides the maximum incentive to develop additional sources of supply in the less developed countries to relieve the pressure of scarcity in the developed countries; furthermore, it provides both incentive and opportunity to shift adversely affected resources in the developed country into more lucrative alternative uses rather than to demand protection against competition from the less developed countries. Conversely, an environment of generally slack demand reduces the incentive to develop new foreign sources of supply, reduces the ability of resources to move out of industries encountering difficulty in competing with foreign producers, and increases both the political pressure for and the political justifiability of protecting such industries.[4]

The less developed countries will obviously benefit from an efficient and rapid process of transmission of economic development. They therefore have a strong interest in the establishment of an international monetary system conducive to the maintenance of full employment in the developed countries and the resolution of international disequilibria by expansion in the surplus countries rather than contraction in the deficit countries. Specifically, they have a particular interest in

[4] In a full employment environment, resources tend automatically to move out of inefficient low-income industries, and the wasteful effects of protectionism become apparent to and are given political expression by the efficient high-income industries whose expansion is hampered by the general scarcity of resources; thus the demand for protection tends to be weakened both economically and politically. In an underemployed economy, by contrast, resources tend to stay in the inefficient low-income industries, providing economic justification for demands for protection, while the availability of resources gives the efficient high-income industries no reason to oppose those demands.

the establishment of a system that will expand international liquidity at a rate great enough to impart an inflationary bias to world economic development. This is so because (it is generally agreed) some moderate upward trend of prices in a developed country induced by demand pressure facilitates the reallocation of resources and the mobility of labor and because the promotion of planned economic development in the less developed countries tends to generate inflationary price movements which tend to cancel out their ability to export unless offset by price increases in the developed countries to which they export.

THE PROBLEM OF INTERNATIONAL MONETARY REFORM

The International Monetary Fund was intended by the planners of postwar reconstruction of the international economy to provide a monetary framework for a liberal international trade and payments system that would be free of the defects of the gold-exchange standard of the interwar period that eventually precipitated the collapse of the international monetary system in the 1930's. Specifically, the Fund was intended to supplement the world's inadequate supplies of monetary gold with international liquidity in the form of drawing rights on the Fund proportioned to the various countries' importance in international commerce; to provide an effective mechanism of international adjustment through internationally agreed and accepted changes in the exchange rates of countries suffering from "fundamental disequilibrium" in their balances of payments; and to distribute the burden of adjustment more fairly between surplus and deficit countries by means of the "scarce currency" clause, sanctioning discrimination by deficit countries against countries in chronic balance-of-payments surplus.

The International Monetary Fund has been thrust from its intended position, however, by the growing use of the U.S. dollar as an international monetary reserve supplementary to gold and by the development of a dollar-exchange standard similar to the sterling-exchange standard that worked successfully up to World War I only to collapse so disastrously in the interwar period. This development has been an unintended but natural consequence of the dominance of the United States in the world economy since World War II and particularly of its role in the prolonged period of dollar shortage as chief world trader and source of external capital for reconstruction and development.

With the emergence of the dollar-exchange standard and the establishment of the United States as the central reserve-currency country of the international monetary system, the international liquidity provided through the International Monetary Fund has been relegated to a role secondary to ad hoc arrangements between the United States and the major European countries important in international finance. For a variety of reasons the other leading countries have become increasingly reluctant to contemplate altering their exchange rates, while the reserve-currency role of the dollar is assumed to preclude alteration of its exchange value. Thus in practice the significant exchange rates have become rigid and alterations of them have been ruled out as a method of settling balance-of-payments problems. The Fund's scarce-currency clause has become a dead letter, while the appropriate division of the burden of adjustment between debtor and creditor countries has become the subject of increasingly acrimonious dispute among the countries concerned.

Like the sterling standard before it, the dollar standard has made an important contribution to the growth of the world economy by providing a reasonably stable monetary environment for conducting international trade and payments on an increasingly liberal basis. With the successful reconstruction of Europe, culminating in the establishment of the Common Market, and the emergence of the United States after 1957 as a country in serious chronic balance-of-payments deficit, however, the dollar-exchange standard has been increasingly subject to internal strains. Both academic observers and officials concerned with the operation of the system, fearing that the dollar-exchange standard may collapse as did its predecessor gold-exchange standard, and believing that the system is in need of fundamental reform, have advanced proposals for basic changes in international monetary organization.

International monetary experts agree that the present dollar-exchange standard suffers from three major problems: the confidence problem, the liquidity problem, and the adjustment problem.[5] The confidence problem derives from the fact that the use of the dollar as an international reserve is currently conditional on its convertibility

[5] See especially Fritz Machlup and Burton G. Malkiel (eds.), *International Monetary Arrangements: The Problem of Choice; Report on the Deliberations of an International Study Group of 32 Economists* (Princeton University Press, 1964).

into gold by central bank holders, and the likelihood that any large-scale attempt to convert dollars into gold would, by threatening the exhaustion of U.S. gold reserves, precipitate a collapse of confidence in the dollar that would wipe out international liquidity and completely disrupt international trade and payments. The fact that the power to precipitate such a collapse lies in the central banks of countries other than the United States (and the United Kingdom, which plays a similar role as a secondary reserve-currency center) has made the continued operation of the system dangerously dependent on voluntary cooperation among national central banks and (especially in the past few years) vulnerable to tactics designed to put pressure on the United States to follow balance-of-payments policies desired by the European surplus countries.

The liquidity problem is the problem of providing for the stable long-run growth of international reserves required to support the steady expansion of international trade and payments associated with the normal growth of the world economy. This problem has two aspects. First, if the required rate of growth of international reserves exceeds the rate of growth of monetary gold stocks provided by the mining of new gold and the difference is made up by a more rapid expansion of outstanding holdings of the reserve currency, either the reserve-currency country suffers a progressive reduction of the ratio of its gold reserves to the claims on those reserves held by other countries (in the form of reserve holdings of its currency) or the other countries must progressively increase the ratio of their reserve-currency holdings to their gold reserves, or both. The former alternative involves a progressive weakening of the international liquidity of the reserve-currency country and increasing danger of loss of confidence in the reserve currency; the latter involves a progressive sacrifice of the monetary autonomy of the nonreserve-currency countries and acceptance of international monetary management by the reserve-currency country. Second, within limits set by the ability of the nonreserve-currency countries to discipline the reserve-currency country by using their option to convert its currency into gold without precipitating a crisis of confidence, the rate of growth of international liquidity is governed by the balance-of-payments deficits of the reserve-currency country and (depending on that country's policies) may be too large or too small for stability and may fluctuate in a destabilizing fashion. This problem is especially acute when, as has been the case for the past eight years, the reserve-currency country runs an abnormally large deficit; the international monetary implications of an unduly small deficit or a surplus could be counteracted by purchases of nonreserve-currency assets by the central bank or treasury of the reserve-currency country.

The third problem of the present international monetary system, the adjustment problem, is one of correcting, by automatic processes or policy measures, the economic forces that give rise to international monetary disequilibrium. This problem is essentially the converse of the confidence and liquidity problems, since the more promptly adjustment can be effected, the less the danger of loss of confidence in the deficit country's currency and the less the need for liquidity to finance transitional deficits (and the less the need for growth of liquidity to finance prospectively larger future deficits). Fundamentally, adjustment entails the alignment of a country's prices and costs with those of other countries so as to make its products competitive enough both internationally and domestically to enable it to finance its capital exports by a current-account surplus or to finance its current-account deficit by normal capital imports.[6]

The present rigidity of exchange rates, associated with the emergence of the dollar as central-reserve currency, rules out the resort to exchange-rate changes in cases of fundamental disequilibrium envisaged in the design of the International Monetary Fund. The effective alternatives are, first, the classical gold-standard mechanism of inflation in the surplus country and deflation in the deficit country and, second, the use of interventions in international trade and payments to conceal the need for adjustment pending solution by automatic forces coming into play with the passage of time coupled with domestic measures to increase international competitiveness. The use of the gold-standard mechanism, however, is severely limited by the adoption in the major countries of the policy objectives of full employment and price stability, which leads deficit countries to resist deflation and surplus countries to resist inflation. The result is sharp controversy between the two parties to international disequilibrium over the equitable distribution of the burden of adjustment. The controversy has been exacerbated in re-

[6] Much analytical confusion has been engendered by the practice in international financial and policy-making circles of regarding both special intergovernmental capital transactions and interferences with private capital movements motivated by the existence of international monetary disequilibrium as measures of balance-of-payments "adjustment." Such measures are not "adjustments," but stop-gaps for "financing" imbalances pending their elimination by other means.

cent years by the fact that the surplus European countries have had
strong historical reasons for disliking inflation, while the deficit United
States has had equally strong reasons for disliking abnormally high unemployment. Both attitudes derive from interwar experience and their
effect has been to make each party unsympathetic to the policy restraints encumbering the other. In effect, adjustment under the present
international monetary system depends on the inability of the policy-
makers in the surplus country to resist inflationary pressure and of the
policy-makers in the deficit country to maintain employment at the desired level. This mechanism of reluctant adjustment is bound to take
considerable time and to generate continual mutual recrimination,
while the size of the payments imbalances inevitably exerts pressure for
the increasing use of interventions in international trade and payments
to reduce the magnitudes of deficits and surpluses and especially for
the use of restraints and controls on private capital movements.

The plans put forward to cope with these problems fall into two
broad categories: proposals to substitute for the present system an automatic self-regulatory system, either by returning to the classical gold
standard or by adopting a regime of floating exchange rates, and proposals for reforming the existing system to improve its functioning.
The former type of proposal has not received serious consideration and
is unlikely to, even though early in 1965 President de Gaulle of France
denounced the financial power that the present system gives to the reserve-currency countries and called for a return to the gold standard.
Among the latter group of proposals, the two alternatives under active
discussion are concerned with the reform of the provision of international liquidity, and hence with the liquidity and confidence problems;
they are concerned with adjustment only indirectly insofar as the crux
of the debate between their proponents is the distribution of the responsibility for and burden of adjustment between deficit and surplus
countries.

The two alternatives in question, favored respectively by the United
States and the United Kingdom and by the Common Market countries
(especially, although sporadically, by France), are to increase the powers of the International Monetary Fund to provide international liquidity, and to create a new type of international reserve asset outside
the Fund, as now constituted, in the form of a "composite reserve
unit" made up of the currencies of the major countries in fixed ratios,
which these countries would be obliged to hold in a more or less fixed

ratio to their gold reserves.[1] Both would diminish the reserve-currency roles of the dollar and the pound and "internationalize" the use of credit money as a substitute for gold, the former indirectly by providing an explicitly international form of credit in substitution for or supplementation of dollars and sterling, the latter directly by sharing the role of international reserve currency between these currencies and the other major national currencies. The significant difference between the two proposals, which reflects the divergent interests of their proponents, is that the former would entail an extension of international control of the international monetary system through the International Monetary Fund, which as presently constituted is dominated by the United States and in which the less developed countries have representation, whereas the latter would increase the dependence of the system on collaboration and agreement among the leading nations of the international economy, which would have to agree on the amount and rate of increase of the stock of composite reserve units and the ratio to gold in which they would be held. In particular, the need for agreement would enable the Common Market countries to insist on sufficient limitation of the stock of composite reserve units to force the deficit country (i.e., the United States) to assume the major part of the burden of adjustment by following deflationary domestic policies. (In European thinking, in fact, the composite-reserve-unit plan is a way of

[1] Under the former scheme, the confidence problem would be mitigated because the growth of reserves in the form of IMF liabilities rather than dollar and sterling balances would avoid the progressive weakening of the liquidity positions of the reserve-currency countries; the long-run liquidity problem would be solved by regular increases in the Fund's liabilities. (Under the more sweeping version of this alternative advocated by some academic experts—to convert the IMF into a world central bank—the confidence problem would be eliminated by converting existing holdings of reserve currencies into liabilities of the International Monetary Fund and gradually liquidating the corresponding dollar and sterling assets; the long-run liquidity problem would be taken care of by appropriate secular expansion of aggregate Fund liabilities through open market operations.) Under the latter scheme the confidence problem would be eliminated by fixing the ratios to gold holdings of the various national currencies held as reserves, and the long-run liquidity problem would be dealt with by periodic increases in the amount of composite reserve units and in the ratio of these to gold reserves required.

Both proposals, by removing the confidence problem, would facilitate adjustment in imbalances of payments by means of exchange-rate changes, especially by changes in the values of the present reserve currencies, the dollar and the pound. Such changes would merely require compensatory transfers of the currency whose value was changed to or from the International Monetary Fund or the holders of composite reserve units.

raising the price of gold among the advanced countries—by tying the purchase of gold to a parallel purchase of composite reserve units—and restoring the discipline of the gold standard.)

The choice between these two alternatives is therefore effectively a choice between an international monetary system that places major responsibility for adjustment on the surplus country, and one which places major responsibility for adjustment on the deficit country—essentially, a choice between a more expansive and a less expansive international monetary system than the present one. The choice evidently will be determined by negotiations among the developed countries, negotiations in which the less developed countries will have little or no participation and over whose outcome they can exercise little influence. Nevertheless, because a decision to reform the international monetary system along the more expansive line could substantially improve the prospects of economic growth of the less developed countries —and especially their prospects of development through trade—it is a relevant consideration for the developed countries engaged in the negotiation of international monetary reform.

REFORMS OF DIRECT BENEFIT TO LESS DEVELOPED COUNTRIES

The fact that both the need for reform of the international monetary system and the need of the less developed countries for increased external resources for development have simultaneously become increasingly apparent in the past six years or so has led a number of economists and international monetary experts to devise and recommend schemes for international monetary reform to solve the two problems simultaneously, by channelling the real saving implicit in the expansion of international liquidity to the less developed countries. Frequently these schemes are based on the notion that it is somehow unfair to the less developed countries to reform the international monetary system without designing the reform specifically to benefit them, on the implicit assumption or explicit assertion that such reforms benefit only the developed countries and even in some unspecified sense damage the less developed countries.

There is no obvious advantage, and much evident and avoidable complexity, in attempting to solve two different and incommensurable problems with one and the same institutional change. There is good reason, moreover, to suspect that the need for reform of the international monetary system is being used as a lever to obtain additional aid for the less developed countries by subterfuge. The assertion that reforms that do not explicitly and directly benefit the less developed countries are inequitable is not at all convincing. In the first place, while most people's ethics would protest a change that benefited the developed countries at the expense of the less developed, it is ethically far more debatable to protest a change that would benefit the developed countries without harming the less developed,[8] let alone one that would benefit the less developed countries as well. In the second place, to judge plans for reform only on the criterion of direct contribution to the less developed countries is to confuse efficiency considerations with distributional considerations and to ignore the fact that the economically most efficient solution to a problem will provide the maximum saving of resources and the maximum possibility of compensation to the less developed countries for any losses they might incur or of additional transfers of external resources to them. In the third place, the question of direct benefits to less developed countries may be irrelevant or misleading, since the developed countries could offset any direct benefit by other policy changes, for example by reducing their bilateral or multilateral foreign aid or by increasing their trade barriers.

These proposals, therefore, must be considered on only one of two alternative criteria: either as a superior solution to rival schemes for international monetary reform, or as a more acceptable means of providing additional external resources and other benefits to less developed countries than alternative direct schemes. The second of these criteria involves the imponderables of political feasibility, but some analysis of the effectiveness of the schemes in achieving their objectives is possible.

The proposals in question fall into two broad classes: a variety of schemes for providing the additional liquidity required by an expanding world economy through loans to the less developed countries, so that the real savings involved in the growth of the international reserves of the developed countries would be automatically channelled into external capital assistance for the less developed countries; and

---

[8] This statement needs qualification to the extent that less developed countries accumulate international reserves over time, and these reserves would be backed by liabilities of the developed countries; the magnitudes involved, however, are not such as to make this a significant source of inequity for the less developed countries.

the Hart-Kaldor-Tinbergen commodity-reserve-currency plan, under which the real savings involved in the growth of international liquidity would be invested in the accumulation of stocks of primary products, mostly produced by the less developed countries. Unlike the first class of scheme, which simply attempts to graft a requirement of additional aid to less developed countries onto reform schemes of the kind that are currently being discussed, the Hart-Kaldor-Tinbergen scheme proposes a fundamental transformation of the present international monetary system.

Advocates of schemes of the first type object to the fact that current reform proposals would provide additional liquidity against assets consisting of the liabilities of the developed countries, thus channelling the implicit saving to the developed countries which would be accumulating the liquidity. This would be the case under the composite-reserve-unit plan and under plans to create additional Fund liabilities for use as reserve assets by the leading developed countries against deposits of their own currencies, as proposed for example by Roosa.[9] It would also probably be the case, indirectly, under proposals for converting the International Monetary Fund into a world central bank operating on traditional central banking lines since, following sound banking principles, such a bank would conduct its open market operations in the securities markets of the developed countries. To avoid this allegedly undesirable feature, this group of plans envisages creating international liquidity directly against loans or grants to the less developed countries.

An alternative and more illuminating way of putting the objection avoids the "something-for-nothing" overtones of the concept of "implicit saving" inherent in the creation of international reserves and also explains why the developed countries concerned with international monetary reform have not found it particularly persuasive. If the developed countries were to pool contributions of their own currencies to back a new international reserve unit (either inside or outside the International Monetary Fund) and were then to withdraw amounts of the new reserve unit exactly equal to their individual contributions of national currencies, international liquidity would be created at no cost in real resources to, and with no need for real saving by, anyone. The

[9] Robert V. Roosa, *Monetary Reform for the World Economy* (Harper & Row, 1965). For a critique of this plan, see Harry G. Johnson, "Roosa on International Monetary Reform," *The National Banking Review*, Vol. 3 (December 1965), pp. 182-92.

P

"implicit saving" involved in holding the additional international reserves would be exactly matched by the "implicit dissaving" involved in creating the domestic currency for deposit in the pool. The objectors assert that this procedure would be unfair to the less developed countries whose currencies are unacceptable to the developed countries as backing for the new international reserve unit, and that instead these countries should receive the new international money in the first instance (or the contributions of national monies) so that the developed countries would be obliged to earn back the new liquidity from them through balance-of-payments surpluses. This would require real saving by the developed countries to match the real investment by the less developed countries that would be financed by the new money creation. The schemes proposed aim in one way or another to achieve this result, by creating new international liquidity directly or indirectly against loans or grants to the less developed countries.

An early proposal for aiding less developed countries along these lines was the first Stamp Plan.[10] According to the plan less developed countries would be given certificates representing purchasing power that could be used for development expenditures in the developed countries; the developed countries would agree to regard the certificates as international reserves to be used in settling payments imbalances among themselves. This plan had a number of obvious defects, stemming from ambiguity about which countries would have to agree to accept the certificates and whether they would be convertible into gold at the International Monetary Fund or not. Essentially, the certificates would have been a means of providing additional aid tied to purchase in the participating developed countries, or the equivalent of a grant of aid from the International Monetary Fund; in either case, the international monetary effects could have been achieved much more efficiently by other means, while the advantages to the less developed countries depended on the developed countries being willing to give aid in this form but not in others.

The proposal to convert the International Monetary Fund into a world central bank, advocated in various forms by a variety of writers, offers a much superior opportunity to channel additional liquidity

[10] For description and discussion of this and alternative plans, see Herbert Grubel (ed.), *World Monetary Reform: Plans and Issues* (Stanford University Press, 1963); also Fritz Machlup, *Plans for Reform of the International Monetary System* ("Essays in International Finance," No. 3; Princeton University Press, 1962).

into aid for the less developed countries. The extent of the opportunity would depend, however, on how far the liabilities of the world central bank merely supplemented, in contrast to replacing, gold as an international reserve money. If gold were to be completely replaced, and the world central bank's liabilities become the ultimate international reserve, there would be no economic restrictions on the assets that it could purchase to increase its liabilities[11] and it would be free to lend or even make grants to the less developed countries as it desired. If, on the other hand, the liabilities of the world bank were substitutes for gold, and countries were free to convert their holdings of these liabilities into gold if they so desired, the bank would have to manage its asset portfolio so as to maintain the confidence of its (national) customers in its liquidity. This would in all likelihood prevent it from giving grants to the less developed countries (though it could probably get away with some concessional loans) and restrict its freedom to purchase the securities of less-developed-country governments. However, it could probably invest a significant part of its funds in securities issued by the International Bank for Reconstruction and Development (IBRD) and by the growing number of regional development banks, or by the International Development Association, as proposed by Stamp in a revision of his original proposal. So long as it kept a substantial proportion of its resources in securities readily marketable in the developed countries it could channel much of the annual increment of its resources into external assistance for the less developed countries. This is the procedure most commonly suggested by those who would like to combine international monetary reform with additional aid to the less developed countries. With international monetary reserves currently in the neighborhood of $70 billion, an increase in international liquidity at the rate of 3 percent per year could channel a maximum of $2.1 billion, and at the rate of 5 percent $3.5 billion, of new loans to the less developed countries; these figures of course substantially overstate the net resource transfer involved, which would depend on the interest rate and repayment period of the loans.

[11] Since an ultimate reserve money cannot be exchanged with its issuer for any other form of money, the issuer need hold marketable assets only to the extent that it envisages desiring to reduce the amount of its liabilities outstanding. The bank's management, however, might restrict its assets to particular types for political or conservative reasons, or be obliged to do so by the representatives of the national states on its directorate.

The foregoing discussion, however, assumes that the aid policies of the developed countries are independent of international monetary operations, so that whatever aid would be channelled by a world central bank to the less developed countries would be a net addition to their aid receipts. Since in the real world the left hand usually knows full well what the right hand is doing (though it may not admit it publicly), this is an unrealistic assumption. A more realistic view suggests two points for consideration: first, if the management of the world bank attempted to give more aid than the developed countries thought desirable, they could offset the bank's efforts by reducing the aid they contributed through other routes; and second, even if none of the annual increase in international liquidity were channelled to the less developed countries through portfolio investment by the world central bank, the bank could nevertheless play an important role in increasing the flow of aid by confining its security purchases to the public debt of developed countries that agreed to match such purchases by increasing their bilateral or multilateral aid to the less developed countries.

Current proposals for expanding liquidity through the International Monetary Fund, however, stop far short of transforming that institution into a world central bank and hence do not encounter the problem of whether new reserve assets would constitute an ultimate reserve money or be convertible into gold and national reserve currencies. Instead, they envisage the creation of a carefully limited type of secondary international reserve asset that would be either convertible at the Fund into currencies supplied to the Fund by participating developed countries under lines of credit, or transferable directly between participating countries within quantitative limits as to the amounts countries would be obliged to accept, or transferable in fixed proportion to other types of international reserve assets, on the lines of the composite-reserve-unit proposal. Under any of these arrangements, the liquidity of the assets held by the Fund against the new monetary liability would be in principle a relatively unimportant consideration, and it would be quite feasible to invest a substantial proportion of these assets in development lending, either directly or through the International Bank.[12]

[12] A carefully considered proposal along these lines has been made by the expert group convened by the Secretary-General of UNCTAD in the autumn of 1965; the proposal envisages the creation of Fund Units against the deposit of national currencies and the investment of the whole of the currencies so deposited in IBRD bonds. See *International Monetary Issues and the Developing Countries* (United Nations Conference on Trade and Development, TD/B/C.3/6, 1 November 1965).

Like the more comprehensive plans for international monetary reform discussed above, however, this scheme would be successful in increasing the overall flow of development assistance only if the developed
countries participating in it were "irrational," in the sense either of
failing to appreciate that the scheme would impose on them a tax for
the finance of development in no way necessary to the objective of increasing international liquidity, or in the sense of being willing to give
in this covert form development assistance that they would not be willing to give overtly as bilateral or multilateral aid. Moreover, because
of the secondary nature of the reserve assets, the amount of development assistance might be both erratic and substantially smaller than
might be forecast from prospective liquidity needs. The amount of
such new assets created would presumably be what was considered necessary to fill the gap between the growth of international liquidity requirements and the growth of the combined total of gold stocks and
reserve-currency holdings. Changes in confidence in the reserve currencies could make the gap to be filled vary erratically, while a recovery of
confidence in the dollar and the pound consequent on improvements
of the balance-of-payments positions of the United States and the
United Kingdom could lead to a sufficiently rapid growth of holdings
of reserve currencies to obviate the need for creation of supplementary
new international reserve assets.[13]

THE COMMODITY-RESERVE-CURRENCY
PROPOSAL

The commodity-reserve-currency proposal of Hart, Kaldor and Tinbergen[14] starts from a rejection of three alternative reforms of the
international monetary system. Extension of the key-currency system is

[13] It is true, as the UNCTAD expert group argues in its report (*ibid.*), that erratic
variations in the rate of creation of Fund Units could be smoothed out in the flow
of development finance and so need constitute no serious problem in that context.
However, insofar as the purpose of the creation of Fund Units is to stabilize the
growth of the world economy by stabilizing the rate of growth of its international
money supply, stabilization of the rate of release of the national currencies deposited in exchange for Fund Units to the less developed countries could have
destabilizing effects on world growth. These would result from the temporary
sterilization of these funds when an abnormally large increase in secondary liquidity
was required for world stability and the release of previously sterilized funds when
an abnormally small increase in secondary liquidity was required.

[14] Albert G. Hart, Nicholas Kaldor and Jan Tinbergen, "The Case for an International Commodity Reserve Currency" (United Nations Conference on Trade and
Development, E/Conf. 46/P/7, 17 February 1964).

rejected on grounds of the difficulty of making additional reserves practically available[15] and the dependence of the system on confidence among the reserve-currency countries in each others' domestic and balance-of-payments policies. Establishment of a credit-creating world central bank is rejected on the grounds that it would conflict with national sovereignty, both because countries would have to maintain confidence in each others' willingness to abide by the agreement setting up the bank and because the bank would have sovereign powers to place the real resources of one country at the command of another through its credit operations, and that therefore the bank would inevitably operate conservatively and for the benefit of the advanced industrial countries to the neglect of the less developed countries. Revaluation of gold is rejected on the usual grounds that it would have to be large to be successful, would increase the costs of operating the international monetary system, would shower uncovenanted gains on a few countries, and would not be justified because the price of gold is already maintained artificially.[16]

The Plan

Instead of these three alternatives, the authors propose an ingenious scheme under which the International Monetary Fund would be converted into a world central bank whose liabilities would be backed (in addition to a fiduciary issue) by gold and by warehouse receipts for a bundle of primary commodities whose aggregate value (not the prices

[15] The argument here relies on the "dilemma-of-the-deficit" reasoning: that for its currency to be acceptable as an international reserve money, a country's balance-of-payments position must be "strong"; yet for the available supply of its currency to expand, its balance-of-payments position must be "weak" (in the sense of requiring a deficit). This reasoning obviously applies only to a "natural" development of a currency as an international reserve money. The difficulty could be avoided by international agreement as in the scheme for a composite reserve unit, under which countries would simply swap their own currencies for an equal amount of reserves, with no effect or a strengthening effect on their balances of payments, depending on the accounting conventions used to define the latter.

[16] As Roy Harrod in particular has pointed out ("A Plan for Increasing Liquidity: A Critique," *Economica*, Vol. 28 [May 1961], pp. 195-202) many of these arguments are beside the point, for they object to features of the proposal that are incidental to its main purpose of strengthening the international monetary system. In addition, most of them—especially the cost-of-operation argument—apply with as much or greater strength to the commodity-reserve-currency plan, unless one shares the authors' view that uncovenanted and arbitrarily distributed benefits secured at considerable cost to the world as a whole are to be welcomed if the beneficiaries are less developed countries but not if they are gold-producing countries.

of the individual commodities) would be stabilized in terms of gold by the Fund's open market operations. Under the scheme, existing holdings of reserve currencies would be liquidated by sales of stockpiled commodities and gold by the reserve-currency countries to the Fund, and all countries would therefore become free to alter the rate of exchange between their currencies and "bancor" (the Fund's liability). The scheme would therefore contribute to the solution of the confidence and adjustment problems in the same way as the more orthodox proposal for a world central bank. The fundamental difference lies in the provision of liquidity, especially in the context of secular growth.

On behalf of the commodity-reserve-currency plan, as opposed to a discretionarily managed world central bank, it is argued, first, that the automaticity of the plan would avoid a bank's susceptibility to conflicts of national sovereignty in its credit operations and so presumably make the plan more acceptable to the developed countries. Second, it is argued that the stabilization of commodity prices in terms of gold would have great economic advantages to both the less developed and the developed countries. This argument derives from a long-recognized feature of the gold standard that has provided the rationale for commodity-reserve-currency schemes past and present: that any commodity-reserve standard tends automatically to stabilize the prices of commodities in general, since a rise in such prices relative to the commodity tends to reduce production of the standard commodity, contract the money supply, and force down prices of other goods, and conversely a fall in such prices tends to be counteracted by the monetary expansion consequent on increased production of the standard commodity. This mechanism operates, it is important to note, both directly, by affecting the generation of income through stimulating or depressing output of the standard commodity, and indirectly, by affecting demand for output through alteration of the money stock; a credit-money standard operates only in the latter way, by discretionary management of the stock of money. The difficulty with the gold standard is that the existing stock is extremely large relative to the flow of new production and that nonmonetary demand for current output is small relative to the monetary demand, so that the stabilization mechanism works extremely slowly. The argument for broadening the gold standard to include a range of primary commodities important in world production and trade is that large current production relative to stocks, and large nonmonetary demand relative to monetary demand, would make the stabilization mechanism operate rapidly.

The authors also argue that the scheme would promote world economic growth. This argument rests on an asserted empirical asymmetry in the mechanism of world economic growth, and an assertion that the commodity-reserve-currency plan would overcome this asymmetry. The empirical proposition is that the rate of growth of world manufacturing production strongly influences the prices of primary products and hence the rate of growth of primary production, but that an increase in the rate of growth of primary production does not call forth an increase in the rate of growth of industrial production. While an increase in primary production permits an expansion of industrial production, the resulting fall in primary product prices reduces demand for industrial products and on balance tends to depress the world economy and retard its growth. The commodity-reserve-currency plan would, it is argued, by maintaining primary commodity prices and thereby increasing the incomes of primary producers through stockpiling, inject the required additional demand for industrial products into the system and promote its growth.

In the contrary case[17] in which commodity prices were rising and sales of primary commodities from stocks were depressing the world economy, the authors argue that the depressive effects could be avoided by devaluation of the currencies of the developed countries. The same remedy is recommended for a fall in prices of primary products relative to prices of manufactures resulting from excessive wage increases in the developed manufacturing countries.[18]

The empirical asymmetry on which this argument is based obviously assumes a naive Keynesian model of the world economy in which less developed countries spend all they earn, whereas developed countries allow their output of manufactures to respond passively to demand. If the developed countries used fiscal and monetary policy to maintain full employment, adjusting their exchange rates as necessary to main-

---

[17] The authors regard this case as much less likely and provide certain safeguards against it by asymmetries in the rules governing eligibility of commodities for the plan. Especially, commodities whose prices rise more than 50 percent above the initial standard price are automatically excluded from the reserve, while the prices of included commodities may fall indefinitely without leading to exclusion.

[18] The authors' argument is marred here as elsewhere by a tendency to confuse money prices with relative prices and to treat money wages in the developed countries as being determined autonomously without reference to productivity and the level of unemployment.

tain international equilibrium, the asymmetry and its retarding effects on economic growth would not arise. The solution to the authors' problem is therefore to establish a properly functioning international monetary system, not necessarily to adopt their scheme for forcing full employment through the operation of the buffer stock. It is a striking peculiarity of their argument that they assume that developed countries will follow rational economic policies in the face of primary commodity prices rising due to excess demand or falling (relatively) due to excess wage increases in the developed countries, but will not follow a rational economic policy in the face of primary commodity prices falling due to excess supply.[19]

Objections to the Plan

Leaving aside the question of promotion of world growth, on which the authors' arguments are not particularly persuasive, the commodity-reserve-currency plan is open to a number of well-known practical and theoretical objections. The first set of practical objections concerns the extent to which the scheme would really contribute to the welfare and development of the less developed countries. The scheme would stabilize the average money price of the commodities included under it; as explained in Chapter V, this is by no means equivalent to stabilizing either the average purchasing power of these commodities over manufactured goods, or the average money or real incomes of the producers or the export earnings of the producing countries. Moreover, since it is the average price of the commodities and not their individual prices

[19] The economic irrationality of the authors' world is further exemplified by their assertion (*op. cit.,* p. 34) that under their scheme devaluation would directly change the terms of trade between manufactures and primary products, whereas under the present system devaluation would leave unchanged the relation between primary product prices and industrial countries' wages. Neither proposition is in general correct. This scheme stabilizes the money prices of primary products, not the terms of trade between these products and manufactures; and while the devaluation of a manufacturing country's currency would initially lower the world market price of its manufactures relatively to the average price of primary products, it might produce a subsequent inflation of domestic wages and prices sufficient to restore the previous terms of trade. Under the present system, such a devaluation would alter the relation between the devaluing country's wages and primary product prices in the world market, providing that a subsequent inflation of domestic wages sufficient to offset the devaluation did not occur. Note that the assumption of unchanged money wages in the devaluing country required to make the first proposition valid would invalidate the second proposition, while the assumption of a compensating wage inflation required to make the second proposition valid would invalidate the first proposition.

that will be stabilized, by purchases or sales of commodities in the fixed ratios composing the bundle, the scheme could well destabilize the prices of particular commodities important to particular countries that happened to be falling while the average price of a bundle was rising or vice versa. Further, the effects of open market operations on the prices of particular commodities would depend on the elasticities of demand for and supply of them, so that such operations might produce sharp variations in the pattern of commodity price relationships disturbing to their suppliers and users.

Since its aim is to stabilize money prices of commodities, the scheme would do little to counteract the alleged long-run tendency of the terms of trade to turn against primary products (which the authors imply is one of its purposes). Generally speaking, that tendency (if it exists) would merely assert itself in a long-run upward trend of the money prices of manufactures, instead of a downward trend of money prices of primary products. The only qualification would be that, since the commercial demand for primary products and the rate of growth of the monetary demand for stocks of primary products would presumably be related to the growth of the money value of total output, the rate of growth of total demand for primary products would be somewhat greater—and consequently the rate of fall of the relative prices of primary products somewhat smaller—than in the absence of the scheme.

A second set of practical objections concerns the cost of operating the commodity-reserve scheme and the implications of the magnitude of its operations. The operating cost would include the resource cost of the required annual additions to the stock, the storage costs of the stock, and the costs of the buying and selling operations. The fact that commodities deteriorate over time would require the managers of the stocks to turn them over periodically, so that gross purchases and sales would be substantially larger than the annual net additions to the stocks, with correspondingly larger expenses for transaction costs. The turnover of stocks would make the International Monetary Fund a much larger participant in the world commodity market than the net annual acquisitions to stocks would suggest, with corresponding power to dominate the market for good or evil.[20] It should be observed that,

[20] Herbert Grubel, "The Case Against An International Commodity Reserve Currency," *Oxford Economic Papers*, N.S.17, No. 1 (March 1965), pp. 130-35, calls

of the total costs of operation of the commodity-reserve-currency scheme, only a small fraction would directly benefit the less developed countries by increasing their export earnings. Much of the cost would be storage and transaction cost; moreover, a substantial part of the net additions to stocks would be supplied by developed countries.[21]

It could be argued that the costs of the commodity-reserve-currency plan, high as they could be, would be of little importance if the plan actually secured a substantial improvement in the international monetary system. But the well-known theoretical objections to a commodity-reserve-currency standard[22] are, briefly, as follows. First, a partial standard of the kind proposed, which is to be grafted onto the international gold standard while the creation of domestic credit money remains under national autonomy, is not truly a reform of the monetary stan-

---

attention to the size of these costs and their growth over time. He estimates that the resource cost (net annual addition plus 6 percent operating cost) would rise from $3.9 billion in 1973 to $12.4 billion (at a 3 percent growth rate) or $20.1 billion (at a 4 percent growth rate) in the year 2000; of these figures, $2.3 billion, $5 billion, and $9 billion respectively represent the cost of net annual acquisitions. These figures may exaggerate the size and growth of resource cost, since his 6 percent operating cost allowance is far above the Hart-Kaldor-Tinbergen estimate of 3-3.5 percent and makes no deduction for the storage and operating costs of existing stockpiles. Grubel reckons that the gross annual purchases for the stocks would rise from $11.5 billion (three-year turnover period) or $7.8 billion (five-year turnover period) to $45.9 billion or $29.5 billion (3 percent growth rate) or $70.7 billion or $46 billion (4 percent growth rate) in the year 2000. Such a vast participation in the market, he points out, entails a Hobson's choice between unwieldy rigid rules and undesirable discretionary power in operations in the market.

[21] For the thirty commodities included in the Hart-Kaldor-Tinbergen scheme, 58 percent of world exports come from less developed countries. Applying this percentage to Grubel's figures for net acquisitions—making the extreme assumption that these purchases increase the total export earnings of the less developed countries by the same amount, and accepting Grubel's cost estimates—it appears that the scheme would expend $3.9 billion to increase less developed countries' export earnings by $1.3 billion in 1973, and $12.4 billion or $20 billion to increase their export earnings by $3 billion or $4.9 billion in the year 2000. The implied cost-benefit ratios are obviously extremely high. Using the authors' own much lower estimate of $200 million for net additional storage costs, it would cost $2.5 billion to increase developed countries' export earnings by $1.3 billion in 1973, still a high cost-benefit ratio. Further, it must be remembered that the net transfer of external resources to the less developed countries is less than the value of the increased export earnings, owing to the resource cost of producing the commodities.

[22] For a full discussion, see Milton Friedman, "Commodity Reserve Currency," *Journal of Political Economy*, Vol. 59 (June 1951), pp. 203-32, reprinted in his *Essays in Positive Economics* (University of Chicago Press, 1953), pp. 204-50.

dard but a scheme for price support of the commodities included combined with a cyclical deficit-surplus fiscal policy mediated through the commodity stocks.[23] Secondly, since the commodities suitable for inclusion by reason of durability, marketability, and conditions of supply are bound to account for only a small part of world output and to be unrepresentative of aggregate output, their costs of production relative to other commodities are likely to change in consequence of uneven technical progress and new resource discoveries; thus stabilization of their money prices is likely to destabilize the general level of prices, perhaps even more than has occurred under the gold standard. Thirdly, because of the small share of these commodities in total output and the limited elasticities of supply and demand for many of them, the automatic stabilizing effects (through direct income effects on their production and indirect monetary effects of automatic variations in stocks) of the commodity-reserve standard are likely to be small and consequently to take considerable time to be effective.[24] Finally, the scheme depends on persuading nations that have already largely abandoned the gold standard, in spite of the historical tradition and symbolism that have supported it, to adopt and live by an untested and unorthodox alternative of an equally arbitrary kind.

In view of all these considerations, and especially of the plan's inefficiency in achieving worthwhile objectives and the deliberate reversal of the historical evolution from the gold standard to intelligent monetary management, the commodity-reserve-currency plan appears to offer little to recommend it as a solution to the problem of international monetary reform. Less developed countries and their sympathizers would be better advised to press for as liberal a credit-based international monetary system as can be achieved, preferably an internationally controlled world central bank.

[23] See Friedman, *Essays*, p. 222. The retention of gold as the basis of the international monetary system under this scheme exposes it to the same possible danger of loss of confidence as might afflict a world central bank obliged to maintain convertibility of its liabilities into gold at a fixed price.

[24] For an illustration of these points, see Appendix F.

VIII

The Study in Retrospect

The convening of the United Nations Conference on Trade and Development reflected the growing belief of the less developed countries that the system of international trading relationships institutionalized in the General Agreement on Tariffs and Trade, based on the principles of nondiscrimination and of trade liberalization through reciprocal tariff concessions, is biased in favor of the developed countries and against their own trading interests, and especially against providing them with adequate opportunities for growth through trade. These countries used UNCTAD as an opportunity to organize themselves into a cohesive political bloc, to express their grievances about the trade and aid policies of the developed countries and the shortcomings of the GATT system, and to press on the developed countries a host of demands for policy changes.

THE MAJOR ISSUES

The most important changes demanded at UNCTAD were an extension of the use of commodity agreements to stabilize and raise commodity prices, and trade preferences in industrial products. The United States strongly opposed most of these demands; in so doing, it appeared isolated from most of the other developed nations of the West, which displayed considerably more sympathy for the problems and proposals of the less developed countries.

The main act of the conference was to establish itself as a continuing organization of the United Nations, under the charge of a Trade and Development Board, and to call for another conference in 1966 (since postponed to 1967). The problems of trade policy raised at UNCTAD have thus been institutionalized; this fact and the deep gulfs which appeared at Geneva between the position of the United States and those of the other developed countries and the less developed country group necessitate a fundamental rethinking of the United States commercial policy as it affects the less developed countries.

The first question is whether there is an issue. Must the United States respond in some way to the criticisms and proposals made at UNCTAD? Or can the proceedings of UNCTAD be dismissed as a blowing-off of steam by the less developed countries egged on by the communist countries and abetted by European countries eager to see the United States embarrassed, an eruption which has left the foundations of U.S. economic policy toward the less developed countries triumphantly unshaken? The central theme of this study has been that there is a real issue, in both political and economic terms. Politically, as the leader of the Western world, the United States cannot ignore the grievances of the less developed countries or the fact that other developed Western nations do not share its attitude toward those countries' demands. If the United States is to maintain its leadership and fulfill the responsibilities it has assumed to both the developed and the less developed countries, it must evolve some positive new approach to the problems aired at UNCTAD. It is not of course obliged to accept the solutions proposed at UNCTAD.

Economically, there is substance in the complaints of the less developed countries about the present system of international trade organization. The techniques of bargaining under GATT for reciprocal tariff reductions on a nondiscriminatory basis have encouraged reductions on commodities of interest primarily to the developed countries, and while the linear technique of the Kennedy Round represents an improvement over the earlier item-by-item bargaining technique, it will not undo the effects of past rounds of bargaining. Moreover, the lists of exceptions from bargaining in the Kennedy Round entered by the developed countries imply that the benefits to the less developed countries will be substantially watered down. Nor will the GATT technique, even if the Kennedy Round is successful, reduce to negligible proportions the barriers to trade in the products in which the less developed countries are most interested; if these are measured by effective rather than nominal rates of protection, these barriers are likely to remain significantly restrictive of trade.

More important in terms of the products the less developed countries now export, GATT has been used by the developed countries to legitimize a steady increase in the protection accorded their producers of primary products. This protection against competition from the less developed world is also reflected in special barriers to the expansion of less developed countries' exports of cotton textiles, the major manufactured product in which they had succeeded in establishing a competitive position despite relatively high tariff barriers imposed by the developed countries.

In devising a positive policy in response to these political and economic considerations, the United States has two main alternatives. One would be to attempt to initiate a major move toward free trade along traditional GATT lines, but aimed specifically at reducing barriers to trade that handicap the less developed countries. While this would be in the spirit of traditional U.S. policy, it would raise two major issues. First, the tariff has traditionally been used to cushion the adjustment of domestic producers to the shifting pressures of international competition. A determined drive toward freer trade would necessitate both developing an alternative (and more effective) system of assisting adjustment and persuading public opinion that adjustment rather than protection is the best policy. Second, the GATT principles of reciprocity and nondiscrimination permit a major trading partner to block any United States-led drive for freer trade by refusing to bargain. The countries of the European Common Market may well desire to call a halt to further trade liberalization under GATT after the Kennedy Round in order to maintain the protected common market they have established and which they consider essential to their broader political and cultural objectives. In that case the United States would be forced to abandon one of the two GATT principles—either reciprocity or nondiscrimination. This choice is essentially a false one, in fundamental economic terms, since the case for freer trade rests on the benefits of reducing one's own tariffs and does not in general depend on other countries reducing theirs. But it is likely to be the choice seen by the policymakers and the public, and in terms of the domestic politics of international commercial relations the decision might well be to abandon nondiscrimination rather than reciprocity.

The other alternative would be to admit the disadvantages of the present GATT system for the less developed countries and to depart from it by following the lines of the policies they proposed at UNCTAD. This would involve both extension of price-fixing agreements for primary commodities and introduction of preferences for trade in manufactures. Commodity agreements are anathema to most international trade experts, for many good reasons well grounded in theory and experience. If, however, it is desired to increase the external resources made available through trade to the less developed countries, and developed countries are unwilling to abandon agricultural policies that progressively strengthen protection against and restrictions on imports of commodities from the less developed countries, agreements to raise commodity prices might prove the most expedient solution. Similarly, preferences for imports of manufactured goods from less developed countries might prove the most expedient compromise between the desire to avoid disruption of established domestic industries by liberalized imports and the desire to help the development of the less developed countries through trade. They might enable those countries both to earn their foreign exchange requirements rather than receive them as charity and to acquire industrial experience and enjoy the economies of large-scale production by exporting to large and rich markets.

The question of expanded opportunities for industrial exports is of great and growing importance to the less developed countries, both for valid economic reasons arising from the implications and requirements of the development process and because they aspire to establish themselves as modern industrial nation-states. In that aspiration they are simply modeling themselves on the example of the developed countries —the United States, Russia, and the European countries of which many of them are former colonies. But they find the achievement of their ambitions frustrated (as they see it) by the protectionist policies of the developed countries in both primary products and manufactures that they can or could export. Having been brought up in a protectionist world, and encouraged in the belief that protectionist policies are necessary to the promotion of economic growth, they naturally hope to solve their trade problems by inverting the protectionist policies of the developed countries in their favor. Those problems could be resolved far more rationally and efficiently, from a strictly economic point of view, by a substantial move toward genuinely free international trade, at least among the developed countries.

The fundamental political choice for the United States and other developed countries lies between meeting the demands of the less developed countries along the protectionist lines they have proposed and initiating new actions along the lines of the free-trade alternative. The

European countries have indicated their willingness to follow the former course; the United States still has a choice to make. There are cogent arguments for and against both alternatives. What the United States cannot continue to do is to follow protectionist policies for itself, while using the language and concepts of the free-trade position to deny that these policies injure the less developed countries whose economic development it has pledged itself to help promote, and to reject their proposals for improvement of their trading opportunities.

SUGGESTIONS FOR SPECIFIC POLICY ACTIONS

The purpose of this study has been to survey the major issues raised by UNCTAD for U.S. policy toward the less developed countries, and to explore the various policy alternatives open to the United States, in order to facilitate the thinking of government officials, academic experts and members of the public who are concerned with the formulation of American trade and development assistance policies. While it was not intended that the study produce a set of recommendations for future policy or formulate a concrete policy program for U.S. dealings with the less developed countries, it is appropriate to present briefly some conclusions about the relative desirability of the various alternatives surveyed and about what concrete policy actions might best be undertaken.

Most of the serious criticisms that can be leveled against the present system of international trading relationships (the GATT system) are criticisms, not of the trade-liberalizing intentions and objectives of that system, but of the ways in which its operating rules and methods have been warped to serve protectionist ends. This is particularly true of the principle of nondiscrimination. Despite the hollowness of that principle as it works in the practical context of bargaining among nations for reciprocal tariff reductions, there is much to be said for it as an established principle that does maintain some semblance of a rule of law in commercial policy dealings among nations and like the rule of law in other contexts provides some constraint on the abuse by the powerful of their power over the weak. That being so, it would seem highly desirable for the United States to respond to the demands of the less developed countries for greater opportunities for development through trade by taking action within the present international institutional

Q

242 ECONOMIC POLICIES TOWARD LESS DEVELOPED COUNTRIES

framework (along the lines explored in Chapter IV) rather than by offering to participate in international commodity agreements designed to raise prices—discussed in Chapter V—and to accord preferential entry to its market to the industrial products of less developed countries on one or other of the schemes surveyed in Chapter VI.

Action along these lines, as mentioned in Chapter IV, would require that the United States substitute domestic adjustment policies for tariffs and other protective devices presently used to shield American producers from the impact of foreign competition. Because other industrial countries might not be prepared to negotiate tariff reductions, U.S. policy would have to concentrate on the unilateral reduction of its tariff and other barriers to the exports of less developed countries.

In this connection, it is relevant to observe that what impedes trade is not only existing barriers but uncertainty about the future level of those barriers, and particularly the suspicion that success in expanding exports to the American market will evoke a countervailing increase in U.S. trade barriers. Moreover, this suspicion is kept alive by the publicity accorded to the few cases where successful exporting has evoked this response—notably the case of the Cotton Textiles Arrangement. It cannot be dispelled by reference to the vastly predominant number of cases in which the United States has in fact accommodated substantial and rapid increases in its imports and allowed its domestic economy to absorb the resulting disturbance unaided by increased trade barriers.

As a first step, therefore, and one which would involve no substantial change in overall policy—though it would involve an important change in principle—the United States could publicly pledge itself not to introduce any new quota or other restrictions, and not to raise any tariff rates, on goods in which the less developed countries already have, or in the course of time develop, an export trade to the United States. The sincerity and credibility of this pledge would be greatly reinforced by the adoption of a detailed program for phasing out the Cotton Textiles Arrangement by increasing the quotas substantially each year. This would probably necessitate the adoption of a special adjustment program for the domestic cotton textiles industry, designed to compensate owners of enterprises for the losses they would incur and to retrain labor for other industries. Such a program might well be expensive, but it would provide the less developed countries with convincing evidence that the United States was prepared to accept a "new international division of labor" based on the principle of competition according to comparative advantage, while at the same time erasing the one important example supporting the allegation that the United States is unwilling to allow them to develop through trade.

At the same time as it pledged itself not to raise any new barriers against imports, the United States could commit itself to a policy of untying aid as it relaxes its present interventions in international transactions in response to the expected rectification of its balance-of-payments deficit in the next few years. This commitment could be strengthened by a pledge not to increase the degree of aid tying in the future. A commitment of this kind, besides promising an increase in the usefulness of aid to the recipient countries, would give the United States the moral advantage—especially by comparison with the other aid-giving countries—of explicitly rejecting the use of aid as a means of giving protection to domestic producers in foreign markets. On the other hand, given its conditionality on improvement in the balance of payments, the commitment might not be credible to the less developed countries, and the making of it might conceivably induce a reduction in the amount of aid Congress would be willing to provide.[1] An alternative possibility in this field would be for the United States to retain aid tying but undertake to provide the difference between the cost of U.S.-supplied aid goods and the world market prices of comparable

[1] As this book is being sent to press, the prospect for an early improvement of the U.S. balance of payments looks extremely bleak, and the value and credibility of the suggested commitments to the less developed countries correspondingly small. The proposed commitments would be greatly strengthened if the United States coupled them with a definite program for relieving itself of the balance-of-payments constraint that now ties its hands in so many fields of economic policy. The following conclusions reached in late 1963 seem particularly relevant at the present time:

". . . the difficulties of the dollar will continue until the U.S. authorities are prepared to face a show-down with Europe over the dollar's key-currency role. To precipitate such a show-down, the United States would have to face Europe with a choice between an agreed devaluation of the dollar supported by central bank co-operation—and a suspension of the convertibility of [dollars into] gold. If the dollar were made non-convertible into gold, the Europeans would be forced to decide what the value of the dollar in terms of their currencies should be: and if they wanted to preserve the present exchange rate out of either regard for the dollar-reserve currency system or desire for an over-valued dollar, they would be obliged to assume the responsibility for supporting their decision by capital movements, thus freeing U.S. policy for the pursuit of . . . domestic objectives. . . ." (Harry G. Johnson, "The International Competitive Position of the United States and the Balance of Payments Prospect for 1968," *Review of Economics and Statistics*, Vol. 46 [February 1964], pp. 14-32.)

goods as a grant and not as a loan. This would eliminate the basis for some, though not all, of the criticisms to which aid tying as presently practiced is subject.

The pledges just described would, of course, be primarily a declaration of the commitment of the United States to the principle of promoting the development of the less developed countries within a genuinely liberal international system of trade and payments. As such it would be no more than a preliminary to policies designed actually to promote development along these lines. These policies would focus on two complementary objectives, increased trade opportunities and increased development aid.

With respect to trade opportunities, the objective consistent with the principle of nondiscrimination and the general commitment of the United States to a liberal international economic order would be the reduction of the high barriers to international trade in certain products or product groups, with special emphasis on those barriers that weigh especially heavily on the less developed countries. This objective could be approached by means of a political determination of the maximum tariff rates—or, with more sophistication, the maximum effective rates of protection—that could be justified given the other economic objectives of the country, and subsequent reduction of those tariff rates that exceeded the maximum. A more far-reaching and economically sensible alternative would be for the Administration to appoint a review committee of economic experts to make a comprehensive study of the economic effects of the United States tariff and the consistency or otherwise of these effects with the domestic and international policy objectives of the United States, including the objective of promoting the economic growth of the less developed countries of the world. Such a review, besides providing guidance for a policy of tariff reduction to benefit the less developed countries, would make the United States legitimately able to demand that the less developed countries review and be able to justify their own protectionist policies. This proposal may seem unduly novel; but in fact some of the smaller developed countries have recently conducted such a review of their tariff policies.[2]

With respect to aid, it is clear from the analysis in Chapter II of the comparative contributions of aid and trade to resources for develop-

[2] See, for example, Swedish Customs Tariff Commission, *Revision of the Swedish Customs Tariff* (Stockholm, 1957); Commonwealth of Australia, *Report of the Committee of Economic Enquiry*, Vol. 1 (Melbourne, May 1965), Chaps. 12-14.

ment and the various estimates of the contribution that changes in trade policy could make to the supply of external resources for development—unsatisfactory as these are—that while the contribution of trade policy changes to development might be very large in the long run, their impact in the short run—say five to ten years—would probably be small and concentrated on the few countries that have achieved some success in development. It therefore appears inescapable that for the short run an increase in the supply of foreign aid would be more effective in supplying external resources for development than would the opening of trade opportunities. The effectiveness of increased aid in promoting growth, however, would depend very much on how the money was used. This consideration suggests that the expansion of aid should be integrated with the expansion of trade opportunities, and that the two together should be used to provide the maximum inducements to the less developed countries to modify the policies of currency overvaluation and import substitution to which they are addicted and to concentrate their efforts instead on economic development through trade with the rest of the world.

THE NEED FOR FURTHER RESEARCH

Scholars in the field of international trade have increasingly become aware of a serious lack of integration among the pure theory of international trade, empirical research on the determinants of international trade patterns and the effects of changes in them, and the "common sense" mixture of political, economic, and institutional considerations in terms of which commercial policy issues are debated. This study has been an exercise in the integration of these three aspects of international economics; it has been enriched by empirical information from a number of recent studies, many of them not yet published when this book was written. Nevertheless, if the quantitative information required to evaluate the importance of particular trade problems and to formulate wise trade policy is to be made readily available to those concerned with policy issues, a great deal of empirical research remains to be undertaken.

The areas of ignorance, or of unsatisfactory knowledge, that remain to be explored may be indicated by the following list of questions that have been posed in connection with the problems discussed in this study:

1. Are barriers to international trade currently rather low, and destined to be reduced to relative unimportance in the Kennedy Round, or are they seriously restrictive of trade, especially that of the less developed countries? Much effort has been devoted in the preparations for the Kennedy Round to debating the merits of different methods of arriving at averages of tariff rates; the more relevant concept of the effective rate of protection of value added has been explored so far by only a few academic specialists and only one has attempted to use it to measure the extent to which national tariff structures restrict trade.[3] Though the problem has been widely discussed in connection with UNCTAD, little serious work has been done on the measurement of effective protection of the processing of primary products. The problem of measuring the restrictive effects of quotas, as distinct from tariffs, has scarcely been broached; and while a great deal has been said about the importance of nontariff barriers to trade, and the discriminatory effects of the policies of international corporations and of the fixing of freight rates by international shipping conferences, the effects of these barriers remain to be quantified.

2. Is the tying of foreign aid a serious source of inefficiency and a burden on the aid-receiving countries, or is competition among aid givers pervasive enough to make the wastes involved in aid tying negligible? The one detailed empirical study bearing on this question strongly suggests the need for more such studies.[4] Some scientific attention should probably be given to quantitative study of the frequently offered justification of tying, that it results in a greater real volume of aid than would otherwise be available.

3. How great is the real flow of resources made available to the less developed countries through foreign aid? Although this empirical question has now been explored fairly thoroughly, the findings need to be extended by further research on the growth of the total flow over time and on the real aid flows received by individual less developed countries. Also, the economic concepts relevant to quantifying the real flow of aid need to be integrated into specialist and popular thinking on the subject.

[3] Bela A. Balassa, "Tariff Protection in Industrial Countries: An Evaluation," *Journal of Political Economy*, Vol. 73 (December 1965), pp. 573-94.

[4] Mahbub ul Haq, "Tied Credits—A Quantitative Analysis," paper for the International Economic Association Round Table on Capital Movements and Economic Development, July 21-31, 1965, Washington, D.C.

4. How great a contribution to the foreign-exchange earnings of the less developed countries could be made by reduction of tariffs on a nondiscriminatory basis? An analysis based on conventional concepts, applying estimated changes in average nominal tariff rates and "reasonable" estimates of elasticities to existing trade or to existing trade divided into a few categories, is virtually certain to result in a relatively small figure as an answer. This approach needs to be refined conceptually to incorporate the effective protection concept and applied in microeconomic detail to the products traded internationally. Even so, it would in all probability be necessary to supplement the answer with the information required to answer other questions posed below.

5. Would the less developed countries be unable to supply additional exports in any significant quantity to exploit expanded trade opportunities, or would they on the contrary flood the markets of the developed countries if given the chance? Some participants in the debate over the UNCTAD issues have come close to arguing in the affirmative to both questions in different contexts. To answer the question properly would require empirical study of the elasticities of supply of existing exports from less developed countries, and of the range and prospective supply elasticities of potential exports currently suppressed by the tariffs of the developed countries. A longer-run answer would also involve the answer to the next three questions.

6. What are the reasons for the existing cost disadvantages of the less developed countries? It has been argued in this study and elsewhere that the inability of the less developed countries to produce at competitive prices is largely due to the protectionist and currency-overvaluation policies they tend to follow. This argument is based on observation and "hunch" and requires comprehensive empirical testing.

7. How much substance is there in the scale-economy and infant-industry arguments for protection? These arguments have been widely used in the contemporary policy debate, to defend existing protectionist policies in the less developed countries and to support demands for temporary preferences. Yet empirical testing of the likelihood and quantitative importance of the possible consequences of temporary protection, by reference to either historical experience or current knowledge about the technology and economics of production, is conspicuously absent from the literature of economic development.

8. More generally, how much protection can be justified by the various rationalizations for protection in less developed countries? Many

writers in recent years have displayed considerable ingenuity in refining the economic arguments for protection, all of which involve some failure of the market mechanism accurately to reflect social values or alternative-opportunity costs. These arguments have been used to defend existing protective policies, without recognizing that they justify protection only to an extent determined by the magnitudes of the discrepancies between market prices and social values on which they are based. Empirical research on the relation of the protection actually accorded to the theoretically justifiable amount is urgently necessary to determine whether the protectionist policies of the less developed countries are rational, and deserving of toleration by the developed countries and even supplementation through trade preferences, or on the contrary are irrational and deserving of criticism.

9. How far would trade preferences assist the less developed countries? Quantitative estimates, based on the distinction between the gains from higher prices and the gains from larger trade volume and taking account of the intricacies of the effects of preferences in a modern input-output system, will obviously be necessary if such preferences are to be seriously considered. It would also be necessary to analyze in detail the commodities on which preferences would be most economically beneficial, or least injurious, to the preference-giving country.

10. How much could be done for the less developed countries through price-raising commodity agreements? This question has been examined in detail by John Pincus,[5] but on the assumption that the problem is to maximize foreign exchange earnings rather than the amount of real resources transferred, an assumption which confines attention to easily manageable commodities with low elasticities of demand. The transfer of real resources demands a more sophisticated economic analysis and the application of it to commodities with elasticities above unity.

To answer these questions in a manner satisfying to the standards of contemporary economic analysis would require a massive research program, including much reformulation of the theory of international trade and refinement of the methods of economic measurement employed in international trade research. But if international economic policy is to be intelligently formulated to serve the fundamental needs of a developing world economy efficiently, such a program is a minimal prerequisite.

[5] John A. Pincus, *Economic Aid and International Cost Sharing* (The Johns Hopkins Press, 1965), Chap. 6.

Analysis of Prebisch's Views
on the Terms of Trade

In *Towards a New Trade Policy for Development*[1] Dr. Prebisch maintains that there is a long-run tendency for the prices of primary products to deteriorate relative to the prices of manufactured goods. The alleged tendency, however, is not consistent with the empirical evidence. It is necessary in this connection to distinguish between two frequently confused but analytically distinct propositions: that there is a long-run tendency for the terms of trade between manufactures and primary products to turn against producers of the latter, and that there is a long-run tendency for the terms of trade between developed and less developed countries to turn against the latter. The most recent empirical study of these issues is by Robert E. Lipsey.[2] On the first proposition, the one under discussion here, Lipsey concludes from his study of the U.S. data for 1879-1960 and previous studies that: "In summary, comparisons with exports of U.S. manufactures strongly contradict the belief in declining relative primary product prices; comparisons with manufactures imported into the U.S. mildly confirm it. On the whole, there seem to be more instances of primary products relatively gaining in price than losing. The scatter around these relationships among totals is large, and supports Kindleberger's view that the primary vs. manufactured product distinction is not a particularly useful one for the analysis of changes in terms of trade."[3]

On the second proposition, Lipsey concludes: "To summarize, among the three industrial areas compared, only one—the United Kingdom—showed evidence of substantial gains in its terms of trade. Neither our new indexes for the U.S. nor Kindleberger's data for continental industrial Europe confirm the belief that industrial countries as a whole have enjoyed large improvements in their trade terms since the 1870's or 1880's. The experience of the U.K. cannot be taken as typical of developed countries."[4]

The short-to-medium-term trend of the terms of trade discernible in the statistics is highly sensitive to the terminal years chosen. The period analyzed by

[1] Raúl Prebisch, *Towards a New Trade Policy for Development* (United Nations, 1964).

[2] *Price and Quantity Trends in the Foreign Trade of the United States*, a study by the National Bureau of Economic Research (Princeton University Press, 1963).

[3] *Ibid.*, p. 23.

[4] *Ibid.*, p. 17.

R

Prebisch, 1950-61, begins with a year in which primary commodity prices had been raised exceptionally high by the Korean War boom and ends with a year in which prices were depressed by relative stagnation in the U.S. economy and by new supplies stimulated by the rise in prices during the Suez crisis. The choice of 1950 as a base year is a United Nations convention, however.

Dr. Prebisch's theoretical explanations are no more satisfactory. A number of standard works on trade and growth have exposed the deficiencies of his theory.[5] The explanation in *Towards a New Trade Policy for Development* of the alleged tendency for relative prices of primary products to deteriorate is confused and obscure. It starts with the proposition that technical progress in primary production in the face of a slowly growing demand requires a shift of the working population out of primary activities; it then calls attention to the high proportion of the economically active population engaged in agriculture and other low-productivity occupations, and asserts that: "All these sectors of the population exert constant pressure on the real level of wages in the developing countries and make it extremely difficult for this level to rise in direct proportion to productivity as the latter improves with technological progress. The increase in income generated by higher productivity in the agricultural sector thus tends to shift to other parts of the domestic market or abroad, as the case may be, provided that the shortage of available land does not absorb the increase in income by raising the rent for the benefit of landowners and provided that the play of market forces is left undisturbed.

"In the industrial countries, on the other hand, the relative shortage of labour and strong trade-union organization allow wages not only to rise as productivity increases but even, as often happens, to outstrip the increase."[6]

The first paragraph seems to be asserting that labor is in infinitely elastic supply to agriculture at a constant wage in terms of manufactured goods or money (perhaps as a result of Malthusian population pressure?), in which case population limitation would seem the only possible policy solution. The second paragraph confuses money with real wages, and does not explain the conditions that allow rising money wages to be translated into rising relative prices of manufactured goods. It may be remarked that if, as Prebisch asserts, the problem is basically the slowness of the shift from primary production to manufacturing, one would expect this to generate a differential between agricultural and industrial wages, so that primary product prices would be relatively lower than they would be if the shift were completed. But one would expect a falling *trend* of agricultural prices only if productivity were rising faster in agriculture than in industry; and it would be the wage differential, not the falling relative price trend, that would measure the compensation due to agricultural producers under a social policy of maintaining parity between agricultural and industrial labor incomes.

[5] The most thorough recent exploration of the theory and the conditions under which it could be valid is by M. June Flanders, "Prebisch on Protectionism: An Evaluation," *The Economic Journal*, Vol. 74 (June 1964), pp. 305-26.

[6] Prebisch, *op. cit.*, p. 15.

UNCTAD Principles
Governing International Trade

In its final act[1] the United Nations Conference on Trade and Development agreed on fifteen general and twelve special principles to govern international trade relations and trade policies in the interest of fostering economic development. Negative votes and abstentions of the major developed countries on these principles are shown in Tables B-1 and B-2.

The United States was alone in voting against General Principle One ("respect for the principle of sovereign equality of states, self-determination of peoples, and non-interference in the internal affairs of other countries"); Four (pledge "to help to promote in developing countries a rate of growth consistent with the need to bring about substantial and steady increase in average income in order to narrow the gap between the standard of living in developing countries and that in the developed countries"); Six (cooperation in creating international trade conditions "conducive in particular to the achievement of a rapid increase in the export earnings of developing countries and, in general, to the promotion of an expansion and diversification of trade between all countries, whether at similar levels of development, at different levels of development, or having different economic and social systems"); and Twelve ("a significant portion of resources released in successive stages as a result of the conclusion of an agreement on general and complete disarmament under effective international control should be allocated to the promotion of economic development in developing countries").

The other General Principles against which the United States voted were Two ("no discrimination on the basis of differences in socio-economic systems"); Three ("Every country has the sovereign right freely to trade with other countries, and freely to dispose of its natural resources in the interest of the economic development and well-being of its own people"); Seven (elimination of barriers to, and positive measures to increase markets for, exports of developing countries; cooperation in international arrangements "to increase and stabilize primary commodity export earnings, particularly of developing countries, at equitable and remunerative prices and to maintain a mutually acceptable relationship between the prices of manufactured goods

[1] *Final Act of the United Nations Conference on Trade and Development* (United Nations, E/Conf. 46/L.28, June 16, 1964).

TABLE B-1

Negative Votes and Abstentions of Major Developed Countries on General Principles in UNCTAD

(*Negative vote indicated by "V"; abstention indicated by "A"*)

Country	General Principle[a]															Total	
	1	2	3	4	5	6	7	8	9	10	11	12	13	14	15	V	A
United States	V	V	V	V	A	V	V	V	-	-	V	V	-	A	-	9	2
United Kingdom	A	A	V	A	A	-	V	V	-	-	V	A	-	V	-	5	5
Canada	-	V	V	A	A	-	V	V	-	-	A	A	-	A	A	4	6
Australia	-	A	V	A	A	-	V	V	-	-	V	A	-	V	-	5	4
South Africa	-	A	A	A	A	-	V	V	-	-	V	A	-	A	-	3	6
New Zealand	-	-	A	-	-	-	A	A	-	-	-	-	-	A	-	0	4
France	-	-	A	A	A	-	A	A	A	-	A	-	-	A	-	0	8
Italy	-	-	A	A	A	-	A	A	A	-	A	A	-	A	-	0	9
Belgium	-	-	A	A	A	-	A	A	A	-	A	A	-	A	-	0	9
Netherlands	-	A	A	A	A	-	A	A	A	-	A	A	-	A	-	0	10
Germany (Federal Republic)	-	V	A	A	A	-	A	A	A	-	V	A	-	A	-	2	8
Sweden	-	A	-	-	-	-	A	V	-	-	A	A	-	A	-	1	5
Norway	-	A	-	-	-	-	A	V	-	-	A	A	-	A	-	1	5
Denmark	-	A	-	-	-	-	V	A	-	-	A	A	-	A	-	1	5
Japan	-	-	A	A	A	-	A	A	-	A	A	-	-	-	A	0	8
Soviet Union	-	-	-	-	-	-	-	-	-	-	-	A	-	-	-	0	1

[a] Key to General Principles:
1. Sovereign equality of nations.
2. Against discrimination by socioeconomic system.
3. Freedom to trade and dispose of natural resources.
4. Acceleration of growth, narrowing of income gap.
5. International division of labor; developed countries help less developed.
6. Increase export earnings of less developed, regardless of system.
7. International arrangements for market access, remunerative prices of primary products.
8. Preferences and nonreciprocity.
9. Regional groupings should not harm outsiders.
10. Encouragement of regional groupings and integration.
11. Increasing aid without political or military strings.
12. Disarmament-freed resources to be used for development.
13. Transit trade of land-locked countries.
14. Complete decolonization necessary.
15. Recognition of differences in stages of development.

and those of primary products"); Eight ("developed countries should grant concessions to all developing countries and extend to developing countries all concessions they grant to one another and should not, in granting these or other concessions, require any concessions in return from developing countries. New preferential concessions, both tariff and non-tariff, should be made to developing countries as a whole; and preferences should not be extended to developed by developing countries. Developing countries need not extend to

TABLE B-2

Negative Votes and Abstentions of Major Developed Countries on Special Principles in UNCTAD

(*Negative vote indicated by "V"; abstention indicated by "A"*)

Country	Special Principle[a]												Total	
	1	2	4	5	6	7	8	9	10	11	12	13	V	A
United States	V	–	A	A	–	V	V	A	–	A	V	A	4	5
United Kingdom	A	–	–	–	–	V	A	A	–	A	V	–	2	4
Canada	V	–	–	A	–	V	A	A	–	A	A	A	2	6
Australia	A	–	–	A	–	V	A	A	–	A	–	A	1	6
South Africa	A	–	–	A	–	V	A	A	–	A	–	–	1	5
France	–	–	–	A	–	A	A	–	–	A	A	–	0	5
Italy	–	–	–	A	–	A	–	–	–	A	A	–	0	4
Belgium	–	–	–	A	–	A	–	–	–	A	A	–	0	4
Netherlands	A	–	–	A	–	A	–	–	–	A	A	–	0	5
Germany (Federal Republic)	A	–	–	A	–	V	–	–	–	A	V	–	2	3
Sweden	A	–	–	A	–	A	A	A	–	A	V	–	1	6
Norway	A	–	–	A	–	V	–	A	–	A	V	–	2	4
Denmark	A	–	–	A	–	V	A	–	–	A	V	–	2	4
Japan	A	–	–	A	–	V	–	–	–	A	A	A	1	5
Soviet Union	–	–	–	–	–	A	–	–	–	–	–	–	0	1

[a] Key to Special Principles:
1. Setting targets for trade expansion.
2. Need for industrialization, modernization of agriculture.
3. Preferences [no action taken].
4. Right to protect infant industries.
5. Domestic support prices should not stimulate uneconomic production.
6. Developed countries help less developed re substitution for their commodities.
7. Compensatory financing of worsening terms of trade.
8. Surplus disposal by international rules.
9. No dumping.
10. Technical assistance.
11. Assistance: more multilateral aid; easier terms; repayment in local currency or commodities.
12. Action to promote invisible earnings.
13. Multilateral trade and payments arrangements among less developed countries.

developed countries preferential treatment in operation amongst them. Special preferences at present enjoyed by certain developing countries in certain developed countries should be regarded as transitional and subject to progressive reduction. They should be eliminated as and when effective international measures guaranteeing at least equivalent advantages to the countries concerned come into operation."); and Eleven (obligation of international institutions and developed countries to provide an increasing net flow of international financial, technical and economic assistance; "such assistance, should not be subject to any political or military conditions"; whatever its form and source it "should flow to developing countries on terms fully in keeping with their trade and development needs. International, financial and monetary policies should be designed to take full account of the trade and development needs of developing countries.")

The United States also cast the only vote against Special Principle Eight (undertaking to apply internationally agreed criteria of surplus disposal in the disposal of agricultural surpluses, primary product surpluses and stockpiles so as to avoid adverse effects on developing countries, and to dispose of such surpluses and stockpiles "for the promotion of economic development of all developing countries whether producers or recipients.")

The other Special Principles against which it voted were One ("Developed countries should cooperate with developing countries in setting targets for the expansion of trade of the latter and in periodically reviewing measures for their achievement"); Seven (whenever international price stabilization arrangements for primary products are inadequate, "arrangements should be made on an equitable and universal basis, and without prejudice to the general level of financial aid to developing countries, to correct and compensate the deterioration in terms of trade and short-term decline in the export earnings of countries exporting primary commodities with a view to facilitating the implementation of economic development plans and programs"); and Twelve (cooperation "in devising measures to help developing countries to build up maritime and other means of transport for their economic development, to ensure the unhindered use of international transport facilities, the improvement of terms of freight and insurance for the developing countries and to promote tourism in these countries in order to increase their earnings and reduce their expenditure on invisible trade").

APPENDIX C

The Real Value of Concessionary Loans

The accompanying table is designed to illustrate the magnitude of the difference beween the actual and nominal value of the loans on concessional terms given as development aid. It shows the present value (either to lender or borrower) of the transfer element in interest-free loans of different maturities at different assumed interest rates, as a proportion of face value, for loans paid in full at maturity (column A), and for loans repaid in equal annual installments (column B).

TABLE C-1

Difference Between Actual and Nominal Value
of Loans on Concessional Terms

Years to Maturity	Assumed Interest Rate in Lending or Borrowing Nation											
	3 Percent		4 Percent		5 Percent		6 Percent		7 Percent		8 Percent	
	A	B	A	B	A	B	A	B	A	B	A	B
5	.137	.087	.178	.110	.216	.136	.253	.157	.287	.180	.319	.203
10	.256	.147	.324	.190	.386	.228	.442	.263	.492	.297	.537	.329
15	.358	.204	.445	.258	.519	.308	.583	.352	.638	.394	.685	.429
20	.446	.257	.544	.320	.623	.377	.688	.427	.742	.470	.785	.509
25	.552	.304	.625	.375	.705	.436	.767	.489	.816	.534	.854	.573
30	.588	.347	.692	.423	.769	.487	.826	.541	.869	.586	.901	.625
35	.645	.384	.747	.467	.819	.532	.870	.586	.906	.630	.932	.667
40	.693	.423	.792	.505	.858	.571	.903	.624	.933	.667	.954	.702
45	.736	.455	.829	.539	.889	.605	.927	.657	.952	.698	.969	.731
50	.772	.485	.859	.570	.913	.635	.946	.685	.966	.721	.979	.755

The present value of a loan at a reduced interest rate repayable in full at the end of the period can be computed by multiplying the figures in the A column by the proportion by which the interest rate is reduced; for example, a 30-year loan at 4 percent when the market rate is 6 percent involves a gift of $2/6 \times 0.826 = 0.275$ of its face value.

The real amount given by the donor will be different from the real amount accruing to the recipient if the rate of return on investment (alternative opportunity cost of capital) is different in the two countries. Wilson E. Schmidt ("The Economics of Charity: Loans versus Grants," *Journal of Political Economy*, Vol. 72 [August 1964], pp. 387-95) has shown how this fact may be used to minimize the burden of aid to the donor. The general principles he establishes are that for a given real present value of aid to the recipient, (1) grants are cheaper to the donor than loans if the yield on capital is higher in the donor country than in the recipient, and vice versa; (2) larger loans with higher interest rates cost the donor less (or earn more) than smaller loans with lower interest rates if the yield on capital is higher in the donor than in the recipient country, and vice versa; (3) smaller loans for longer periods cost the lender less (or earn the lender more) than larger loans for shorter periods if the yield on capital is higher in the donor country than in the recipient, and vice versa. These rules suggest that if (as is more likely) the yield on capital is higher in the donor country, grants are to be preferred to loans, larger higher-interest to smaller lower-interest loans, and smaller longer-period to larger shorter-period loans. Schmidt's calculations assume, however, that recipient countries assess grants and loans by their present value, which implies that they can invest and disinvest freely at the yields on capital prevailing in their own countries; in fact, since the investments financed by aid are usually relatively large and "lumpy," the value of particular loans may not be assessable independently of the profile of material yields on the project financed.

APPENDIX D

Sugar Protectionism and the Export Earnings of Less Developed Countries

An article by R. H. Snape relating to the international sugar situation in 1959 contains some interesting figures on the effect of sugar protection in raising the prices of protected sugar production above world market prices, the effect that replacement of protection and heavy excise taxes by deficiency payments would have on sugar consumption, and the effect these changes would have on the international trade in sugar.[1] Although the estimates are subject to certain reservations, which Snape carefully records, they illustrate the contribution that might be made to the export earnings of the sugar-producing less developed countries by changes in the policies of the developed (and some of the developing) countries of the world such as were recommended at the 1964 United Nations Conference on Trade and Development.

Table D-1 shows the extent to which returns to sugar producers in protectionist countries exceed the world market price. The table gives some indication of the extent to which the export earnings of the less developed countries producing for the free world market could be increased if they were accorded the same prices as their protected competitors, a type of policy advocated by Dr. Prebisch in his report *Towards a New Trade Policy for Development*.[2] According to Table D-1 prices received by protected producers of raw sugar in the main consuming markets are 60-105 percent higher than the free world market price. Some of this excess price advantage is currently channelled to less developed countries through the U.S. Sugar Act, the British Commonwealth Sugar Agreement, and the association of the overseas territories with the Common Market. But the free market accounts for some 40 percent of total international trade in sugar and, estimated from Snape's figures, in 1959 it

[1] R. H. Snape, "Some Effects of Protection in the World Sugar Industry," *Economica*, Vol. 30 (February 1963), pp. 63-73. This appendix is based on Snape's article. It is a revised version of Harry G. Johnson, "Sugar Protectionism and the Export Earnings of Less Developed Countries: Variations on a Theme by R. H. Snape," *Economica*, Vol. 33 (February 1966), pp. 34-42.

[2] Raúl Prebisch, *Towards a New Trade Policy for Development* (United Nations, 1964). Prebisch's actual concrete proposal is for some sort of parity price scheme; the version examined here is in the spirit of Prebisch's suggestion that the developed countries accord the less developed countries the income-redistribution treatment they accord their own primary producers.

TABLE D-1

Estimated Average Receipts from or Costs of Home-Produced Raw Sugar, 1959

Country[a]	Estimated Average Receipts or Costs (in U. S. Cents per Pound)	*Average Receipts or Costs as Percent of Import Parity or Export Parity Price*[b]
CANE		
Argentina	4½	120
Australia	4½	150
Brazil	4¾	160
British Guiana	4½	150
British Honduras	5¼	140
British West Indies:		
Antigua	4¼[c]	140
Barbados	5	165
Jamaica	4½	150
St. Christopher-Nevis	4¾	160
Trinidad-Tobago	5	165
Cuba	4	135
Dominican Republic	2¾	90
Fiji	5	165
Hawaii	7[d]	235
India	6¼	165
Indonesia	6	185
Mauritius	4½	150
Mexico	5¼	175
Peru	3¼	110
Philippines	5½	170
Puerto Rico	7[d]	235
South Africa	3¾	125
Taiwan	3¼	100
United States (cane and beet)[e]	7½[d]	200
BEET		
Belgium-Luxembourg	5½	145
France (Metropolitan)	6	160
Germany (Federal Republic)	7¾	205
Italy	7	185
Netherlands	5	135
United Kingdom	6	160

Source: Snape, *op. cit.*, Table 1.

[a] For countries in italics, average receipts are based on export parity; in roman, on import parity.

[b] Import parity taken as 3¾ cents per pound; export parity taken as 3 cents per pound (except for Indonesia, Philippines and Taiwan, taken as 3¼ cents per pound).

[c] Average for 1958 and 1959.

[d] Includes conditional payments to farmers.

[e] Does not include Hawaii.

accounted for some 5.3 million metric tons worth in the neighborhood of $347 million.[2] Arrangements that would give the less developed countries prices equal to those paid by the protectionist countries to their own producers would therefore increase the export earnings of the less developed producers for the free market by $208-$347 million; that is, between a fifth and a third of a billion dollars. These earnings would constitute an additional net flow of resources to these countries, at the expense of the taxpayers or consumers of the importing countries, almost all of which rank as developed countries.

Secondly, using an elaborate econometric estimate of the demand function for sugar developed by Viton and Pignalosa, Snape estimates the increase in the quantity of sugar demanded by the noncommunist countries that would have resulted from the replacement of present tariff and nontariff barriers to sugar imports by protection in the form of deficiency payments, together with the removal of the excise taxes that in some countries now fall so heavily on sugar consumption. These changes would have allowed domestic consumers in all countries to purchase sugar at export parity or import parity prices (depending on whether the country is or would be a net exporter or importer), estimated by Snape respectively at 17¢ and 19¢ per kilogram (estimates include refinery and distribution costs). On the assumptions made, the increased consumption would be supplied by less developed countries now largely dependent on the free world sugar market. Snape also ventures the suggestion that if these policy changes had been introduced, the free market price of sugar would have risen by about ½¢ a pound.

Snape estimates that the resulting increase in consumption would have been 3.9 million metric tons, about 30 percent of net total world trade and over 70 percent of free world net trade in sugar; if the communist countries had increased their consumption in the same proportion, the increase in consumption and trade would have been 5 million metric tons. Table D-2 shows that on the alternative assumptions the value of the increase in trade (exports of the sugar-producing less developed countries) would have been either a quarter or a third of a billion dollars, at the price of 3¢ per pound (f.a.s. Cuba) used by Snape; had the price risen as he suggested it might to 3½¢ per pound, the increase in export earnings on sugar would have ranged from slightly over a third to over a half of a billion dollars, depending on whether the increase was confined to the free world sugar trade or extended to all sugar exports and whether or not the communist countries made changes allowing their imports to expand to the same extent as those of the noncommunist countries.

Confining attention for comparability to the assumption that any price increase would apply only to the free sugar market, it appears that the policy of more rational protection of domestic sugar producers in the protectionist countries would increase the export earnings of the less developed free market producers by substantially more than would the policy of extending to their existing trade the subsidies provided by protection to national producers. To obtain these extra earnings, however, the exporters in question would have to

[2] For the basis of calculation, see Table D-2, note a.

Estimated Effects of Replacing Sugar Protection by Subsidies and Eliminating Sugar Excises

(In millions of dollars)

Item	Noncommunist Countries	World[a]
Estimated expansion of consumption (in metric tons)[b]	3.9 million	5 million
Value of additional trade (at 3¢ per pound, equals $66 per metric ton)	$256.7	$327.6
Increased value of existing trade (at 3½¢ per pound)[c]		
Net total trade	$142.6	$142.6
Free market trade only	$ 57.9	$ 57.9
Increased value of additional trade	$ 42.8	$ 54.6
Estimated rent on new trade		
At ¼¢ per pound[d]	$ 21.4	$ 27.3
At ½¢ per pound[e]	$ 42.8	$ 54.6
Increase in trade value		
Net total trade	$442.2	$524.9
Net free trade only	$357.4	$440.1
Increase in exporters' gain from trade		
Net total trade		
Rent estimate ¼¢	$164.0	$169.9
Rent estimate ½¢	$185.4	$197.2
Net free trade only		
Rent estimate ¼¢	$ 79.3	$ 85.2
Rent estimate ½¢	$100.7	$112.5

Source: Snape, op. cit., Table 2, p. 69; figures shown in Snape's table have been rounded.

[a] Equal expansion of consumption in communist and noncommunist countries is assumed.

[b] Total net trade is estimated at 12.9 million metric tons from Snape's statement (p. 71) that the estimated increase in consumption is 30 percent of net international trade; net free international trade is estimated at 5.3 million metric tons from Snape's statements (p. 71 and p. 71, n.1) that the estimated increase in consumption in noncommunist countries is more than 70 percent of net free international trade and for the world more than 90 percent of net free international trade.

[c] The estimated increase in price of 3½¢ per pound is due to Snape (p. 72); his argument on this point is not entirely satisfactory, since it rests on an "increase in confidence on the part of exporters."

[d] Rent estimate at ¼¢ per pound assumes that half the increase in the price of marginal supplies is rent, corresponding to the assumption of a linearly rising cost curve.

[e] Rent estimate at ½¢ per pound assumes that rent is equal to the increase in price, and corresponds either to Snape's "confidence" rationale or to the fact that production was restricted in the free market supplying countries, implying marginal costs less than price (it would reflect the assumption of a marginal cost of 2½¢ per pound and a linearly rising cost curve).

produce the additional sugar, at a cost in real resources. The net benefit accruing to them would not be the total increase in export earnings, but the sum of the increase in the price of existing exports and the rent earned on the additional supplies. The calculations of this net benefit presented in Table D-2 show results ranging from $164 million to $197 million if the increase in price affected all sugar traded, but of only $79 million to $112 million if it affected only sugar traded in the free market—either about two-thirds or about one-third of the net gain under the Prebisch policy.

In the third place, Snape's estimates permit a calculation of the consumption costs imposed on consumers in the various countries studied by existing protection and excises. This calculation is presented in Table D-3. These costs could be thought of as the amounts of resources that the protective developed countries could release by the relevant policy changes and contribute to the less developed as additional foreign aid, without making themselves worse off, or that the protective less developed countries could release for their own development or increased consumption by appropriate policy changes. The table shows that in the aggregate $193 million could be so released, and that the developed countries could release from $70 million to $148 million, depending on which countries are included in the classification of developed countries. Adding this avoidable consumption cost as prospective additional development resources to the net benefits to the less developed countries that would accrue from the associated expansion of export earnings, it appears that a policy of "scientific" protection combined with contribution of the resulting savings to development resources would make a contribution to the free market sugar exporters of the same order of magnitude as the Prebisch-style scheme and on some alternative assumptions would make a significantly larger contribution.

A "scientific" protectionist policy, however, is by no means the outer limit of what could be done to increase the export earnings of the less developed sugar producers. Snape estimates that in the absence of protection the free market price of sugar would have been 4 to 4½¢ per pound (f.a.s. Cuba)—an increase of 33⅓ to 50 percent. This would have meant increased export earnings of $285-$428 million had it applied to net total international trade, and $116-$174 million had it applied to net free market trade, at the volumes actually realized in 1959, the latter figure being the more relevant one. The establishment of such a higher price, however, would have been the result of a contraction of sugar production in the protectionist countries and an expansion in the free market producing countries (and in some of the least protectionist countries), so that the latter would have benefited additionally by expanded exports substituting for protected production—and also by an increase in total consumption on a somewhat smaller scale than Snape's estimates.

Unfortunately no estimates are provided by Snape, or available elsewhere, on the difficult question of what the resulting changes in national production levels and trade would have been. An illustrative calculation is presented in Table D-4. The table is based on the assumption that resources in the major sugar-protectionist countries are perfectly mobile out of sugar production in

Estimated Consumption Cost of Sugar Protection and Excise Taxes[a]

Country	Export or Import Price (Per Metric Ton)	Estimated Increase in Consumption (Thousands of Metric Tons)	Tariff Equivalent of Estimated Price Decline (Percent)[b]	Estimated Consumption Cost (Thousands of Dollars)[c]
Group A				
Australia	$170	37	0.2048	$ 644
Austria	$190	19	0.2048	370
Belgium-Luxembourg	$190	26	0.4925	1,216
France (Metropolitan)	$190	91	0.2500	2,161
Germany (Federal Republic)	$190	205	0.5625	10,955
India	$190	505	0.1964	6,544
Italy	$190	300	1.1277	32,139
Netherlands	$190	51	0.3514	1,703
Sweden	$190	35	0.4286	1,425
Switzerland	$190	8	0.0989	75
United Kingdom	$190	60	0.0753	429
United States	$190	588	0.3333	18,618
Venezuela	$190	28	0.4085	1,087
Ten Other Countries[d]	$180[e]	216	0.5456[f]	10,606
Total, Group A	—	—	—	$ 87,973
Group B				
Algeria	$190	11	0.0870	91
Canada	$190	33	0.1494	468
Cuba	$170	3	0.0309	8
Iran	$190	93	0.3333	2,945
Japan	$190	674	1.0408	66,642
Pakistan	$190	146	0.6129	8,501
Philippines	$170	37	0.2658	836
Spain	$190	20	0.0638	121
Turkey	$170	114	1.1277	10,927
Total, Group B	—	—	—	$ 90,540
Group C				
All Other Noncommunist Countries	$180[e]	582	0.2681[f]	$ 14,043
Total Groups A, B, and C	—	—	—	$ 192,556

TABLE D-3 (CONTINUED)

Country	—	—	—	Estimated Consumption Cost (Thousands of Dollars)[e]
Addendum				
Groups A and B, less Ten Other Countries				$167,906
Group A, less India, Venezuela and Ten Others				$ 69,736
Group A, less India, Venezuela and Ten Others, plus Canada and Japan				$136,847
Group A, less India, Venezuela and Ten Others, plus Canada and Japan, plus Spain and Turkey				$147,895

Source: Snape, *op. cit.*, Table 2, p. 69. Countries were grouped by Snape according to the data used in calculating price elasticities of demand. Columns may not sum to totals due to rounding.

[a] Snape employs a price of 17¢ a kilogram for exporting countries and 19¢ for importing countries.

[b] Snape gives the estimated percentage price fall. The tariff equivalent to the price fall is $t = p/1-p$, where p is the proportional price fall.

[e] The consumption cost is estimated from the usual formula, cost $= \frac{1}{2} t \cdot P \cdot dQ$, where P is the parity price and dQ the change in consumption resulting from its establishment. It is equal to half the product of the first three columns.

[d] Ceylon, Finland, Greece, Guatemala, Ireland, Israel, Norway, Portugal, Puerto Rico, and the Federation of Rhodesia and Nyasaland.

[e] Price is the average of Snape's two prices for exporters and importers.

[f] A price elasticity of demand of 0.5 is assumed; division of the proportional increase in consumption predicted by Snape by 0.5 yields the implicit proportional price reduction, from which the tariff equivalent is computed.

the long run, so that free trade would completely eliminate such production if the country were uncompetitive at the free trade price. It presents computations of the saving of resource cost in the protectionist countries that would ensue on free trade, and of the resulting increase in the trade of the exporting countries and their net gain from trade.

The table shows that in the major (Western) protectionist countries, substitution of imports for protected domestic production, allowing for the effects on sugar prices of world free trade in sugar, would have saved the expenditure of real resources worth $319 million. The additional export earnings of the exporting countries due to this substitution would have been worth $675 million—over two-thirds of a billion dollars—and the estimated net benefit from this additional trade would have been worth nearly $120 million. Altogether, with respect to substitution in production alone and entirely ignoring the effects of the expansion of consumption that would have ensued on the adoption of free trade in sugar, $438 million additional resources could have been freed for development purposes from these seven countries alone through the abandonment of protection.

TABLE D-4

Effects on Trade of Major Protectionist Countries of Substituting Imports for Domestic Production

(Dollar items in thousands, tonnage in thousands of metric tons)

Item	Germany (Federal Republic)	United States	Italy	France (Metropolitan)	United Kingdom	Belgium-Luxembourg	Netherlands	Total
1959 production tonnage	1,390	2,682	1,000ᵃ	1,051	855	224	499	7,701
Proportional excess of domestic price or costs over 5¢ per poundᵇ	0.55	0.50	0.40	0.20	0.20	0.10	0	—
Saving of resource costᶜ	$82,271	$147,818	$44,092	$23,170	$18,849	$2,469	0	$318,670
Value of increased trade by exportersᵈ	$130,237	$251,291	$93,696	$98,474	$80,110	$20,988	0ᵉ	$674,795
Estimated net benefit to exportersᶠ	$22,983	$44,346	$16,535	$17,378	$14,137	$3,704	0	$119,081
Resource cost saving plus net benefit to exporters	$105,254	$192,164	$60,627	$40,548	$32,986	$6,173	0	$437,772
1959 import tonnage	203.9	4,116.4ᵍ	33.2	534.5	2,578.5	65.9	158.1	7,690.5
Increased cost of 1959 importsʰ	$5,619	$113,438	$915	$14,729	$71,057	$1,816	$4,357	$211,931
Net savings (loss) to importers	$76,652	$34,381	$43,177	$8,441	-$52,208	$653	-$4,357	$106,739
Gross benefit to exportersⁱ	$28,602	$157,783	$17,449	$32,107	$85,194	$5,520	$4,357	$331,012

Source: Food and Agriculture Organization of the United Nations, *The World Sugar Economy in Figures, 1880-1959*, Commodity Reference Series 1 and Table 1. ᵃ Italy's production is recorded as 1,408,000 metric tons in 1959, far above previous years' production and above the year's consumption of 1,000,000 tons, and the discrepancy is not accountable for by exports. Production has therefore been set equal to consumption in 1959 for the purposes of this table. ᵇ The import price of 5¢ corresponds to an export price of 4¼¢ (the mid-point of Snape's range) plus Snape's figure of ¾¢ for transportation. ᶜ At 5¢ a pound, a thousand metric tons are worth $110,250; this figure is used in calculating resource saving. ᵈ At 4¼¢ a pound, a thousand metric tons are worth $93,695.50; this figure is used in calculating the value of the additional trade to the exporting countries. ᵉ The Netherlands is assumed to be marginally competitive, at 5¢ per pound, so that no increase in trade results from its dropping protection. ᶠ For the purpose of calculating net gains, the rent element in marginal production is assumed to be ¾¢, i.e., half the difference between 2¾¢ and 4¼¢; this amounts to $16,594.50 per thousand metric tons. ᵍ Imports for the United States exclude imports from territories (1,756,600 metric tons). ʰ The increased cost of imports is taken to be 1¼¢ per pound (the difference between 5¢ and 4¼¢ per pound), and worth $27,557.50 per thousand metric tons. ⁱ Net benefit plus increased import cost.

As they stand, the foregoing calculations are somewhat misleading, since they imply that the saving in resource cost from the elimination of protected production accrues to the importing country as a gain that must be deliberately transferred to the less developed exporting countries through additional foreign aid. In fact, a part, and in some cases more than the whole, of this saving would be automatically transferred to the exporting countries through the assumed increase in the prices of existing imports, involving a reduction of the resources freed for additional aid and in some cases requiring a reduction of existing foreign aid if the importing country concerned is to be made no worse off than at present.

Table D-4 includes calculations of the increased cost of imports, the net saving of resources to the importing countries, and the gross "automatic" gains to exporters that would result under free trade, abstracting from any increases in consumption and trade that would ensue on the lowering of prices to consumers. These calculations, it should be noted, are overestimates, since they assume that all 1959 imports (except U.S. imports from associated territories) were imported at the world market price, whereas a substantial part of the imports of most of these countries entered under one form or another of preferential arrangement, and therefore probably at prices above the world level, so that the extent of the automatic transfer of resource savings on protected domestic production is exaggerated. Nevertheless only two countries—the United Kingdom and to a much smaller extent the Netherlands—would incur a net loss of resources under free trade, and the loss to the United Kingdom in particular may be seriously exaggerated.

For the seven countries shown in Table D-4, Table D-3 shows an expansion of consumption of 1.3 million metric tons and an estimated saving of consumption cost of $67 million. At the prices used in Table D-3, the expansion of consumption would mean an increase in the value of less-developed-country exports of $124 million, entailing an estimated benefit (rent) of $22 million, making a total of resources freed of $89 million (on the inconsistent assumptions of the same expansion of consumption at a higher world price). Assuming as a rough approximation that half of this amount ($45 million) would be realized under free trade with the higher world price it would entail, the total resources that restoration of a freely competitive world market in sugar would release to the less developed countries from these seven countries alone would be in the neighborhood of half a billion dollars ($482 million).

These calculations, while admittedly rough and tentative, and deficient inasmuch as no account has been taken of the possible contribution that existing protection makes to important groups of less developed countries and the losses to them that might result from the universal abandonment of protection, do tend to support two general conclusions.

The first, and firmer, is that the prevalence of sugar protection has substantial effects both in wasting resources and in reducing the earnings of the less developed countries that have a comparative advantage in sugar production. According to the rough estimates presented here, replacement of the present national systems of protection by deficiency payments (scientific protectionism) would increase the export earnings of these countries by about half a billion dollars, and free trade would increase their export earnings fom the seven major countries alone by about three-quarters of a billion dollars (to be compared with the widely cited estimated "trade gap" of ten billion dollars for all less developed countries in 1970). Free trade would free resources that would go automatically or could be contributed as foreign aid to the less developed countries to an amount around half a billion dollars (to be compared with the current foreign aid total from all countries and international organizations of about ten billion dollars, a figure probably nearly double the net transfer of real resources actually involved). In addition, the free market producers would undoubtedly benefit in terms of economic welfare from the reduction in price fluctuations now associated with the marginal nature of their sector of the market.

The second conclusion, less sure because of the lack of quantitative information on the effects of existing preferences for important groups of less developed countries, is that the abandonment of sugar protectionism in favor of free world competition in sugar could increase the resources available to the less developed countries by more than could a Prebisch-type policy of "internationalizing" sugar protection. Moreover, in contrast to the latter policy, which would merely transfer resources from developed to less developed countries through an increase in prices, a policy of free trade would make the additional resources available without cost to anyone[4] as a consequence of the increased efficiency of resource allocation it would produce.

[4] In the short run there would be some costs involved in shifting resources out of sugar production, but it seems reasonable to assume that resources are mobile enough in the developed countries to absorb a shift out of sugar production without intolerable social strains (as has indeed been assumed in computing Table D-4). In the long run there would be distributional effects insofar as some consuming countries benefit from the low world price associated with protection.

Earnings Response to Price Stabilization

The effects of commodity price stabilization on the earnings of producers can be illustrated by the accompanying diagram. The broken line SS represents the supply curve, OQ and OP the equilibrium constant average supply quantity and price, P' and Q' the low and P'' and Q'' the high prices and quantities. ($P'P = PP''$, $Q'Q = QQ''$, by the simplifying assumption of a linear supply curve and a constant average output.) Demand is assumed to alternate in a two-period cycle, producing successively the prices OP' and OP'' in the absence of stabilization. If supply responds to current price, output is successively OQ' and OQ'' in the absence of stabilization. Thus, earnings in the first period are $OP' \times OQ'$ (represented by the area A) while in the second period they are $OP'' \times OQ''$ (represented by the entire bounded area). Over the two periods together, therefore, earnings are $2A + 2B + 2C + 4D$ in the absence of stabilization. This compares with earnings of $2(A + B + C + D)$ under the buffer stock, and ex-

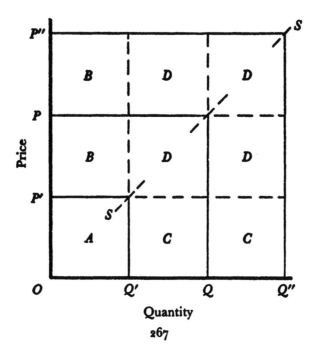

Quantity

ceeds them by $2D$. If, instead, supply responds to price with a one-period lag, income over two periods is $A + 2B + A + 2C$ as compared with $2(A + B + C + D)$ under the buffer stock—a decrease of earnings of $2D$. Note that the diagram assumes a metastable cobweb cycle (neither damped nor explosive); also that while, on the average, producers can earn only $A + B + C$ per period when supply responds with a one-period lag, in place of the $A + B + C + D$ they would earn with stabilization, this does not necessarily mean that they incur losses, in the sense of earning negative rents. They would only lose if their average uncompensated marginal production costs D exceeded their average rents, equal to B plus the portion of A above the supply curve; the probability of loss obviously increases with the elasticity of supply.

Stabilizing Effects
of a Commodity-Reserve Standard

For reserve commodities whose elasticities of supply and demand are low, the stabilizing effects of a commodity-reserve standard are likely to be small and to take considerable time to be effective. To illustrate these points, consider first a static equilibrium system with a fixed nominal quantity of money M and a desired ratio of money to income k; in such a system the price level p is determined by the equation $M = kpY$, where Y is real output, and the effect of a change in k is $dp/p = - dk/k$. Now consider a similar system producing a commodity whose quantity is represented by C and whose price is fixed at one unit of money by a commodity-reserve system and another commodity whose quantity is represented by X and whose (variable) price is p. Let the desired ratio of money to income again be k, the desired money stock being $M^* = k\,(pX + C)$ where $pX + C = Y$ and initially $M^* = M$. The expenditure equation of the system is

$$Y = E + S = pX' + C' + S,$$

where E is total expenditure, S is saving (initially equal to zero), and primes denote quantities consumed (initially equal to quantities produced). Differentiating by p,

$$Xdp = X'dp + pdX' + dC' + dS$$

or

$$0 = pdX' + dC' + dS$$
$$= - dC + dC' + dS$$

(since initially $X = X'$, p must change to make $dX' = dX$, and on the production side $pdX + dC = 0$). The first term is a production substitution effect dependent on the change in p; the second term is a combination of the effect of increased saving in reducing expenditure on C, representable by a marginal propensity to consume, and a substitution effect dependent on the change in p. Hence the equation may be rewritten (using the fact that initially $C = C'$) as

$$0 = (\epsilon + \eta)C(dp/p) + (1 - c)dS,$$

from which

$$\frac{dp}{p} = -\frac{1-c}{(\epsilon + \eta)C} \, dS, \tag{1}$$

where ϵ and η are respectively the elasticity of supply of and (compensated) elasticity of demand for the commodity with respect to its own price.

To introduce monetary behavior, assume that any imbalance between actual and desired money stocks is adjusted according to the equation

$$dS = a \, dM^*$$
$$= a \left[M \frac{dk}{k} + kp \, X\frac{dp}{p} \right]. \tag{2}$$

Substituting in (1),

$$\frac{dp}{p} = \frac{(1-c) \, aM}{(\epsilon + \eta)C + (1-c)akpX} \cdot \frac{dk}{k}$$
$$= -\frac{(1-c) \, a \, k}{(\epsilon + \eta)\check{c} + (1-c)ak(1-\check{c})} \cdot \frac{dk}{k} \tag{3}$$

where $\check{c} = C/(pX + C) = C/Y$

$$dS = aM \frac{(\epsilon + \eta) \, C}{(\epsilon + \eta) \, C + (1-c)akpX} \cdot \frac{dk}{k}$$
$$\frac{dS}{M} = \frac{a(\epsilon + \eta) \, \check{c}}{(\epsilon + \eta)\check{c} + (1-c)ak(1-\check{c})} \cdot \frac{dk}{k}. \tag{4}$$

From these equations it is evident that if $\epsilon = \eta = 0$, $dp/p = -[1/(1-c)] \, [dk/k]$ and $dS = 0$, that is, the result would be the same as in the static system first considered except for the rigidity of the money price of the standard commodity. Any stabilizing effect on prices depends on the existence of some elasticity of demand for or supply of the standard commodity. It is obvious from inspection of (3) that the fall in the price of the nonstandard good is smaller, the larger are the elasticities of demand for and supply of the standard commodity. It can also be verified that the price fall will be smaller, the larger is the marginal propensity to consume the standard commodity, and the smaller are the adjustment coefficient and the desired ratio of money to income (a and k). The magnitude of the price fall will vary inversely or directly with the share of the standard commodity in total output, depending on whether $\epsilon + \eta$ is greater or less than $(1 - c)ak$; the probable magnitude of the parameters makes the former the more likely case. From inspection of (4) it is obvious that dS/M will be closer to dk/k (i.e., the addition to money stocks will be closer to the desired increment, and therefore the economy will be returning more rapidly to its initial price level) the larger are the average and marginal propensities to consume the standard commodity (the larger the ratio of production of that commodity to total output and the higher the marginal propensity to consume it), the higher the elasticities of demand for and supply of the standard commodity, the lower the desired ratio of money to income, and the higher the adjustment coefficient.

To obtain an impression of the stabilizing effect that might obtain in practice, one might plausibly assume that $c = \bar{c}$, and that $\bar{c}$ is in the neighborhood of 0.05. The quantity η is likely to be under unity for primary products, probably in the neighborhood of 0.4; given that many of the commodities covered in the proposed scheme are agricultural products, whose supply is fixed within the crop year, ϵ would be very small, probably no more than 0.1. More difficulty is encountered with k and a, which require specification of the period of the analysis; this might be taken as one year for $a = 1$, with k probably around 0.05 (given that it is international reserves and not money in the hands of the public with which the scheme is concerned). With these figures the results are:

$$dp/p = -0.677 \ (dk/k) \tag{5}$$

$$dS/M = 0.356 \ (dk/k). \tag{6}$$

These figures indicate a significant but not a very high degree of stabilization.

Index

Africa, 200

Agricultural products (*See also* Commodities): price supports on, 10, 11, 28, 29, 79, 85-86, 94, 117, 130, 138; surpluses, 4, 70, 85 92-93, 94; taxation of, 71; trade restrictions on, 10, 21, 28, 71, 84, 85-89, 129-31

Aid. *See* Foreign aid.

American Farm Economic Association, 86

Australia, 87, 165

Automobile industry, 128

Balance-of-payments problems: during development, 53-55; effect of tariff reduction on, 133-34; inflation-caused, 17, 58, 74; and international monetary system, 212, 213; in reserve-currency country, 219-20; restriction of capital movements because of, 215; restriction of foreign aid because of, 213-15; restriction of imports because of, 58, 214, 215, 221

Baranson, Jack, 77n, 78n

Basevi, Giorgio, 97

Bauer, P. T., 3n

Balassa, Bela A., 27, 98, 103, 205n, 246n

Bilateralism: in foreign aid, 9, 23, 24, 80, 81 112, 113, 115-16, 124, 125; in tariff reduction, 15-16, 41

Blau, Gerda, 136-37n, 144, 158-59

Bloch, Henry S., 26n, 33n

Boissonneault, Lorette, 151n

Brasseur plan, 197

Canada, 21, 42, 89, 128, 138, 165

Capital investment. *See* Investment, domestic *and* Investment, foreign.

Capital mobility, 48-49, 50, 97, 102, 117, 195

Commodities (*See also* Agricultural products *and* Commodity agreements, international): demand for, 28, 49; domestic price supports on, 10, 11, 28, 29, 85, 94, 117, 138; export earnings from, 28, 140-42; as monetary reserves, 230-33, 236; price fluctuations of, 141-46; stabilization of prices of, 5, 6, 29, 35, 41, 138, 139, 140, 144, 154, 157, 159, 161-62, 231-34, 235-36; substitutes for, 28, 71; surplus, disposal of, 4, 70, 85, 92-93, 94; terms of trade on, 28-29, 234; trade restrictions on, 28, 29, 35, 84-90, 129, 238-39

Commodity agreements, international: existing, 112, 113, 138-39; history of, 138-39; limitations of, 137, 139-40; reactions to, 6, 10-11, 35, 153, 237, 239-40; use to control commodity prices, 5, 6, 29, 138, 139, 140, 144, 154, 157, 159, 161-62; use to increase export earnings, 140, 152, 155, 158-59, 161-62, 248; use to increase market share, 29, 115, 157-59

Commodity Credit Corporation, 93, 121

Common Market. *See* European Economic Community.

Comparative costs: and competitive position, 77; effect of reduced tariffs on,

273

For Product Safety Concerns and Information please contact our EU
representative GPSR@taylorandfrancis.com
Taylor & Francis Verlag GmbH, Kaufingerstraße 24, 80331 München, Germany

www.ingramcontent.com/pod-product-compliance
Ingram Content Group UK Ltd.
Pitfield, Milton Keynes, MK11 3LW, UK
UKHW021012180425
457613UK00020B/914